fP

OBJECT RELATIONS THEORY AND SELF PSYCHOLOGY IN SOCIAL WORK PRACTICE

EDA G. GOLDSTEIN, D.S.W.

THE FREE PRESS

NEW YORK LONDON TORONTO SYDNEY

*f*P

THE FREE PRESS

A Division of Simon & Schuster, Inc.
1230 Avenue of the Americas
New York, NY 10020

Copyright © 2001 by Eda G. Goldstein

For information about special discounts for bulk purchases, please
contact Simon & Schuster Special Sales: 1-800-456-6798 or
business@simonandschuster.com

Designed by Lisa Chovnick

Manufactured in the United States of America

10   9   8   7   6

Library of Congress Cataloging-in-Publication Data is available.

ISBN 0-684-84009-X

CONTENTS

ACKNOWLEDGMENTS   *ix*

PART I   HISTORICAL, THEORETICAL, AND CLINICAL
PERSPECTIVES

1   Object Relations Theory and Self Psychology: Their Scope
and Significance   3

The Assimilation of Psychoanalytic Theory into Social Work

The Expansion of Psychodynamic Theory

Object Relations Theory and Self Psychology Defined

Significance for Social Work Practice

Impetus for the Book

The Focus and Plan of the Book

2   The Evolution of Object Relations Theory and Self Psychology   15

Classical Freudian Theory

Ego Psychology

American Object Relations Theory

The British School of Object Relations Theory

Self Psychology

Extensions and New Directions

Further Considerations

Summary

3   Object Relations Theory: Major Concepts   53

Basic Terminology

Structure, Development, and Psychopathology

Summary

4   Self Psychology: Major Concepts   79

Basic Terminology

Perspectives on Psychopathology

Emerging Research and Theory

Summary

5 Treatment Principles   96

    Object Relations Treatment

    Self Psychological Treatment

    Summary

PART II   SOCIAL WORK TREATMENT: Principles
            and Applications

  6 Assessment and Treatment Planning   125

    The Nature of Assessment

    Planning Treatment

    Case Examples

    Summary

  7 The Beginning Phase   155

    Establishing a Therapeutic Holding Environment

    Overcoming Obstacles to Forming a Positive Relationship

    Selective Techniques

    Summary

  8 Middle Phase Issues   186

    Repairing Disruptions of the Selfobject Transference

    Case Examples

    Addressing Projective Identification and Enactments

    Case Examples

    *Understanding Similarities and Differences Between Client
    and Worker*

    Recognizing Other Forms of Object Relating

    Summary

  9 Treatment of Clients Undergoing Stressful Life Events   216

    Death of Significant Others

    Illness and Disability

Midlife Issues

Treatment Emphases

Countertransference Issues

Case Examples

Summary

10 The Treatment of Clients with Special Problems   241

   Substance Abuse

   Child Maltreatment

   Adult Survivors of Childhood Sexual Abuse

   Countertransference Issues

   Case Examples

   Summary

11 Couple and Family Treatment   267

   Object Relations Perspectives

   Self Psychological Perspectives

   Treatment Principles

   Countertransference Issues

   Case Examples

   Summary

REFERENCES   287

INDEX   297

ACKNOWLEDGMENTS

Writing this book has provided me with the opportunity to integrate different phases of my education, training, and professional life. In my undergraduate days, the University of Chicago introduced me to a vast body of knowledge and imbued me with the importance of critical thinking. I began to recognize that the search for absolute truth is elusive and to appreciate the value of remaining open to new knowledge rather than of being wedded to one way of viewing people and the world. Later, my graduate work at both the School of Social Service Administration of the University of Chicago and at the Columbia University School of Social Work instilled me with a respect for the social work profession's history, values, and commitment to practice. Many remarkable individuals have inspired me, including Helen Harris Perlman, Friedericka Mayers, Dorothy Large, Rebecca Cohen, Janet Korman, Lila Swell, Florence Hollis, Carel Germain, and Carol Meyer. Their spirits linger on.

Initially, my understanding of clients and my clinical work were heavily influenced by Freudian theory and ego psychology, but during the course of my career, I became conversant with other psychodynamic and psychosocial theoretical frameworks and their practice applications. I shall always be grateful to Dr. Otto Kernberg for affording me the opportunity to work closely with him when he was conducting research on borderline disorders. I grew professionally during the seven-year collaboration in which we co-led an intellectually stimulating interdisciplinary clinical research group at both the New York State Psychiatric Institute and the New York Hospital–Cornell Medical Center, Westchester Division. During this time, our research tried to operationalize many Kernbergian concepts and treatment principles. We vigorously debated the utility of a range of theoretical and treatment frameworks within American and British object relations theory and self psychology.

After leaving my position as Assistant Director of Social Work at New

York Hospital to become a faculty member at New York University in 1981, my clinical work expanded and I experimented with different approaches. I shall always be indebted to Dr. Marjorie Taggart White, a courageous and generous woman and a creative clinician and scholar, who helped me to grasp the significance of self psychology and to understand and implement its core concepts and treatment principles in depth.

As a faculty member at the New York University Shirley M. Ehrenkranz School of Social Work, I chaired the Social Work Practice Curriculum Area for fourteen years and then was appointed Director of the Ph.D. Program in Clinical Social Work in 1997. In these roles, I have tried to help social work students, practitioners, and supervisors to gain knowledge of and to apply a range of contemporary psychodynamic concepts and treatment principles to social work practice with a broad range of clients. Much of my teaching, writing, speaking, and dissertation advisement has been related to this challenge. I am particularly appreciative of my colleagues, professors Jeffrey Seinfeld, Rose Marie Perez Foster, Judith Mishne, Carol Tosone, Theresa Aiello, Barbara Dane, Lala Straussner, and Judith Siegel. I also am grateful to the late Dean Shirley M. Ehrenkranz and former Deans Tom Meenaghan and Eleanore Korman for their encouragement and provision of a facilitating environment.

Over the years, I have learned a great deal from my students, supervisees, and clients. They have made the theories and treatment principles that this book addresses come alive. Likewise, I have had the opportunity to meet with social work practitioners and faculty, both locally and nationally, and in some instances internationally. I am grateful for the warm welcome that I have received in many settings and for the rich dialogue that I have been able to have with numerous individuals and groups across the country about the current state of clinical theory and practice.

The task of writing a book is lonely and arduous. I want to thank the wonderful friends who have been a source of support along the way, Enid Ain, Norma Hakusa and Robert Counts, Dick Rizzo, Lucille Spira, and especially Patricia Petrocelli. I have also been fortunate in having the expert assistance of Mr. Philip Rappaport, senior editor at The Free Press.

PART I

HISTORICAL, THEORETICAL, AND CLINICAL PERSPECTIVES

1

OBJECT RELATIONS THEORY AND SELF PSYCHOLOGY

THEIR SCOPE AND SIGNIFICANCE

A person-in-situation perspective has been a defining characteristic of social work practice historically. The social work profession has relied on numerous distinctive theoretical frameworks that help to explain the nature of person-environmental transactions during the lifelong developmental process (Goldstein, 1983). Psychodynamic theory has occupied a prominent position in this knowledge base. Although its place as an underpinning to social work practice has waxed and waned over the years (Goldstein, 1996; Specht & Courtney, 1994; Strean, 1993), it has provided practitioners with important insights into human motivation, needs, capacities, and problems and has played a major role in shaping social work practice from the 1920s to the present.

As we begin the twenty-first century, psychodynamic theory is by no means the only theoretical paradigm that is available to social workers, but it continues to have significance for social work practice. It has moved far beyond its Freudian and ego psychological base, however, and reflects newer and more diverse views of personality development and the nature of human problems. Psychodynamic thinking and treatment principles are applicable to a broad range of clients, in both short-term and long-term intervention, and across a variety of treatment modalities. This broad and varied framework can be used to complement other formulations that inform social work practice, such as ecological, cognitive-behavioral, family systems, and group theories. Evidence that psychodynamic theory has stood the test of time can be found in a study of practitioners drawn from the 1991 National Association of Social Workers Register of Clinical Social

Workers. Respondents said they utilized 4.2 theoretical bases in their work, but 83 percent reported using psychodynamic or psychoanalytic theory (Strom, 1994: 80–81). Additionally, it is common for social work students and practitioners to seek to advance their knowledge of psychodynamic theory and treatment principles by taking academic courses, participating in in-service training programs, enrolling in psychotherapy institutes, and attending professional workshops and conferences.

THE ASSIMILATION OF PSYCHODYNAMIC THEORY INTO SOCIAL WORK

Sigmund Freud's classical psychoanalytic, or drive, theory was the first psychodynamic framework that was introduced into social work during a period called "the Psychiatric Deluge" in the 1920s (Woodroofe, 1971: 118–51). Throughout the next several decades, Freud's writings had a dramatic impact on social workers, particularly on the East Coast, who belonged to the diagnostic school associated with Mary Richmond, Gordon Hamilton, Lucille Austin, Annette Garrett, Florence Hollis, and others (Goldstein, 1995a: 31–33). Many social work practitioners underwent psychoanalysis and sought supervision from psychoanalysts, some of whom had recently emigrated from Europe. Enthusiastic about their own treatment and educational experiences, social workers began to employ Freudian theory and psychoanalytic treatment principles in their practice (Hamilton, 1958). The only competing psychodynamic framework at this time was Rankian theory, which provided the theoretical underpinnings to the functional school associated with Jessie Taft and Virginia Robinson and the Pennsylvania School of Social Work (Brandell & Perlman, 1997; Goldstein, 1995b).

THE EXPANSION OF PSYCHODYNAMIC THEORY

Beginning in the late 1930s and especially after World War II, Freudian theory underwent major modifications and transformations as social workers began to become familiar with ego psychological writings. Throughout the 1950s to the 1970s, ego psychology, which focused on the more autonomous and rational aspects of the ego, led to major changes in the diagnostic approach and its successor, the psychosocial model. It also contributed to Perlman's problem-solving approach, crisis intervention, the task-centered approach, and the life model (Brandell & Perlman, 1997; Goldstein, 1995a & b; and Strean, 1973).

In the last several decades, psychodynamic frameworks and treatment models that present alternatives to Freudian theory and ego psychology have captured the attention of social workers and other mental health professionals. Among the most significant of these formulations in today's practice arena are object relations theory and self psychology, which arose in reaction to and have a different philosophical base from Freudian drive theory and ego psychology. They have expanded psychoanalytic thinking to encompass the whole person rather than the drives or ego functions alone, a person's here-and-now functioning as well as childhood fantasies and experiences, the strengths and resilience of people alongside or in addition to their areas of pathology or weakness, and the impact of interpersonal, social, and cultural as well as intrapsychic factors on development and personality functioning.

Object relations and self psychological treatment approaches have moved traditional psychoanalytically informed treatment beyond its earlier rigidity and narrowness of focus and in some ways, they have provided a theoretical basis for many of the tried and true principles that have been characteristic of clinical social work practice. These newer frameworks have led to ten important changes in the ways in which psychodynamically oriented treatment is carried out.

1 Treatment has moved away from the traditional psychoanalytic stance that requires that the therapist be neutral in his or her interventions, abstinent with respect to gratifying patients' needs, and anonymous in terms of revealing personal information. Therapists are encouraged to be more empathic, involved, real, and genuine in their responses.

2 The treatment structure is more flexible and individualized.

3 The use of the therapist's self in engaging the patient and in pro-

viding a safe and accepting therapeutic holding environment and a reparative and facilitating relationship that offers opportunities for participation in new, more positive interactions is a crucial component of treatment.

4 The repertoire of treatment interventions has expanded beyond the use of insight-oriented techniques to encompass a broad range of developmentally attuned interventions that include active efforts to meet some of the patient's developmental needs, to facilitate and support the patient's growth, and to provide environmental supports. It is recognized that insight-oriented techniques, such as confrontation and interpretation, too early in treatment are not suited to work with many patients.

5 The therapist pays greater attention to the patient's subjective experience and personal narrative than previously and is advised to adopt a collaborative rather than authoritarian stance in the treatment relationship.

6 Treatment is based on revisions and expansions of personality theory so that it considers the impact of early relationships and self-development in influencing the nature of a patient's strengths and pathology.

7 The concept of transference has been expanded to include more recent views on the type of relational patterns and selfobject needs that patients bring into the treatment relationship.

8 The concept of resistance has been broadened to encompass the fact that many factors may be influencing what appear to be patients' difficulties in using treatment. These may stem from their efforts to maintain safety in the face of fear, hold on to coping mechanisms that have seemed to work for them in the past, sustain their attachment to internalized relations with others, and deal with what they feel to be realistic threats to their well-being. Moreover, impasses in the treatment may reflect a therapist's lack of correct attunement and responsiveness to the patient's concerns.

9 The concept of countertransference has been reconceptualized to encompass not only the therapist's reactions that stem from unresolved unconscious conflicts and other developmental issues but also those that stem from the impact of the patient's personality on the therapist. Additionally, there is recognition that the therapist always brings his or her own personality and organizing prin-

ciples to the treatment relationship and this affects how he or she perceives and interacts with the patient.

10 There is greater appreciation of the need to understand patients' total biopsychosocial situation, which includes the nature of their cultural and other types of diversity, the effects of oppression, and the impact of the difficult and sometimes traumatic and tragic circumstances of life that patients have experienced.

OBJECT RELATIONS THEORY
AND SELF PSYCHOLOGY DEFINED

Like Freudian theory and ego psychology, object relations theory and self psychology are developmental in nature and view adult personality characteristics as dependent upon early childhood experiences. In contrast, however, to Freud's emphasis on biological instincts as the driving force behind personality development, all object relations formulations are relational—that is, they share the view that human beings are social animals and that interpersonal relationships have a major impact on development (Aron, 1996). They describe the process by which the infant takes in (internalizes) the outside world, thereby acquiring basic perceptions of and attitudes toward the self and others that become structuralized within the person. Many object relations theorists have put forth somewhat different formulations, so that there is not a fully unified set of concepts.

Although the term object relations originally referred to the quality of a person's actual or *external* interpersonal relationships (Bellak, Hurvich, & Gediman, 1973), it was later used to describe the *internal* images or representations of the self and others (objects) that a person acquires in the course of early development. As noted by Greenberg and Mitchell (1983: 10), "people react to and interact with not only an actual other but also an internal other, a psychic representation of a person which in itself has the power to influence both the individual's affective states and his overt behavioral reactions."

The following six propositions characterize object relations theory's view of human development, psychopathology, and treatment.

1 Early infant-caretaker interactions lead to the person internalizing basic attitudes toward the self and others, characteristic relational patterns, and a repertoire of defenses and internal capacities. Important developmental processes involve attachment, separation-individuation, early object loss, experiences with frustrating or bad objects, and the move from dependence to independence.

2 Characteristic underlying problems that result from early object relations pathology include maladaptive attachment styles, separation-individuation subphase difficulties, borderline, narcissistic, paranoid, and schizoid disorders, severe and chronic depressive reactions, and false self disturbances. These difficulties also may present in clients who show a variety of clinical symptoms and syndromes.

3 Patients bring their pathological internalized object relations, primitive defenses, developmental deficits, as well as their capacities and strengths to the treatment situation.

4 Treatment can modify pathological internal structures or create facilitative and reparative experiences in which new and stronger structures are acquired.

5 Change processes in treatment result from both reparative and new experiences within the treatment relationship itself and from insight into and modification of entrenched object relations pathology.

6 Providing a therapeutic holding environment, pointing out dysfunctional relational patterns and defenses, engaging in a range of developmentally attuned techniques, and focusing on transference-countertransference dynamics, particularly with respect to what the client "induces" in the therapist or is "enacting" in the relationship are important components of treatment.

In contrast to object relations theory, self psychology places the self rather than internalized interpersonal relationships at the center of development. Whereas object relations theories tend to view the self as reflecting what the child takes in or internalizes from the outside, self psychology defines the self as an innate and enduring structure of the personality that has its own developmental track. It views the self as possessing organization, initiative, and potentialities, regulating self-esteem, and giving purpose and meaning to the person's life (Wolf, 1988: 182).

The following six propositions characterize self psychology's view of human development, psychopathology, and treatment.

1   Infants are born with innate potentialities for self development but require the responsiveness of the caretaking environment in order to develop a strong, cohesive self. The individual needs to have idealizable caretakers, experiences of validation, affirmation, a sense of feeling like others, and other forms of empathic selfobject responsiveness.

2   When the self-structure is weak and vulnerable as a result of unattuned, neglectful, or traumatic caretaking, both the self-concept and self-esteem regulation become impaired. The person may be at risk for developing self disorders and narcissistic vulnerability that lead to chronic problems or to periods of acute disruption later in life.

3   Clients bring their early unmet or thwarted selfobject needs to treatment, which provides them with a second chance to complete their development.

4   Treatment aims at strengthening self-structures, creating greater self-cohesion and self-esteem regulation, and enabling increased self-actualization and enjoyment of life.

5   Change results from the worker's empathic attunement to the client's subjective experience, optimal responsiveness to the client's needs, and empathic interpretations of the link between the client's current needs and problems and his or her early experiences with unattuned caretakers.

6   Engaging in empathic attunement and responsiveness, helping the client to develop and maintain a selfobject transference, exploring past caretaker failures and their sequelae, and removing obstacles to the worker's ability to be empathic to the client's selfobject needs and their manifestations, even when they appear to be demanding or unreasonable, are important components of the treatment.

Because both object relations and self psychological theories address the impact of interpersonal relationships on personality development, there are those who do not view these two frameworks as fundamentally different from one another (Greenberg & Mitchell, 1983; Bacal, 1991). Nevertheless, Kohut, who originated self psychology, saw his formulations as distinctive from those of object relations theory, and many of his followers have continued to hold to his position (Ornstein, 1991). Throughout the book, however, I shall strive to show how both theories can contribute to understanding and working with particular individuals.

Object relations theory and self psychology are not unitary frameworks. Object relations theory is a broad term that encompasses diverse concepts, and it has generated different and sometimes conflicting treatment approaches. For many years, the American object relations theorists such as Edith Jacobson and Margaret Mahler—who showed loyalty to Freud and his daughter, Anna—were highly critical of the writings of the British object relations theorists such as Melanie Klein, W. R. D. Fairbairn, D. W. Winnicott, and Harry Guntrip for rejecting many Freudian tenets. More recently, other theorists such as Otto Kernberg and Stephen Mitchell have attempted to put forth integrative models. Likewise, since the death of Heinz Kohut, who originated self psychology, some of his associates and followers, including Daniel Stern, Michael Basch, Arnold Goldberg, Howard Bacal, Joseph Lichtenberg, Robert Stolorow, Frank Lachmann, Beatrice Beebe, and Morton and Estelle Shane, have extended his ideas, and others have branched into different directions that have led to refinements and modifications of his views on development and the nature of treatment.

SIGNIFICANCE FOR SOCIAL WORK PRACTICE

Object relations theory and self psychology are holistic frameworks that are consistent with the humanistic stance, values, and person-environmental focus of the social work profession and fit well with the existing body of clinical social work theory and practice.

1 They are biopsychosocial theories that address the interplay among a person's innate endowment and interpersonal, familial, environmental, and cultural factors in shaping behavior.

2 They focus on a person's here-and-now functioning as well as on how past development has contributed to a person's capacities, talents, ambitions, values, patterns of relating, and sense of self.

3 They recognize the strengths and resilience of people and their push for growth as well as what goes wrong in the course of development.

4 The treatment approaches that stem from object relations theory and self psychology require a more human therapeutic environment and are optimistic about the reparative and facilitating role of the treatment relationship. They emphasize the importance of an individual's subjective experience, the therapist's need to be where the client is, and the mutual and reciprocal impact of client and worker.

5 Object relations and self psychological concepts apply to a broad range of problems, including life crises and transitions, the effects of physical and sexual abuse and other types of trauma, emotional disorders, substance abuse, physical illness, disability, loss of loved ones, violence, parenting and family problems, and work issues. They have implications not only for individual long-term treatment but also for crisis and short-term intervention and work with couples, families, and groups.

Along with Freudian drive theory and ego psychology, object relations theory and self psychology comprise the contemporary psychodynamic base of social work practice. Because of their divergent elements and emphases, no simple theoretical integration of these four frameworks is possible at present (Phillips, 1993; Pine, 1988). Yet, it is likely that each formulation has some value and no one particular perspective constitutes the only truth about human behavior. Consequently, it is important for practitioners to be competent in their understanding and use of diverse theoretical formulations and treatment models so that they can utilize them differentially depending on the needs of a given client. This eclecticism is necessary because it is likely that clients have difficulties at multiple and different levels, that some aspects of their problems may be more prominent at one time than another, and that some of their problems may be more readily explained and worked with from one framework than another. The need for flexibility in the use of a particular approach may result in confusion and stress for the practitioner because it is difficult to decide when to do what to whom.

IMPETUS FOR THE BOOK

There are numerous reasons for my choosing to write about object relations theory and self psychology despite my having been associated with
ego psychology for over fifteen years. The book received its impetus from
my long-standing interest in demonstrating the applicability of the major
concepts and treatment principles of contemporary psychodynamic theory to social work practice. In the years following the publication of the first
edition of *Ego Psychology and Social Work Practice* (Goldstein, 1984), which
became a widely used social work text and resource, object relations theory
and self psychology gained popularity in the social work and therapeutic
community. The second edition (Goldstein, 1995a) commented on new
directions in personality theory but it was beyond its scope to consider
these fully. The growing interest in object relations theory and self psychology has generated numerous books by social work authors (Applegate &
Bonovitz, 1995; Berzoff, Flanagan & Hertz, 1996; Brandell & Perlman,
1997; Edward & Sanville, 1996; Elson, 1986; Jackson, 1991; Levine, 1996;
Mishne, 1993; Rowe & MacIsaac, 1989; Seinfeld, 1990, 1991, 1993; Siegel,
1992). In most instances, these are geared to more advanced clinicians
engaged in psychotherapeutic work. Despite their value, there is a need for
a basic social work text that describes the main concepts and treatment
principles of object relations theory and self psychology and shows their
application to a broad range of problems encountered by social work practitioners.

A second reason for undertaking the task of writing this book arises
from my own interest in and use of object relations theory and self psychology in my work with clients and supervisees. Employing these frameworks has expanded my ability to understand and relate to a wide range of
clients and has produced fundamental changes in the ways in which I listen, what I observe, where I focus, and how I use myself in the treatment
process. I cannot imagine working without drawing on these perspectives
and believe that a knowledge of these frameworks will help other social
work practitioners.

A third motivation for writing this book stems from concerns about the
current state of education for direct practice. In contrast to earlier times,

currently there is little, if any, curriculum space allocated to the teaching of psychodynamic theories. Consequently, students graduate without acquiring even basic understanding of this body of thought. Upon graduation, many social workers take courses at psychodynamically oriented training institutes, but they are taught by members of other disciplines who are not conversant or identified with the nature of social work practice and with the types of clients that social workers generally see in agency practice. It is my hope that a basic social work text that describes the major concepts of object relations theory and self psychology and their implications for social work practice will provide trainees and instructors with a resource that can guide their learning and teaching of these important frameworks.

There is an old joke that aptly conveys one of the consequences for the practitioner of the multiplicity of psychodynamic theories that exist at present. As the story goes, a man visits a psychiatrist and complains of stress at his place of employment, explaining that his job is to sort the oranges, grapefruits, and melons that roll down a chute by putting each type of fruit in an appropriate container. When the psychiatrist asks, "But what is hard about that? It seems so simple," the client replies, "Doctor, you don't understand. All day long it's decisions, decisions, decisions."

Although this book may not make treatment decisions any easier, I hope that it will enrich practitioners' knowledge base and that it will be read not only by those social work practitioners, students, and instructors who are interested in working within an object relations or self psychological framework but by all those who are committed to direct practice. The ideas generated by these theories offer new ways of understanding the needs and problems, struggles and triumphs, of our clients and open exciting and creative approaches to the interventive process.

THE FOCUS AND PLAN OF THE BOOK

This book is written primarily for social work students, practitioners, and educators as well as for trainees and members of other mental health disciplines. It will focus on the practical use of the concepts and treatment principles of object relations theory and self psychology to the clinical situation. Although it presents these two frameworks as distinctive, it attempts to show how they each can be used in a complementary way to work with a broad range of clients and client problems. I have tried to write in a hands-on, user friendly style. In most instances, the numerous case examples and excerpts that I have utilized throughout the book are based on my own practice, supervisory, and teaching experience. They have been disguised and edited and sometimes reflect composites of similar client situations.

The book is divided into two parts as follows:

Part I first describes the significance of object relations theory and self psychology and traces the evolution of this body of knowledge, considering both the similarities and differences among these frameworks and their recent trends and new directions. It then describes their major structural and developmental concepts, views of psychopathology, and treatment principles and techniques.

Part II discusses and illustrates the implications of object relations theory and self psychology for social work practice. It starts with a discussion of the nature of assessment and treatment planning and moves to a consideration of beginning phase issues, particularly the establishment of a therapeutic holding environment, overcoming obstacles to developing a positive relationship, and the use of selective techniques. It then discusses important middle phase issues, including the ways in which the worker addresses disruptions, enactments, and resistances that arise in the course of treatment. The book shows the application of object relations and self psychological concepts to the treatment of clients who are undergoing life transitions, illness and disability, loss of significant others, and other stressful life events, and to those manifesting special problems such as substance abuse, child maltreatment, and the effects of childhood sexual abuse. It concludes with a chapter on couple and family treatment.

Although the process of helping clients to improve their lives has been challenging, it has been personally gratifying. It has expanded my "self" more than I could ever have imagined. It is my hope that this book will prompt students and practitioners to try out some new ideas and to enrich their work with clients.

2

THE EVOLUTION OF OBJECT RELATIONS THEORY AND SELF PSYCHOLOGY

In order to understand the evolution and significance of object relations theory and self psychology, it is necessary to set the stage for their emergence by reviewing earlier formulations. This chapter first will briefly review the development of Freudian classical psychoanalytic theory and ego psychology and then it will trace the evolution of object relations theory and self psychology.

CLASSICAL FREUDIAN THEORY

Sigmund Freud, the originator of classical psychoanalytic theory, was born in Moravia in 1856 but spent most of his life in Vienna. Wanting to be a scientist, Freud underwent medical training in neurology but entered private practice for economic reasons and because of the limited opportunities for academic advancement for Jews. In Paris, he studied with Jean Charcot, a French psychiatrist who utilized hypnosis in the treatment of mental disorders, and soon began to experiment with Joseph Breuer's talking methods for relieving symptoms. Freud gradually evolved his own views about the origins of mental symptoms and their treatment.

Freud began writing when Darwin put forth his theory of evolution, which linked human beings to their animal ancestry. Medicine was emerging as a science and was dominated by the mechanistic and energic principles of the Helmholz School, which viewed mental disorders as organic in nature (Wyss, 1966: 45–145). The psychology of the day focused on consciousness; philosophical writings prized rationality; and society reflected the aftermath of a repressive and restrictive Victorian period with respect to sexuality and the role of women.

Freudian theory derived largely from accounts of childhood related to Freud by his adult patients during the course of their treatment. His beliefs about the importance of the unconscious and the "seething caldron" of a person's instinctual life were revolutionary and represented a radical departure from prevailing views about consciousness and rationality. Likewise, his views about the significance of infantile sexuality shocked many people in the lay and scientific communities. Despite the controversy Freudian theory engendered, it gathered numerous followers. Nevertheless, criticism and rejection of Freud's ideas both by those outside and within his inner circle contributed to his feelings of depression and embitterment. During his lifetime, Freud experienced anti-Semitism, witnessed the devastation of World War I and the rise of Hitler, withstood many losses, and suffered from cancer of the jaw, for which he took pain-relieving drugs for many years. He continued to do research and to write extensively, however, until his death in 1939 in London, where he had fled to escape the Nazis (Jones, 1953; Gay, 1988).

Freud's writings reflected his pessimistic view of human nature (Horney, 1945: 19). He viewed infants as innately pleasure-seeking and as driven by sexual and aggressive instincts, which sought immediate discharge. He placed considerable importance on psychic determinism (that all behavior is motivated and does not occur by chance); the role of unconscious fantasies, wishes, fears, prohibitions, and conflict in the genesis of emotional disorders; the experience of anxiety and the resultant defenses utilized to protect against it; and the impact of fixation and regression points related to childhood sexuality (psychosexual stages) in the development of personality traits and psychopathology (Mishne, 1993: 147–168; Mitchell & Black, 1995: 1–22; Greenberg & Mitchell, 1983: 21–78).

Unlike the theorists who followed, Freud did not believe that human life was motivated by an innate tie to others. He saw interpersonal relationships or object relations as a by-product of the child's growing libidinal (sexual) investment in others and use of others and inanimate objects to discharge or relieve instinctual tension (Mitchell & Black, 1995: 39). Thus, he minimized both the relational aspects and impact of the child's actual interactions with others on personality development.

In Freud's early topographic theory, he divided the mind into the regions of the unconscious, preconscious, and conscious (Freud, 1900). Later, in what became known as structural theory, he classified the mind into the id (the seat of the drives), the ego (the executive arm of the personality), and the superego (the conscience and the ego-ideal) and revised his thinking about the ego's role in perceiving anxiety and mediating conflict among these internal structures (Freud, 1923, 1926, 1933, 1940).

A significant aspect of Freud's developmental theory was his description of the psychosexual stages (oral, anal, phallic or oedipal, latency, and genital). He focused particular attention on the controversial oedipal period, when the child was 5 to 6 years of age and already possessed a more intact intrapsychic structure. He argued that the child's fantasies connected to the Oedipus complex, in which the parent of the opposite sex is desired and the parent of the same sex is feared, result in anxiety and conflict (Freud, 1905). According to Freud, when this stage is resolved optimally, superego development, gender identification, and sexual object choice ensue, but when it is not, the basis for later neurotic symptoms is laid down. This view replaced an earlier one in which Freud thought that parental seduction or other types of sexual trauma were at the root of adult neuroses. In abandoning his so-called seduction hypothesis, Freud opted in favor of fantasy rather than the objective realities of the child's life in explaining adult psychopathology.

Consistent with Freud's ideas about development and psychopathology, psychoanalytic treatment aimed to relieve neurotic symptoms by making the unconscious conflicts that were thought to underlie them conscious. Freud thought that once conscious, these conflicts would come under the ego's control. Psychoanalytic treatment attempted to stimulate a therapeutic regression in which patients would come into contact with their early childhood experiences and conflicts and relive these in the treatment relationship (transference) and to enable patients to recall their childhood wishes, fantasies, and fears. The procedures and techniques that Freud and his later followers recommended included free association; the patient's lying on a couch; dim lighting; frequent sessions (as many as five a week); a focus on the patient's dreams, fantasy life, and early childhood memories; the analyst's abstinence or non-gratification of the patient's expressed wishes; the analyst's anonymity with respect to aspects of his or her personal feelings, attitudes, and personal life; and the analyst's neutrality and reliance on interpretation. In order to tolerate the demands of the treatment and use it optimally, patients needed to possess personality strengths, psychological-mindedness, and the ability to engage in an often lengthy and intense process. Thus, psychoanalysis favored those whose difficulties were at the higher end of the health-illness spectrum and who were self-reflective and verbal.

EGO PSYCHOLOGY

The writings of the ego psychologists—including Anna Freud, Heinz Hartmann, David Rapaport, and others—introduced expansions and revisions of Freudian psychoanalytic theory beginning in the late 1930s and continuing through the post–World War II period. The table on pages 23–25 compares the major components of classical Freudian theory and ego psychology.

It is noteworthy that ego psychology originated in Europe but quickly took root in the United States, to which many European psychoanalysts immigrated in order to escape Nazi persecution. They found the intellectual climate in the United States to be stimulating and open. No doubt the resilience necessary for many of these individuals to survive and relocate to a different country contributed to a respect for human strength under conditions of adversity, and the freer American atmosphere generated hopefulness (Hamilton, 1958: 22).

Ego psychologists attempted to correct for Freud's instinctual emphasis, minimization of the strength of the ego, focus on the unconscious, and inattention to the impact of reality. Ego psychology drew attention to the individual's more innate and autonomous capacities, the more conscious, rational, and problem-solving capacities of the ego, and the individual's active attempts to adapt to the environment. It also incorporated new ideas regarding the impact of interpersonal relationships, the environment, and the culture.

ANNA FREUD

Freud's oldest daughter, Anna, who is known for her major contributions to the study of child development and treatment, was among the first psychoanalysts to strengthen and elaborate on his conception of the ego. She became a significant and forceful proponent and advocate of psychoanalytic ego psychology both within the British Psychoanalytic Society and the United States. Anna never married, was fiercely loyal to her father, and at different times served as his secretary, companion, business and personal courier, colleague, and nurse. She died in 1982 (Dyer, 1983: 1–44).

In *Ego and the Mechanisms of Defense* (1936), Anna Freud described the adaptiveness of the ego's defenses in helping the individual cope with external reality, delineated a greater repertoire of defenses, and showed how their origins were linked to specific developmental phases. Also elaborating on the role of the defenses, Wilhelm Reich (1949), another psychoanalyst, described how character traits and defenses become crucial components of a person's personality.

In keeping with these new emphases, psychoanalytic treatment expanded its focus to working with the ego's defenses—which Anna Freud believed were the major resistances in treatment—strengthening more adaptive defenses, and modifying pathological character traits. It is noteworthy that in her work with children, Anna Freud also began to use environmental interventions as part of her own adaptation of psychoanalysis (Levine, 1996: 42).

HEINZ HARTMANN

Heinz Hartmann generally is considered to be the father of ego psychology. Born in Vienna in 1894 to a prominent, politically active, and intellectual family, Hartmann was exposed to a range of people and ideas. He studied medicine, became a psychiatrist, and entered analysis with Freud. Having a wide range of interests and educated broadly, Hartmann became a synthesizer of many diverse areas of knowledge. His goal was to transform classical psychoanalytic theory into a more general psychology of human behavior and to address the impact of the real world on development. He collaborated extensively with Ernst Kris and Alfred Lowenstein, and their collective writings were seminal in the development of ego psychology. Hartmann died in 1970 (Mitchell & Black, 1995: 34–35).

In *Ego Psychology and the Problem of Adaptation* (1939), Hartmann proposed that the ego is an innate and autonomous structure with its own energy source. He argued that human beings possess inborn rudimentary capacities and are born "preadapted" to an "average expectable environ- ment" for the species as a result of evolution. He described a set of ego func- tions that are "conflict-free," having a "primary autonomy" from the drives, and wrote that "apparatuses of perception, thinking, object-comprehen- sion, intention, language, recall-phenomena, productivity, motor develop- ment (grasping, crawling, and walking), maturation, and learning processes generally develop outside the area of conflict" (Guntrip, 1973: 107). Hart- mann believed that these capacities mature during the course of develop- ment given certain basic environmental conditions. He also viewed the ego as having an organizing or synthetic function and emphasized how all ego capacities can be used for the purposes of adaptation to the outside world.

Following Hartmann, numerous authors delineated the concept of ego functioning more systematically and attempted to integrate ego psycho- logical concepts with Freudian theory. For example, Bellak, Hurvich & Gediman (1973; Goldstein, 1995a: 53–71) delineated twelve ego functions and traced their development, and David Rapaport (1960) described six vantage points from which the personality could be viewed, including the topographic (conscious, preconscious, unconscious), the structural (id, ego, superego), the genetic-developmental (historical), the dynamic (the drives), the economic (distribution of energy), and the adaptive (relation- ship to reality).

ERIK ERIKSON

Although Hartmann recognized the role of interpersonal and environ- mental influences on development, his writings tended to be abstract and theoretical rather than specific and personal (Guntrip, 1973: 103–144). In contrast, Eric Erikson, another prominent ego psychologist, described human interactions in more real and human terms. His writings were philosophical and humanistic in tone, highly readable, and achieved con- siderable popularity.

Born in 1902, Erikson never had a formal education beyond high school but nevertheless became a prominent psychoanalytic author. He was brilliant, creative, and artistic and was invited to teach at a school based on psychoanalytic principles that was headed by Anna Freud and her close friend Dorothy Burlingham. Erikson also entered analysis with Anna. He moved to the United States in 1933, where he lived until his death in 1994 (Mitchell & Black, 1995: 142–143).

In *Childhood and Society* (1950) and *Identity and the Life Cycle* (1959), Erikson portrayed ego development as biopsychosocial in nature. He was among the first theorists to describe the nature and process of forming and maintaining an identity and to portray adulthood as a period in which people were capable of growth and change. Erikson described how progressive mastery of developmental tasks in each of eight successive stages of the human life cycle resulted in a solid sense of identity. He also showed how the transition from one stage to another constituted a "healthy" crisis or period of instability. He called attention not only to biological and psychodynamic factors but also to interpersonal, environmental, societal, and cultural influences in the developmental process.

Erikson's views, along with those of Robert White (1959, 1963), who postulated that a person is born with a drive toward mastery and competence, had considerable impact on social work practice. They emphasized the importance of early developmental task mastery in the acquisition of a solid ego identity and showed how the caretaking and social environment provide the conditions that foster mastery, competence, and a positive or healthy identity all through life. Erikson's ideas also contributed to the use of more supportive treatment strategies aimed at helping caretakers to meet children's needs more optimally and enabling clients to deal with the problems engendered by life-cycle transitions and failures in mastering previous life stages.

Psychoanalytically oriented treatment following ego-psychological principles expanded to encompass patients whose egos were less intact and who showed developmental arrests prior to the oedipal stage. A more supportive treatment approach, which attempted to use a patient's strengths in order to address and alleviate certain problems and to strengthen, build, or facilitate a person's ego functioning or coping, evolved alongside a modifying approach that aimed at structural or personality change. Supportive treatment might employ encouragement, ventilation, reassurance, and suggestion instead of insight-oriented techniques, and focus on a person's current life situation and his or her more conscious thoughts and feelings and problem-solving capacities rather than on childhood conflicts. Even in more modifying treatments, there was greater attention to the more here-and-now aspects of the patient's life situation, including the real relationship in contrast to an exclusive focus on the transference relationship with the therapist (Greenson, 1974).

AMERICAN OBJECT RELATIONS THEORY

Despite ego psychology's potential in bridging the individual and the environment, most early ego psychologists retained Freud's instinctual and mechanistic emphasis and, with the exception of Erikson, tended to minimize the more personal impact of the caretaking and social environment. They viewed object relations as an ego function that referred to a person's capacity for mature interpersonal relationships.

Numerous theorists began to expand and revise their conception of object relations, often in response to the findings of studies of infants and their mothers. Rene Spitz, Edith Jacobson and Margaret Mahler were developmentalists who were trained in classical psychoanalytic theory and ego psychology. In contrast to many of the British object relations theorists, who will be discussed later in the chapter, Jacobson and Mahler adhered to Freud's dual instinct and structural theory but focused attention on how the developing infant builds up *internalized* representations of self and others that form the core of one's identity, view of the world, relationships with others, and personality traits and capacities. Jacobson and Mahler usually are credited with building object relations thinking into ego psychology. These two women, along with another prominent theorist, Otto Kernberg, who attempted to integrate Freudian theory and ego psychology with Kleinian object relations theory, sometimes are referred to as American object relations theorists.

The writings of the American-born psychiatrist Harry Stack Sullivan (1953, 1956) also reflected an interpersonal view of personality that anticipated later theoretical developments in many respects. Although attracting a core of followers, Sullivan's work remained outside of mainstream psy-

COMPARISON OF CLASSICAL FREUDIAN THEORY AND EGO PSYCHOLOGY

	Classical Freudian Theory	Ego Psychology
Focus of Theory	Inborn instincts and their vicissitudes; unconscious childhood conflict; neurotic symptom formation and personality traits	Innate ego functions and the role of past and present person-environmental transactions on ego development and adaptation throughout life
Factors Influencing Theory	Freud's scientific bent	Reaction to Freud's emphasis on instincts and minimization of ego and reality
	Medicine in its infancy; organic view of mental disorders	Interest in making psychoanalysis a psychology of normal development
	Emphasis on rationality	Interest in impact of interpersonal, social, and cultural factors
	Darwin's theory of evolution	Focus on adaptive capacities
	Helmholtz school of medicine—man is like a machine	Development of behavioral and social sciences
	Victorian society	Effects of emigration from Europe and of new United States culture
	Freud's personality and long illness	
	Defections by members of Freud's inner circle	
	World War I and Hitler's rise to power	
Nature of Individual	People are driven by sexual and aggressive drives and unconscious wishes and fears; people are doomed to suffer or destroy unless impulses are tamed; behavior is strictly determined; childhood events are important	People are born with innate adaptive capacity; the person is a biopsychosocial being; early childhood and adult life events all through the life cycle are critical
Structural Concepts	Id, ego, and superego	The ego's numerous functions are described and emphasized
Developmental Concepts	Infantile sexuality and psychosexual stages	The maturation of conflict-free or autonomous ego functioning
	Fixation and regression	The role of the average expectable environment
	Identification	Psychosocial stages
	Anxiety, conflict, and defense	The importance of stage-specific parenting
		The process of coping and adaptation
		Person-environmental mutuality
		Stress and crisis

	Classical Freudian Theory	Ego Psychology
Nature of Problems	Individual neurotic symptoms Neurotic characters Unconscious oedipal conflict Fixations, regression, and defenses Compromise formations	Individual problems in ego functioning stemming from developmental difficulties Life transitions and stressful events Ego deficits Maladaptive defenses Lack of fit between inner capacities and external resources or conditions Maladaptive coping
Nature of Change	Insight and conflict resolution	Ego mastery Learning and problem solving Emotionally corrective experiences Better person-environmental fit
Treatment Goals	To cure symptoms To modify pathological character traits and patterns To make the unconscious conscious To increase rational choice and behavior To develop insight into childhood conflicts and how they are influencing current behavior	To increase the individual's adaptive capacities or ego functioning To neutralize conflict To modify maladaptive defenses and personality traits and patterns To build ego where deficits exist To improve the fit between individual capacities and environmental conditions
Treatment Principles and Techniques	Catharsis Free association Therapeutic regression Focus on dreams, fantasies, and childhood past Analysis of defense and resistance Analysis of transference Reliance on insight-oriented techniques: clarification, confrontation, and interpretation	*Ego-Supportive* Here-and-now and reality oriented Focus on conscious thoughts and feelings Reliance on more sustaining and structured techniques; ventilation; reassurance; advice; rational discussion; education; reflection Experiential use of relationship geared to developmental needs Selective focus on past Environmental provision or restructuring *Ego-Modifying:* Greater reliance on insight-oriented techniques and interpreting the transference

	Classical Freudian Theory	Ego Psychology
Nature of Relation-ship	Therapist anonymity	Genuineness, realness, and support important
	Therapist neutrality	
	Transference relationship important	Real relationship and positive transfer-ence important
	Non-gratification or frustration of needs	Use of the relationship to provide correc-tive emotional experiences and to facili-tate development
Applicability	Neuroses and neurotic character types	Most problems in coping
	Those with ego strength	Those with a range of ego strengths and weaknesses
	Those with stable lives	
		Those in most life circumstances
	Those with ability to make financial and time commitment	

choanalysis for many years because he rejected Freudian drive theory (Aron, 1996: 2). It has been suggested that other, more personal reasons also contributed to the dismissal of Sullivan as a theorist (DeLaCour, 1996: 217). Nevertheless, many of his ideas were appropriated by others and were a precursor to current relational theory.

RENE SPITZ

Little is written about Rene Spitz's (1897–1974) early life, but he became a seminal researcher and attachment theorist. Although preserving Freud's view that infants are pleasure-seeking, his research provided grounding for the emerging emphasis on the importance of interpersonal relationships. According to Mitchell and Black (1995: 40), "Spitz cut a conceptual course for theory-building midway between Freud's drive theory and radical object relations theories . . . The libidinal object provides the essential human connectedness within which all psychological development occurs."

Throughout his life, Spitz devoted himself to the study of early mother-child relationships and their impact on ego development (Spitz, 1945; 1946a, b & c; 1959, 1965). At the beginning of his professional career, he observed the harmful effects on children who were left in foundling homes from birth of being deprived of human touch and nurture even if their physical survival needs were met. As a result of what he named "hospital-ism," Spitz described the development of a condition called "marasmus," in which children became depressed and withdrawn, failed to thrive and develop, and in many instances became sickly and died. He thought that this condition could be reversed if the children were reunited with their mothers within the first three months of life. Spitz concluded that children needed social stimulation in order to develop optimally, and his early work shed light on the nature of children's depressive reactions when separated from their mothers.

Spitz's later studies produced a wealth of data on the specific effects of maternal attitudes and behavior on the child's normal ego development and on the importance of the mother's ability to regulate herself in accordance with the child's needs. He identified critical periods in early childhood during which children acquire important building blocks of personality functioning (organizers of the psyche) that form as a result of adequate caretaking and showed how the failure to meet certain needs at the right time leads to developmental deficiencies that cannot be corrected later (Goldstein, 1995a: 11).

EDITH JACOBSON

Born in 1897 and trained in medicine and psychoanalysis in the 1930s in Germany, Edith Jacobson became a member of the Berlin Psychoanalytic Society. Known as a courageous woman with strong convictions, Jacobson, like Hartmann, Mahler, and many others, was among those analysts who immigrated to the United States to escape Nazi persecution, but not before she was imprisoned briefly (Mitchell & Black, 1995: 49). Settling in New York, she became a private practitioner and a prominent member of the New York Psychoanalytic Society. From the 1940s to the early 1970s, she demonstrated her brilliance as a thinker. Although her writings are very abstract and theoretical, she was known for developing a "seamless, coherent model that accounts for the traditional elements of id, ego, superego, and instincts, as well as object relations" (St. Clair, 1996: 91). Thus, without officially abandoning Freudian theory, Jacobson managed to show the effects of interpersonal relationships and their internalization on the psychic structure. Jacobson's description of the complexity of the internalization process was comprehensive, and her writings about superego formation and feeling states were extremely helpful in understanding severe depression and other types of affective disorders (Jacobson, 1971). She died in 1978 after having a very rich and rewarding professional life.

In Jacobson's seminal book, *The Self and the Object World* (1964), she reworked many basic Freudian concepts to include an object relations component. Jacobson distinguished the actual self and object from the internalization of self- and object-images. She showed how infants acquire self- and object-images or representations based on their relationships with others and how these affective experiences are linked to and consolidate libidinal and aggressive drives. For example, pleasant and loving relationships will reinforce libidinal instincts and result in positive images of the object and the self. Jacobson was the first theorist to describe the infant's acquisition of an affective repertoire of feeling states based on his or her early caretaking experiences. She also delineated the evolution of superego development and put forth a new perspective on the origins and nature of depressive and manic-depressive disorders.

MARGARET MAHLER

Born in Hungary in 1897, the same year as Jacobson, Margaret Mahler trained in Vienna and became a pediatrician and child analyst. She immigrated to the United States in 1938 and worked with emotionally disturbed children before eventually establishing a center for observational studies of children and mothers. Mahler's early work dealt with what she called childhood autistic and symbiotic psychoses (1968). When Mahler began to study more normal children, she put forth her own distinctive views based on naturalistic studies of child-mother interactions as well as her clinical work (Mahler, 1951, 1968, 1971, 1972; Mahler, Pine & Bergman, 1975). Her ideas evolved in harmony with those of Edith Jacobson. Mahler died in 1985.

Like Jacobson, Mahler believed that the drives were important and adhered to many of Freud's psychosexual concepts, but she viewed the child's relationship with the primary love object, the mother, rather than the child's drives per se as central to human development (Settlage, 1994: 21). She thought that a child's psychological development begins through the process of attachment to the mother and proceeds by means of a progressive detachment from her (St. Clair, 1996: 110) and that sexual and aggressive drives are shaped within the context of early interpersonal relationships. She called this process *separation-individuation,* in which the term *separation* refers to the infant's gradual disengagement from a fused state with the primary love object, and the term *individuation* signifies the development of the child's unique characteristics (Goldstein, 1995: 117–127). Although separation-individuation issues reverberate all through life, successful progression through the separation-individuation process results in the development of self-regulatory functions, the capacity for engaging in more mature relationships with others, and an intact and integrated intrapsychic structure.

Separation-individuation deals with the preoedipal period and consists of the four main subphases of differentiation, practicing, rapprochement, and on the way to object constancy, each of which consists of developmental tasks. Because there is a need for mutual regulation, the child and mother negotiate each subphase together, and the mother must encourage and support the child's separation-individuation. The child's progression from one subphase to the next involves loss for mother and child, which is counterbalanced by their pleasure and satisfaction in the child's newfound achievements (Settlage, 1994: 22).

Because Jacobson and Mahler focused on preoedipal development, their writings shed light on the severe problems manifested by those suffering from early object relations and separation-individuation difficulties. They contributed to the development of new treatments for individuals with depression (Jacobson, 1971) and borderline and narcissistic pathology (Adler, 1985; Blanck & Blanck, 1974, 1979; Kernberg, 1975, 1976; Masterson, 1972, 1976; Masterson & Rinsley, 1975). Some authors recommended the use of more specific techniques geared to the particular subphases at which developmental lesions occurred and to a reparative use of the therapeutic relationship to build or facilitate higher levels of ego functioning and object relations.

OTTO KERNBERG

Otto Kernberg was born in Vienna in 1928 and his family immigrated to Chile when he was a young boy. There he was trained as a physician and psychoanalyst and became familiar with the work of Melanie Klein and other British object relations theorists, who will be discussed later in the chapter. When Kernberg moved to the United States, he occupied both clinical and administrative positions at the Menninger Foundation in Topeka, Kansas before settling in New York in 1973. Although he began to put forth his own distinctive ego psychological-object relations approach when still in Kansas, he became more prolific as a writer, presenter, and theoretician when he arrived in New York. He was appointed director of an inpatient psychiatric unit at New York State Psychiatric Institute and then Medical Director of New York Hospital–Cornell Medical Center's Westchester division. Although retired from that position, Kernberg is still active professionally. He has had a long-standing marriage with Paulina Kernberg, a child analyst, and has three grown children.

Although Kernberg adhered to Freudian drive and structural theory and credited Jacobson and Mahler for their contributions, his writings show a strong Kleinian influence (1975, 1976, 1984). Thus, many writers consider Kernbergian theory to be a bridge between frameworks, which were polarized at the time he began to write (Mitchell & Black, 1995: 172–174). As will be discussed below, Kernberg, like Klein, tended to minimize interpersonal and environmental influences on personality development and favored the view that instincts—particularly innate aggression, and primitive fantasies and defenses—shape the internalization of infants' self- and object-representations. He described a series of sequential stages that trace the infant's acquisition of internal self- and object-representations and affect dispositions under the influence of libidinal and aggressive drives (St. Clair, 1996: 133). Consequently, his writings have a very different emphasis than those of Mahler, who focused upon the impact of the *actual* interpersonal transactions between caretaker and child.

Kernberg's writings covered a variety of clinical and theoretical topics, but his major contribution was his systematic work on the delineation, diagnosis, and treatment of borderline and narcissistic disorders, which has been very influential and controversial. The Kernbergian approach to the treatment of borderline conditions is highly interpretive and confrontative, sometimes utilizing strict limits and structure. Kernberg advised therapists to refrain from actively providing an ego-supportive or reparative experience. His particular views on narcissistic pathology and its treatment in particular often have been contrasted with Kohut's more empathically based self-psychological approach. Followers of these two vastly different frameworks continue to debate their relevance and efficacy (Consolini, 1999).

THE BRITISH SCHOOL OF OBJECT RELATIONS

The British object-relations theorists constituted a group of analysts, including Melanie Klein, W. R. D. Fairbairn, D. W. Winnicott, Harry Guntrip, Wilfred Bion, Michael Balint, John Bowlby, and others, who began to put forth their views well before Freud's death in 1939. They wrote in reaction to Freudian classical psychoanalytic theory and ego psychology and thus comprised a different theoretical current from American object relations theory.

MELANIE KLEIN

The youngest of four children, Melanie Klein was born in Vienna in 1882 of Jewish parentage. Her father, a physician, worked as a dentist, and her mother also was employed. Although wanting to be a doctor, Klein never completed medical training. She married and had three children. After moving to Budapest, she entered treatment for depression in 1914 with Sandor Ferenczi, a somewhat radical disciple of Freud, and at Ferenczi's urging, Klein became a child psychoanalyst. In 1924 and 1925 in Berlin, she underwent a second analysis with Karl Abraham, a close associate of Freud, and after Abraham's untimely death, Freud's biographer Ernest Jones invited her to London, where her writings became more innovative. Klein treated severely disturbed children, many of whom were offspring of her colleagues, and she became interested in the contributions of the early mother-infant relationship to their pathology. She wrote and presented papers extensively, and her ideas gathered adherents but also became controversial in European psychoanalytic circles. A deep and long-lasting schism developed in the British Psychoanalytic Society between Klein and her followers and Anna Freud and her group. Their fight widened into a more general philosophical and theoretical battle that spread to the United States. Klein was denounced for betraying Freudian principles (Hughes,

1989: 21–26) and her writings were considered to be heretical among American psychoanalysts until recently.

In considering the impact of Klein's life experiences on the development of her ideas, it is noteworthy to acknowledge the major personal losses that she experienced, including the deaths of her sister when Klein was a child, her brother when she was 20, her father soon after she met her husband, her mother when Klein was 32, one of her two sons when he was a young man, and her analyst, Abraham, while she was in treatment. Moreover, Klein's marriage ended in divorce, and her daughter, Melitta Schmideberg, also a psychoanalyst, attacked her views publicly. Klein herself died in London in 1960 (Hughes, 1989: 8–14).

In the first phase of her writing, which adhered to Freudian theory for the most part, Klein laid down the principles of child psychoanalysis, reworked Freud's developmental timetable by arguing that the child was capable of certain types of mental activities at an early age, and elaborated on the importance of the child's fantasy (in Klein's writings referred to as phantasy) life (Segal, 1974). In the second and third phases of her work, which began in 1934, Klein put forth many original ideas that departed from Freudian theory significantly (Burch, 1988; Greenberg & Mitchell, 1983: 119–150; Mitchell & Black, 1995: 85–111). One contemporary author (Burch, 1988: 125) observed that "at first encounter Melanie Klein's work reads like an exploration of the bizarre, even the psychotic elements of the human psyche. . . . She is concerned, perhaps more than other psychoanalytic theorists, with the negative side of human emotions. . . . [The] psychic life of babies is detailed as a series of frightening, sadistic, and repellent fantasies."

Like Freud, Klein emphasized the power of the instincts, particularly the aggressive drive, but unlike him, she argued that the goal of life was relationships with others (objects) rather than instinctual gratification. She believed that infants possess an innate awareness of objects, and that their fantasy life is about their relationships to such objects or part-objects, since the infant may not be able to perceive or imagine the whole object (Klein, 1948, 1957).

Klein gave a more significant role to the impact of fantasied rather than actual relationships in the development of internalized object relations but allowed for the impact of real objects in confirming or modifying the infant's views (Segal, 1974: 15–16). She believed that the infant's early fantasies about the object were filled with envy, greed, and destructive impulses and that the infant's ego, from birth, was capable of organizing experience and using defenses such as splitting, projective identification, idealization, and denial to protect the infant from resultant anxiety.

Klein originated the concept of the paranoid/schizoid and depressive positions, to which she gave precedence over Freud's emphasis on psychosexual stages. She showed how these two positions, which form the basis of personality and psychopathology, arise early in development as a result of repetitive cycles of projection and introjection. Paranoid and depressive states may cripple the person or—as Wilfred Bion, an analyst and student of Klein's, speculated—the infant's capacity for relating and ability to perceive and understand reality may be destroyed (Mitchell & Black, 1995: 102–106). This occurs because the infant's fantasied relationship to objects may be so painful that he or she not only angrily attacks the object but also his or her own mental processes that link the infant to others.

Klein regarded the transference, or relationship between the analyst and patient, as activating the patient's inner world, resulting in the experience of intense primitive fantasies, impulses, fears, and defenses. She advocated interpretations of the deepest layers of the patient's inner states and defenses and believed that all individuals experience similar thoughts and fears, and she did not differentiate from patient to patient according to the severity of their problems.

Klein saw children's play as reflecting their disturbing inner states and believed it was important to communicate her understanding of these through interpretations aimed at the point of the child's maximum anxieties. It was this approach that angered Anna Freud and others, who favored more supportive interventions that respected the fragility of the child's ego. They accused Klein of bypassing the ego and assaulting the child (Greenson, 1974: 133–135, 169–170).

W. R. D. FAIRBAIRN

William Ronald Dodds Fairbairn was born in Scotland in 1889. An only child, he was lonely and isolated. His parents were quite religious, austere, and strict and he was sent away to school when he was nine years old. He studied philosophy in college and became a minister briefly before entering medical school after World War I. Fairbairn read psychoanalytic writings extensively, and in 1923 he underwent treatment for a year with a relatively unknown Jungian analyst and then established a practice in psychotherapy. At one point in his career, he worked with delinquent youth who had been severely abused in childhood. He married in 1926 and had three children. His first marriage ended when his wife died in 1952 and he remarried in 1959. During his life, Fairbairn had serious bouts with depression and alcoholism and died in 1964 from a combination of these maladies and Parkinson's disease (Hughes, 1989: 14–17).

Because he lived in Scotland all of his life, Fairbairn remained isolated from and did not have personal allegiance to other psychoanalysts and maintained his independence intellectually. In Fairbairn's early papers, he showed some allegiance to Freud and Klein. By 1946, however, his massive revision of Freudian theory based on his extensive work with schizoid patients and his own intellectual differences with Klein became more apparent. Despite becoming a member of the British Psychoanalytic Society, he was not regarded as well-trained and analyzed. He and Winnicott formed an independent or middle group (between the Freudians and Kleinians) within the British Psychoanalytic Society (Hughes, 1989: 21–26).

Fairbairn's theory (1952, 1954) has been described as the most "pure" object relations model because of its emphasis on psychological and environmental and minimization of biological factors in development (St. Clair, 1996: 55). Arguing that human beings possess a primary drive toward relating to others, Fairbairn totally rejected Freud's concept of an innate aggressive drive and instead argued that the frustration of not feeling loved or lovable, or that one's love is welcome and valued, results in aggressive impulses.

Fairbairn envisioned the ego as a holistic and intact structure that possessed its own energy and potentialities and that was directed at object-seeking rather than pleasure-seeking. He also disagreed strongly with Klein's assertion that personality develops as a result of *fantasied* interactions with objects and chided her for not going far enough in her thinking.

Instead, he argued that it was *real* rather than fantasied objects that result in personality development, and that if such relationships with others are positive generally, the ego remains whole. He believed that it was the inability of external objects to provide for the infant's needs, and the frustrations that the child experiences in significant early relationships, that thwart development.

Fairbairn focused on the results of severe environmental frustration and explained how children deal with the presence of "bad" external objects by taking on the burden of being bad themselves rather than seeing the parents as bad. This "moral defense" allows them some hope and a sense of outer security at the price of inner insecurity . . . since it is better to be a sinner in a world ruled by God than to live in a world ruled by the devil (Fairbairn, 1943:66–67).

Fairbairn also argued that when infants are unable to escape from their bad experiences in reality, they withdraw from the external world of real objects psychologically for the purpose of protection. But this withdrawal is terrifying because of the aloneness that accompanies it. Consequently, infants compensate for the disconnection from others by building up a world of internal bad objects that are based on what was once external. In this way, they maintain a sense of connection to, while seemingly freeing themselves from, the control of others. In this process, the ego and internal objects become split and repressed and constitute a closed system (the endopsychic structure) that takes on a life of its own. They cannot relinquish the tie to their bad internal objects for fear of being alone, progress from infantile dependence to mature dependence, or establish loving and satisfying bonds with others. Instead they repetitively engage in relationships that reflect an internal world of bad objects.

Although Fairbairn wrote that therapy should provide a secure environment and a good object experience that enable patients to restore their capacity to make full and loving contact with others, he stressed the use of interpretation to make the patient conscious of the presence of his or her bad internal objects and their impact, thereby divesting them of their power and lessening splitting. Fairbairn thought that patients would likely resist this process out of fear that relinquishing these *internal* bad objects would make the patient vulnerable once again to bad *external* objects and to the pain of total aloneness or loss of identity. According to some accounts, Fairbairn's behavior in the therapeutic situation tended to be formal, conservative, and orthodox in practice and appearing to give more credence to interpretation than to being a good object (Guntrip, 1975: 145–156).

D. W. WINNICOTT

Donald Woods Winnicott was born in the town of Plymouth in Devon, England in 1896, the youngest child and only son in a prosperous Methodist family. Because his father was often preoccupied with local politics, Winnicott was left to the care of his mother, sisters, and nanny. Accounts of his life suggest that his experiences with women led him to become sensitive to the feminine and maternal as well as to issues of maternal depression and withdrawal and the child's dependency (Applegate & Bonnovitz, 1995: 14). When he was 13, Winnicott was sent away to school. He eventually graduated from medical school after World War I and worked with children as a pediatrician in both hospital and private practice settings. He discovered psychoanalysis through his personal experiences with James Strachey and later Joan Rivière and began to engage in child psychotherapy, often treating his colleagues' children—for example, Melanie Klein's son, Erich (Hughes, 1989: 19). Later, as a result of his work during World War II, Winnicott became more concerned about the effects of environmental failure and the issues of family fragmentation, homelessness, neglect, and deprivation. He was an advocate for the rights of the mentally ill, dependent children, delinquents, and other vulnerable groups and a vocal opponent of dehumanizing treatment procedures (Applegate & Bonovitz, 1995: 16–24).

As a young man, Winnicott has been described as pleasant, kindly, timid, and emotionally and sexually inhibited but as taking pride in his independence (Hughes, 1989: 17–21). He married twice but never had children. His first wife was emotionally disturbed and eventually institutionalized. They divorced when he was 53. Winnicott's second wife, Claire Britton, whom he met while when he was working in London's poverty-stricken East End, was a psychiatric social worker who entered analysis with Melanie Klein. The

Winnicotts shared many interests and collaborated professionally (Applegate & Bonnovitz, 1995: 16). Winnicott remained energetic and optimistic, spiritual and playful, until he died in 1971 at the age of 75.

Winnicott's (1965, 1975) extensive contributions to psychoanalytic theory and treatment technique were based largely on his 60,000 consultations with children and their parents (Applegate & Bonnovitz, 1995: 8) and his treatment of children, many of whom suffered from severe emotional difficulties and environmental deprivation and trauma. His highly accessible and creative writings contain numerous rich examples drawn from his clinical experience. Winnicott was convinced that his ideas were consistent with those of Freud and Klein, the latter being his mentor. Nevertheless, his writings were original and more radical than he stated and he was not trusted with being able to train students in the British Psychoanalytic Society despite his being elected president twice.

Winnicott's writings vividly and cogently describe the mother-infant dyad, which he regarded as the center and foundation of the developmental process (Cheschier, 1985: 218). He wrote that "there is no such thing as an infant; there is only an infant and its mother" (Winnicott, 1960: 39ff). More than other theorists of his time, Winnicott linked the child's development to the social environment. " . . . he attended to the complexities of real caregivers and their real interactions with real babies in various physical settings" (Applegate & Bonovitz, 1995: 22). He viewed women as having a biological preparedness (maternal preoccupation with fantasies about her baby during pregnancy) to perform "good-enough" mothering and to provide a "maternal holding environment." He described the "good-enough" mother as exquisitely attuned to and at the disposal of her child's needs and traced the acquisition of positive personality attributes such as the capacity to be alone and the capacity for concern to sensitive mothering and saw ego defects resulting from maternal failures. Winnicott also drew attention to the significance of transitional objects as a bridge between infants and mothers and the importance of social provision in nurturing the family and to the infant's progression from dependence to mature independence.

In contrast to Fairbairn, who emphasized how the child builds up an internal world of bad objects, Winnicott focused on the child's acquisition of positive attributes as a result of "good-enough" mothering. Winnicott described a significant development with respect to the child's coherent and positive sense of self. He thought that the self required confirmation or mirroring of its aliveness and vitality from the environment and that maternal deprivation or "impingement" resulted in the erection of a "false" self, which is a facade that comes into being to please others. Winnicott's major contribution to understanding the development of psychopathology centered on his delineation of the origins and manifestations of the false-self phenomenon.

In Winnicott's view, psychoanalytic treatment must provide the physical and human conditions that resemble the maternal holding environment and that support the development of the true self. He thought that patients should be allowed and helped to use the treatment to seek what they need in order to resume development and that the therapist must grasp and be responsive to the patient's needs (Mitchell & Black, 1995: 133–134).

HARRY GUNTRIP

Harry Guntrip was born in England in 1900. His father was a Methodist minister and an eloquent public speaker, and the family was religious, politically active, and well-connected. Guntrip described the first seven years of his life as a "grossly disturbed" period (Guntrip, 1975: 148–149). Although the sudden death of his two-year-old brother when Guntrip was three and a half years old was a significant event and resulted in his being sent away to the care of a maternal aunt for a time, Guntrip also appeared to have a mother who was emotionally and physically absent both before and after his brother's death. He suffered from bouts of a serious and mysterious exhaustion illness at points in his life

More of a humanist than a scientist, Guntrip became a minister after attending university. Looking for a more psychologically sophisticated understanding of human beings, he studied psychoanalytic writings but became disillusioned with and critical of what he felt to be Freud's negative view of religion and his dehumanizing account of human nature (Greenberg & Mitchell, 1983: 210). At the age of 49, he entered a ten-year analysis with Fairbairn and then later had a second but less frequent analysis with

Winnicott when Guntrip was 62–68 years of age. The account of these two treatments (Guntrip, 1975: 145–156), about which Guntrip took extensive notes, reflects not only his inner struggles but shows the two very different therapeutic styles of Fairbairn and Winnicott in their later years. It is note-worthy that despite his many years of treatment, it was only after Winni-cott died that Guntrip finally overcome his amnesia for the traumatic events of his first three and a half years of life. He attributed this to his hav-ing acquired a stable internal good object as a result of his work with Win-nicott, which enabled him to face the desolation of his early childhood. Guntrip died at the age of 75.

Guntrip's contributions (1961, 1969, 1973) stemmed not only from his own original thinking but also from his ability as an historian, a synthesiz-er, and a popularizer of the object relations theories of Klein, Fairbairn, and Winnicott (Greenberg & Mitchell, 1983: 209–210). He agreed with the criticism of Freudian psychoanalysis as having broken people into parts without putting them back together again. "You cannot understand a human being by an analysis of his parts, mechanisms, and so on. . . . A per-son is a whole self and so unique that it is impossible to find . . . any two who are exactly alike. When a baby is born, he contains a core of unique-ness that has never existed before. The parents' responsibility is not to mold, shape, pattern, or condition him, but to support him in such a way that his precious hidden uniqueness shall be able to emerge and guide his whole development" (Guntrip, 1973: 181). Like Fairbairn and Winnicott, Guntrip believed in the impact of early mothering and the deleterious effects of parental failure in shaping the personality. Like Fairbairn, he was interested in the nature, origins, and treatment of what he called "the schizoid problem," which he saw as the basis of all psychopathology. Some have suggested that Guntrip's emphasis on the pull or wish to withdraw from relationships is more central in his thinking than the pull toward objects that is characteristic of Fairbairn and Winnicott (Greenberg & Mitchell, 1983: 214–219). Guntrip argued that the schizoid person, in withdrawing from others as a result of extreme frustration, becomes alien-ated from himself or herself and shows a lack of any capacity to love or to experience understanding, warmth, and personal concern for others.

Guntrip shared Winnicott's view of the treatment process. He thought that the analyst's role in the treatment process is to create a holding and facilitating environment that permits the patient to reemerge from his or her withdrawn state. Guntrip opposed the idea of employing a fixed technique and stressed the therapist's ability to be real in the therapeutic interaction. His account of his own analyses with first Fairbairn and then Winnicott contrast the two very different styles of these two men and show how much Guntrip valued what he experienced as Winnicott's human presence in contrast to Fairbairn's formality and interpretive stance (Guntrip, 1975).

OTHER CONTRIBUTORS

Of the numerous theorists who made important contributions to British object relations theory in addition to Klein, Fairbairn, Winnicott, and Guntrip, the work of Balint, Bion, and Bowlby are noteworthy.

Born in 1896 in Budapest, Michael Balint moved first to Berlin and then England to escape the Nazis. A psychoanalyst and writer, he argued that object relations are present from the beginning of life and are independent of the drives. He believed that as a result of a rupture in the relationship with the mother, the child develops a "basic fault," a fragmentation in the core sense of self, that forms the basis of later psychopathology and that the individual longs to heal (Balint, 1968). Consequently, Balint thought that the therapeutic situation provided the patient with an opportunity to repair derailed development (Greenberg & Mitchell, 1983: 182–184).

Wilfred Bion was born in 1879, raised in colonial India, and lived in London for most of his life. As an adult he became both an analysand and a student of Klein, to whom he was very loyal. In numerous writings, Bion (1952, 1954) built on her ideas, highlighting the powerful impact of the infant's internal states on the mother and of the patient's intense feelings on the analyst. Bion did not view the analyst in as neutral or detached a manner as is true of Freudian analysis and recognized that, just as infants are able to rid themselves of intolerable feeling states by getting the mother to feel what they are experiencing through the process of projective identification, patients are able to induce feelings in the analyst. Thus, Bion thought that the analyst constituted an important source of data and that his or her role was to contain what was evoked in the transference-countertransference situation so that it could be understood and interpreted (Mitchell & Black, 1995: 106–111). Seinfeld (1993: 46–50) notes that modern Kleinians, such as Betty Joseph, rely on Bion's concepts of projective identification and containment extensively and pay careful attention to the here-and-now, moment-to-moment shifts in the transference and countertransference in making their interpretations. In 1968 Bion immigrated to the United States, where he lived until just prior to his death in 1979 (Mitchell & Black, 1995: 102).

John Bowlby (1907–1990) became a child psychiatrist, psychoanalyst, and researcher who took issue with many aspects of Freudian theory. His seminal work (1958, 1969, 1973) focused on the child's evolving tie to the mother and contributed to what became known as attachment theory. Bowlby based his views on studies of infants and animals who became separated from their mothers. He documented the mourning reactions that occurred as a result of a child's separation from and loss of the mother, the stages of protest, despair, and detachment that are used to cope with such experiences, and the anxiety about future separations that often ensue. More important, Bowlby concluded that the infant's innate push toward attachment is an aspect of human evolution and endowment that arises in the course of adaptation because it enhances the infant's chance for survival. He believed that secure attachment builds up gradually as a result of the ongoing availability of the mother and, along with Ainsworth (1973), described different types of early attachment patterns that come about when the child internalizes his or her interaction with the mother or primary caretaker. These working models are carried into all later relationships (Sable, 1995: 92). Bowlby's findings were consistent with many of the British object relations theorists and had a far-reaching impact on our understanding of early bonding experiences and their sequellae.

SELF PSYCHOLOGY

Like British object relations theories, Heinz Kohut's self psychology developed in reaction to classical psychoanalysis and ego psychology. There are some important similarities between Kohut's views and those of Fairbairn, Winnicott, and Guntrip (Bacal & Newman, 1990). Nevertheless, Kohut viewed self psychology as distinctive. The chart on pages 45–47 shows a comparison of some of the major concepts and principles of object relations theory and self psychology.

HEINZ KOHUT

Heinz Kohut was born in Vienna in 1913. His father was a successful and cultured man but was often away from home and died when Kohut was 23 years of age. He described his mother as an obscure figure who alternated between closeness and distance and recalled himself as having had a sad and intensely lonely childhood. Kohut had a rigorous and classical education and trained in medicine at the University of Vienna. He became interested in psychoanalysis and entered analysis with August Eichhorn, a close associate of Freud's. After some brief experiences in Paris and London, including a six-month stay in a camp for émigrés in 1939, Kohut was able to move to the United States in 1940. He had a residency in neurology at the University of Chicago, which was known for its highly stimulating intellectual environment, and eventually became a faculty member in neurology and psychiatry in 1944. Subsequently, Kohut sought analytic training and in 1948 graduated from the Chicago Institute for Psychoanalysis, a place that had produced Franz Alexander earlier and had generated its own controversies over the years. He also engaged in a second analysis with Ruth Eissler.

Until the mid-1960s, Kohut identified himself as a classical analyst and was well-respected by Anna Freud, Hartmann, and other more orthodox psychoanalytic theorists. He was even elected president of the American Psychoanalytic Association. Many who knew him described Kohut as a gifted teacher and speaker, possessing great charm and enthusiasm, as having an impressive knowledge base, and as an articulate spokesman for classical psychoanalysis. Although he did not publish extensively during this period, Kohut produced a groundbreaking paper, "Introspection, Empathy and Psychoanalysis" (1957), which discussed the nature and significance of empathy as the main psychoanalytic tool for understanding the patient. This publication was a harbinger of the change in his thinking.

In 1966, when Kohut was 53 and had reached a high point in terms of his reputation and leadership, he appeared to have a burst of creativity, and his seminal paper, "Forms and Transformations of Narcissism" (Kohut, 1966), heralded the beginning of self psychology. Subsequently, he elaborated his views in numerous papers and books (Kohut, 1971, 1977, 1984). He gathered a close circle of ardent supporters around him, including John Gedo, Arnold Goldberg, Michael Franz Basch, David Marcus, Paul and Marian Tolpin, Paul and Anna Ornstein, Ernest Wolf, and others. Kohut lived in Chicago with his wife until his death in 1981 (Strozier, 1985: 3–12). He was deeply affected by the severe criticism of and outright disdain for his views by many members of the psychoanalytic establishment. Nevertheless, self psychology had a significant impact both on psychoanalysis and the broader professional community both before and after his death (Fosshage, 1998: 1–18).

In the process of analyzing individuals with narcissistic disorders, who were previously thought to be untreatable in psychoanalysis because of their inability to form classical transference reactions, Kohut discovered what he believed to be their unique patterns of relating during the treatment process. To explain these reactions, or what he termed the selfobject transferences, which reflected the activation of early developmental needs in the treatment relationship, Kohut (1971) began by proposing that there was a separate line for self-development and envisioned narcissism and many of its forms as resulting from healthy strivings.

In *The Restoration of the Self* (1977), Kohut broke completely with classical psychoanalytic thinking and articulated his theory of self-development. He relegated the drives and Freud's structural model of the mind (id, ego, and superego) to the background. Instead, he argued that the individual is born with an innate sense of self, which is the central organizing and motivating force in the personality but also requires an empathic and responsive selfobject environment in order to unfold optimally.

Kohut placed considerable importance on the role of selfobjects, which he viewed as those persons who are able to perform vital functions for the newborn child, such as soothing, that it cannot carry out itself or who support the self in certain important ways all through life. He identified three main types of selfobject needs: the need for mirroring, the need for an idealization of others, and the need for a twin, or alter-ego (Wolf, 1988: 50–64). Although not all of these selfobject needs may be gratified in a particular child's life, rewarding experiences with at least one type of selfobject give the child a chance to develop a cohesive self through the process of transmuting internalization. Without these experiences or in the face of frustrations that are too abrupt, ongoing, ill-timed, or chronically unattuned to the child's needs, optimal self development is derailed and weakness in the self or narcissistic vulnerability, if not outright self disorders, develop. Kohut challenged the view that the capacity for total autonomy is the hallmark of health and thought that even those individuals who undergo optimal self-development nevertheless continue to need others to provide validation, admiration, support, and sustenance all through life.

Kohut viewed aggression and narcissistic rage as reactive to the unattuned and frustrating responses of others and saw all psychopathology as reflecting self deficits—that is, gaps, missing, or underdeveloped elements in self structure that come about as a result of traumatic or severe and protracted empathic failures with respect to the child's emerging needs. Thus, he regarded the caretaking environment as responsible for producing deficiencies in the structuring of the self and more-pronounced self disorders. He did not believe that all structural defects in the self result in pathology because a child might be able to acquire compensatory structures that strengthen the self and make up for or repair deficits in one aspect of the self through successful development of other facets. Certain self deficits, however, might show themselves in chronic problems or in vulnerability to life situations that lead to crisis proneness. Moreover, many patients who present with problems in their social functioning or with DSM IV disorders might actually have underlying narcissistic vulnerability that is at the root of their difficulties.

Because of Kohut's emphasis on self deficits instead of internalized pathological object relations structures and his view of aggression and narcissistic rage as reactive to frustration and unattunement rather than being innate, some theorists have criticized self psychology for not addressing the presence of entrenched pathology associated with the internalization of bad objects and role of innate aggressive impulses in personality development and the origins of psychopathology.

Kohut argued that treatment must build and strengthen the personality and that individuals with self deficits or what is termed narcissistic vulnerability require a treatment relationship that is more empathic, human, experiential, and reparative than is characteristic of traditional psychotherapy. The therapist's use of empathy with the subjective experiences of the patient as the major way of knowing and responding to the patient is a major feature of the self-psychological treatment approach (Fosshage, 1998: 1). Self psychology also reframed many aspects of traditional psychoanalytic treatment. For example, Kohut defined the concept of transference differently, seeing the selfobject transferences as reflecting the revival of frustrated early mirroring, idealization, and twinship needs in a new, more empathic and nonjudgmental context. He also reconceptualized the concept of resistance as the patient's efforts to maintain self-cohesion and to avoid disappointment and disillusionment. Likewise, he viewed patients' rage reactions as reactive to frustration and narcissistic injury rather than as an expression of innate aggression and saw what others might label drive-related conflicts as disintegration products caused by environmental failures in meeting selfobject needs. He advocated interpretations that emphasize the linkages between the clients' dysfunctional traits, personality patterns, and defenses to early parental empathic failures and their impact but also stressed the importance of the therapists' use of themselves in the treatment relationship in ways that show acceptance of a patient's selfobject needs. Kohut's view of successful treatment was that it results in a patient's showing more stable self-esteem regulation, increased creativity, freer self-expression, the capacity for pleasure and joy, pride in finding one's own way, and the ability to seek out more mature and responsive selfobjects.

EXTENSIONS AND NEW DIRECTIONS

Both object relations theory and self psychology have generated newer formulations in recent years. Some of these involve postmodernist thinking, which rejects the philosophical stance of logical positivism that is present in most earlier theories. "Postmodernism can be thought of as a group of approaches that hold that there is no fixed reality, only constructed versions of reality determined by the perspective of the one doing the describ-

COMPARISON OF OBJECT RELATIONS THEORY AND SELF PSYCHOLOGY

	Object Relations Theory	Self Psychology
Focus of Theory	Interpersonal relationships and their internalization and impact on psychic structure	The unfolding of self potentialities and the role of the selfobject milieu on self-development, self-esteem regulation, and healthy narcissism
Factors Influencing Theory	Disappointment in results of Freudian psychoanalysis	Rejection of Freudian orthodoxy
	Clinical work with individuals who suffered from early developmental problems	Interest in applying psychoanalytic theory to very disturbed "unanalyzable" patients
	British intellectual tradition of openness and tolerance of diversity	Intellectual ferment at University of Chicago
	Interest in role of early relationships	Earlier theorists at Chicago Institute of Psychoanalysis
	Observational studies of infants and infant-mother interactions	Kohut's late life burst of creativity
	Reaction to Freud's narrow instinctual focus	The hostile reception of his ideas
		Interest in creativity
		Interest in the development of the self and its innate potentialities
	In U.S., British object-relations school was not accepted, but some theorists began to formulate object relations concepts within ego psychology—e.g., Jacobson, Mahler, and Kernberg	Interest in subjective experience
		Interest in parenting and social milieu
Nature of Individual	Individual seeks objects from birth	Individual born with innate potentialities that form nuclear self
	Individual internalizes relationships with others	Self has basic needs
	Difference of opinion as to whether aggression is innate or caused by early frustration	Attuned parenting essential
		Individual needs others all through life
	Individual needs others all through life	Frustration causes aggression
Structural Concepts	Objects and part-objects	Nuclear self
	Self- and object-representations	Grandiose self
	Primitive defenses	Bipolar self
	Affects	Cohesive self
	Ego and superego	Compensatory structures
	Types of personality organization	Stern's four senses of the self
	Paranoid/schizoid and depressive positions	
	Endopsychic structure (split ego and internal objects)	
	True self	
	The regressed ego	

	Object Relations Theory	Self Psychology
Developmental Concepts	Innate push to relate to others	Selfobject needs for mirroring, idealization of others, and twinship
	Introjection, identification, and internalization	Impact of attuned, empathic, and responsive parenting
	Patterns of attachment	
		Optimal frustration and responsiveness
	Mature dependence	
		Transmuting internalizations
	The separation-individuation process	
		Narcissistic rage
	Sequential stages in the development of internalized object relations	
Nature of Problems	Attachment difficulties	
	Depression and early object loss	Persistent problems in self-cohesion and self-esteem regulation as a result of early parental empathic failures
	Separation-individuation subphase deficits	
	Borderline and narcissistic personality	Transient problems in self-esteem resulting from current situational stresses
	Paranoid/schizoid and depressive problems	
	Problems related to "bad" objects	
	The schizoid problem	
	The false self	
Nature of Change	Insight	
	Therapeutic relationship experiences	Strengthening self-structures through transmuting internalization and optimal responsiveness
		Insight through empathic interpretations
Treatment Goals	Modification of pathological defenses, intrapsychic splits, and self-and object-representations, including "bad" objects	Developing self-cohesion and self-esteem
		Building self-structures
	or	
	Providing facilitative reparative experiences and building new internal structures	Locating better selfobjects
Treatment Principles and Techniques	Confrontation and interpretation of primitive defenses and pathological internalized object relations	Empathic attunement to patient's selfobject needs and subjective experience
	Neutrality and abstinence	Empathic understanding and explanation of patient's selfobject needs and their link to past selfobject failures
	Systematic focus on transference-countertransference dynamics, particularly projective identification in the therapeutic relationship	Overcoming resistance to development of selfobject transferences
	or	

	Object Relations Theory	Self Psychology
Treatment Principles and Techniques (cont.)	Creation of a therapeutic holding environment	Repairing disruptions in the selfobject transference
	The use of developmentally attuned techniques	Meeting selfobject needs
	Provision of new object experiences in the therapeutic relationship	Encouragement of the expression of healthy narcissism
	Containment	Encouragement to find new selfobjects
Nature of Relationship	Emphasis on transference and countertransference	Allowing emergence of selfobject transferences and the repair of disruptions
	or	Emphasis on empathic understanding and optimal responsiveness
	Therapist as a new and good object	Removing countertransference impediments to empathic attunement
Applicability	Those who have severe developmental arrests but can be used with a range of problems	Those who have self disorders and narcissistic vulnerability; those who have transient problems

ing" (DeLaCour, 1996: 214). Postmodernism includes social constructivism, narrative, recent feminist thought, and intersubjectivity.

A prominent and articulate proponent of what is termed the relational approach, Stephen Mitchell (1988, 1993) has been a major synthesizer of diverse formulations that share the underlying view that intrapsychic structures drive from transactional patterns and always interact with the interpersonal field (Aron, 1996: 1–30). Mitchell "brings together within one model those theorists, like Winnicott and Kohut, who emphasized the self; those theorists, like Fairbairn and Klein, who focused on the object; and those theorists, like Bowlby and Sullivan, who attended to the interpersonal space between self and other. He has brought into one relational confederation a wide variety of alternative (nonclassical) analytic schools, in the hope that, even with their individual weaknesses, together they would be able to overcome the force of classical theory" (Aron, 1992: 33).

Although Mitchell's formulations do not constitute a systematically developed theory, his writings have contributed to a movement away from the way psychoanalytic theory and practice have been conceptualized and practiced traditionally (Ornstein & Ganzer, 1997). Because of its stance and wide umbrella, relational theory has attracted many contributors, including those who represent postmodern feminist and social constructivist viewpoints. Treatment based on a relational perspective focuses on both the patient's and therapist's contribution to the therapeutic interaction and their shared construction of the patient's reality.

Self psychology continued to flourish after Kohut's untimely death in 1981, but because he was no longer present to provide leadership and many aspects of the theory were not thoroughly worked out, it was inevitable that diverse points began to emerge (Galatzer-Levy, 1991: xi). The self psychological community today is more diverse than it was initially and reflects different subsets: 1) the self psychological "purists," such as Paul Ornstein and Ernest Wolf, who have remained allied with Kohut but who have extended and refined his original ideas; 2) others, such as Michael Franz Basch, Arnold Goldberg, and Joseph Lichtenberg, who share some of self psychology's basic ideas but who have ventured in new directions; 3) those such as Daniel Stern, Beatrice Beebe, and Frank Lachmann, whose studies of infants have lent support to self psychological concepts; 4) those such as Howard Bacal and Morton and Estelle Shane, who have tried to bridge self psychology and object relations theory; and 5) those such as Robert Stolorow and his collaborators, who call themselves "intersubjectivists" and who have criticized self psychology's narrow focus as a "one-person psychology" and have tried to evolve an integrative theoretical framework based on a "two person" psychology (Teicholz, 1999: xxi–xxv; Shane, Shane & Gales, 1997: 33–35).

In contrast to Ornstein (1991) and Wolf (1988, 1991), whose writings have remained true to Kohut's formulations, Basch (1988) enlarged upon Kohut and argued for the relevance of data from outside of the empathic-introspective treatment relationship, particularly from infant observation; research on perception, cognition, and affect; neurobiology; and cybernetics. He also was intrigued by the role of the brain's ordering activity and its effect on complex mental states and attempted to integrate neurobiological data with psychological theory (Shane, 1991: 159–160). Likewise, Goldberg (1988), who contributed to a greater understanding of the structure of the self, agreed with Basch on the importance of scientific data rather than empathy-introspection alone in theory development (Shane, 1991: 160–163). Joseph Lichtenberg (1989) became interested in motivational theory and described five different motivational systems, reformulating both self psychology and classical psychoanalytic theory (Shane, 1992: 216).

Daniel Stern, who was not a member of Kohut's inner circle, was a psychoanalyst and researcher who made a significant contribution that supported many of Kohut's ideas about self-development. Using systematic observations of infant-caretaker interaction, Stern (1985) produced evidence that the infant is born with an innate sense of self which is present in a rudimentary form at birth, exhibits an awareness of being separate from others, and that the child's self evolves as a consequence of complex and recurrent interpersonal transactions. His findings contradicted many aspects of Mahler's separation-individuation theory (Weinberg, 1991). Stern delineated four phases of self-development (the sense of emergent self, the sense of core self, the sense of subjective self, and the sense of verbal self), which he called "domains of relatedness." He viewed each domain as codetermined by the growing infant's innate maturational capacities and the nature and degree of caretaker attunement. Stern and others, including Beatrice Beebe and Frank Lachmann (1988a & b, 1994), have continued to engage in studies of infant-mother interaction that have contributed to knowledge about the origins and nature of early personality structures.

Howard Bacal and his collaborator (Bacal & Newman, 1990) explored the historical antecedents to self psychology in British object relations theory, compared Kohut's formulations with those of the numerous British object relations theorists, and tried to create an "object-relations-informed" psychology of the self (Shane, 1992: 216). Bacal is among those writers who argue that self psychology is a form of object relations theory and that object relations theory also requires a psychology of the self (Bacal, 1991: 37). More recently, the self psychologists Morton and Estelle Shane, along with Mary Gales (1997), also have attempted to accommodate relational thinking.

Associated with self psychology for a time, Robert Stolorow and others (Stolorow & Atwood, 1979; Stolorow & Lachmann, 1980; Stolorow, Brandchaft & Atwood, 1987; Stolorow & Atwood, 1992; Stolorow, Atwood & Brandchaft, 1994) have evolved a theory of "intersubjectivity," which is a "two-person" rather than a "one-person" psychology. It deals with the mutual interplay and influence of the two subjectivities present in the therapist-patient interaction. According to Stolorow, his views arose independently of self psychology and reflect a more radical overarching perspective that encompasses but goes beyond self psychological concepts (Stolorow, 1992: 241–250). He stated emphatically that any characterization of his theories of the subjective world and intersubjectivity as deriving from self psychology "would be quite inaccurate" (Teicholz, 1999: 244).

FURTHER CONSIDERATIONS

Although object relations theory and self psychology link the individual to the interpersonal and social environment and are more psychosocial than traditional psychodynamic theory, they have not fully integrated recent developments in the study of trauma, gender, many types of diversity, and the impact of oppressive societal attitudes and policies.

TRAUMA

There has been growing recognition that many patients who seek treatment have experienced traumatic events, such as severe physical and sexual abuse, repeated abandonments, parental death and loss, natural disasters, wars, dislocation, domestic and other forms of violence, and combat, in the recent or distant past. Such traumatic events, particularly when they occur early in a person's life, may become structured in certain ways internally and affect the person's personality functioning, symptoms, and problems. They also may result in post-traumatic stress disorders (Gunderson & Chu, 1993; Herman, 1992; Herman, Perry & van der Kolk, 1989; Corwin, 1996; Kroll, 1993). Because many trauma survivors are highly distrustful of relationships, use defenses and engage in behaviors that protect their traumatic memories and that have helped them to survive, and tend to become involved in situations in which they experience repeated revictimization, treatment requires special sensitivity and skill (Goldstein, 1999: 95–96).

DIVERSITY AND OPPRESSION

Most personality theories have neglected full consideration of the unique development, experiences, characteristics, and strengths of women, gays and lesbians, people of color, and members of certain ethnic and religious groups (Mattei, 1996; Berzoff, 1996). Chodorow (1978) and Gilligan (1982) were early writers who argued that females had a different individuation process than males because of their primary attachment to a same-sex rather than opposite-sex parent. Members of the Stone Center for Developmental Services and Studies at Wellesley College in Massachusetts, including Jean Baker Miller, Judith Jordan, Alexandra Kaplan, Irene Stiver, and Janet Surrey, have developed what they call self-in-relation theory (Jordan, 1990; Kaplan & Surrey, 1984; Miller, 1977). Applying object relations and self psychological theories to the unique development of women, they argue that women, in contrast to men, thrive on enhanced connection rather than increased selfobject differentiation and separateness. They also believe that non-responsive relationships and disconnection rather than problems in separation-individuation per se are at the root of psychopathology in women. Jessica Benjamin (1988), another prominent woman theorist, has viewed women's optimal development as involving both self-assertion and mutuality, separateness and sharing, and that the woman's inability to reconcile dependence and independence leads to patterns of domination and submission.

Some writers have utilized these newer theories to suggest that a more affirmative view of gay and lesbian object relations and self-development arises as a variant of positive developmental experiences, in contrast to the traditional belief that they reflect arrested, immature, narcissistic, and undifferentiated object relations (Burch, 1997; Drescher, 1998; Glassgold & Iasenza, 1995; Isay, 1989).

Knowledge about people of color and multiculturalism is accumulating rapidly and must be integrated into the assessment and treatment process (Perez Foster, Moskowitz & Art, 1996; Perez Foster, 1999). African Americans, Latinos, Asians, and other people of color are major examples of groups within the society who are vulnerable to identity diffusion resulting from cultural conflict, feelings of dissonance or difference with respect to others, and the taking in of unfavorable societal attitudes. Clinicians must be aware of their own attitudes and biases, possess knowledge of different cultural backgrounds and lifestyles, and utilize interventions that are responsive to patients' diverse life experiences. The newer perspectives on object relations and self-development have major implications for understanding patients' strengths and needs throughout the life cycle. They also illuminate the causes of certain symptoms and difficulties and the special treatment needs of those who have been deprived of social conditions that are growth enhancing or who have experienced a stigmatizing, exclusionary, and oppressive environment.

SUMMARY

After discussing classical psychoanalytic theory and ego psychology, this chapter has traced the origins and evolution of the object relations theory and self psychology. It has shown how American object relations theory emerged as an effort to build a more interpersonal focus into classical psychoanalytic theory and ego psychology and to integrate research findings on mother-infant interaction, whereas British object relations theory and self psychology arose in reaction to the limitations of more traditional formulations and the need for new treatment approaches with seriously disturbed patients. This review has described some important similarities and differences among object relations theories and between object relations theories and self psychology. It also has pointed to new directions that both frameworks have taken. The various approaches that have been put forth complement one another and constitute a broadened perspective on human behavior and a greatly expanded repertoire of treatment approaches. They also show how far psychodynamic theory has changed since Freud's time.

3

OBJECT RELATIONS THEORY

MAJOR CONCEPTS

Because each of the object relations theorists discussed in Chapter 2 put forth somewhat distinctive ideas about the main structures that make up the personality and the major developmental processes that account for normal and pathological outcomes, there is no completely integrated set of object relations concepts. Additionally, different terms may be used to refer to similar ideas, and conversely, the same term may have various meanings. This chapter first will define some key terms and then will consider selected structural, developmental, and psychopathological processes that are associated with object relations theories.

BASIC TERMINOLOGY

There is some basic terminology associated with object relations theory that is useful to review and define.

THE OBJECT AND PART-OBJECTS

Although a somewhat mechanistic and impersonal term, "object" refers to persons in the external world with whom the infant, child, and adult interacts and relates. Some theorists believe that initially the infant is only capable of perceiving and relating to others as part- rather than whole objects. For example, Klein wrote that the infant first interacts with the mother through the breast, which becomes a part-object, and the infant comes to associate the mother's breast with other parts of the mother's body. Part-objects are associated with either "good" or "bad" experiences. The infant is not able to recognize the mother in totality and that the breast or other parts of the mother can be both good and bad until a later time. An important developmental achievement is the young child's ability to bring together his or her experiences of others as part-objects into a coherent and three-dimensional whole object. This occurs when the child is able to recognize that good and bad experiences are associated with the same object or person.

Because Klein and Kernberg believed in the importance of the drives, particularly the death instinct and aggression, as motivating infants' relationships with others, their theories depicted infants' earliest fantasies and relationships to part-objects as filled with devouring images of the infant in relationship to parts of the mother's body and its contents. They also described the infant's terrifying fears of retaliation for angry fantasies and impulses by these part-objects.

THE REAL OBJECT AND THE FANTASIED OBJECT

It is possible to distinguish between the *objective* characteristics of those in the external world (real objects) and the infant's *subjective* experiences of or fantasies about others (fantasied objects). Theorists such as Mahler, Winnicott, Fairbairn, and Guntrip viewed the real people in the infant's environment as exerting important influences on personality development. In contrast, such writers as Jacobson, Klein, and Kernberg, who believed in the power of the drives, tended to minimize the impact of the real people in the child's environment in favor of emphasizing the child's fantasies about and subjective perceptions of objects or others. These latter theorists, however, did acknowledge that real objects played a role in reinforcing or challenging the infant's fantasies or perceptions. For example, an infant who projects his or her own violent impulses onto the maternal object and then views her as frightening and destructive might temper his or her perceptions if the mother is calming and basically responsive.

SELF- AND OBJECT-REPRESENTATIONS

Infants begin to form images of themselves (self-representations) and others (object-representations) by taking in experiences with those close to them. Once formed, self- and object-representations are fundamental internal structures that affect the ways in which individuals view themselves and others. Because relationships with external real objects are experienced subjectively and may be affected by fantasy, it is possible that a developing child's self- and object-representations do not actually reflect the objective situation. For example, the presence of aggressively-tinged or frustrating interactions with the mother may make her appear more "monstrous" than she is in reality. Likewise, highly intelligent people may come to view themselves as not very smart despite their objective capacities if they felt inadequate or stupid in their early relationships with significant others.

Likewise, because early self- and object-representations are based on part-object experiences, they do not result in a coherent conception of the self and others until later in the developmental process. An important milestone is the child's ability to integrate his or her part-object experiences.

AFFECTS

Jacobson's writings introduced the idea that infants experience certain feeling states (affects) that are linked to their interaction with others. When their external relationships are internalized, the resultant self- and object-representations and the relationships between them contain affective colorations. For example, the infant may internalize an object-representation of a loving mother in relation to a positive self-representation of the infant's own loving and dependent feelings. The infant also takes in a self-representation that is positive with respect to loving and dependent feelings. Alternatively, an infant might internalize an object-representation of an angry mother in relation to a negatively tinged self-representation involving the infant's neediness, which becomes equated with "badness."

THE EGO

The ego is the structure that is responsible for dealing with the world, for instituting defense mechanisms, for internalizing external objects, and for integrating and synthesizing self- and object-representations. The ego is not the primary focus of attention in object relations theories, and there is some confusion and inconsistency in how the term is even used. Some American object relations theorists, such as Jacobson, who gave a more prominent role to the ego, viewed self- and object-representations as part of the ego. Some British object relations theorists, such as Fairbairn and Winnicott, however, blurred the distinction among the infant, the ego, the self, and self- and object-representations, sometimes using them interchangeably. Object relations theorists also differ with respect to whether they viewed the ego as an innate and intact structure that is present in a rudimentary or undifferentiated form from birth or whether it develops as a result of the introjection of positive experiences with caretakers.

INTROJECTION, IDENTIFICATION, AND INTERNALIZATION

The ego is responsible for the process of internalization in which infants and children take in the outside world and make it a part of their inner life. The ego mechanisms of introjection and identification are key in this development. In introjection, which arises earlier than identification, images of fantasied or real frustrations and dangers in relationships with others are taken in under the impact of highly charged primitive impulses and affects. These images often are experienced as consuming and frightening. For example, the infant may take in an ominous and powerful image of the mother's angry face that is associated with the infant's intense hunger. This part-object image may terrify the infant. Likewise, the infant may introject an image of the mother's smiling face that is associated with soothing and warmth and that exerts a comforting influence. Introjects begin to cluster into "good me" and "bad me" depending on whether the infant is experiencing pleasurable or frustrating interactions with the environment.

Identification, the second and later mechanism that affects the internalization process, rests on the child's ability to recognize his or her separateness from the mother and to take on or model the different roles that the caretaking object plays in important interactions. For example, a little girl whose mother sings to her in a loving and soothing way when she is going to sleep takes in a positive image of the mother in relation to the child's fatigue and bedtime routines. Later she may take on the mother's role by singing to her doll when she imagines the doll is tired. Her imitation of the mother's interaction with her may eventually become a more stable part of her internal organization and repertoire of behavior. The child acquires many diverse introjects and identifications based on his or her interactions with others. The completion of the internalization process involves a consolidation of self- and object-images into a stable and coherent whole that is constituted by selective introjects and identifications.

PROJECTION

Just as infants take in external experiences through introjection, they also project certain internal states onto others. When good or pleasurable feelings are projected, infants experience the object of their projections positively. Alternatively, when infants expel bad, unpleasurable, or frightening feelings and impulses, they experience the object of their projections as threatening and persecutory. Repetitive cycles of introjection and projection result in the building up of internalized object relations.

PRIMITIVE OR LOWER LEVEL DEFENSES

According to Klein and Kernberg, an infant's ego, from birth, has the capacity to organize experience and to protect the infant from the anxiety arising from his or her destructive fantasies and impulses. Primitive ego defenses, such as splitting, projection, and projective identification are erected. In splitting, two contradictory states, such as love and hate, are compartmentalized and not integrated. The infant's positive fantasies about and experiences with "good" objects are separated from frightening and painful interactions with "bad" objects. It was thought that infants engage in splitting because it is too frightening to think of the object upon whom they are dependent as both good and bad. When splitting decreases, the infant becomes capable of experiencing external objects as both good and bad. When splitting does not decrease and continues to operate as a major defensive operation, an individual's self- and object-representations remain separated or compartmentalized, and this distorts relationships with others.

Another important early defense mechanism is projective identification, which is more extreme than projection. In projective identification, not only is an aspect of the person put onto an external object but the object begins to feel or behave in ways that are in keeping with what has been projected. The person who engages in projective identification may then try to control the projected impulses that the object displays. Thus, a woman may experience her rageful impulses as intolerable. Although she does not express her rage directly, she may act in ways that induce her husband to behave in a very angry manner, to which she then feels justified in responding with retaliatory anger. She may feel that her rage is not her own but is a response to her husband's behavior.

In addition to splitting and projective identification, the infant also utilizes the defenses of idealization, in which the object is highly overvalued in order to protect the object from destructive impulses, and denial, in which there is a lack of acknowledgment or nonacceptance of important aspects of reality or of feelings, impulses, thoughts, or experiences.

THE SUPEREGO

The superego establishes a person's conscience, values, ethical guidelines, and ideals and plays an important role in the development of psychopathology. The American object relations theorists, in particular, revised and expanded Freud's view of the origins, development, and importance of the superego. According to Jacobson, who presented the most well-developed view of superego formation, the superego begins much earlier than Freud thought and is built up of many levels of internalization as the infant introjects images of others and the self based on both fantasied and real object experiences. Initially, the child builds up highly idealized views of the parents and takes in their standards without question.

Two important concepts involved in Jacobson's view of early superego formation involve the *ego ideal* and the mechanism of *reaction formation*. Early in development, the child merges with the idealized and omnipotent loved object so that his or her self- and object-representations become fused. The idealized image of the object combines with the child's early grandiose images of the self into an ego ideal, which he or she strives to be.

Growth allows the child to give up some aspects of this ego ideal and to identify with the more realistic aspects of the parents. When the person lives up to his or her ego ideal, self-esteem ensues. When the child feels angry at the frustrating love object, however, the aggression toward the object is turned against the self through the mechanism of reaction formation. Self-esteem fails when the aggression felt toward objects is vented onto the self.

A necessary part of the developmental process is the gradual moderation of these early images in accord with more realistic perceptions of the parents. The child's taking in of more loving, accepting, three-dimensional, and human relationships with others may result in a tempering of the strict and relentless aspects of the ego ideal and the superego. Optimally, the child continues to strive to be like the parents but not to be a carbon copy of them. The superego becomes less rigid. Eventually, when the child is approximately 6 to 7 years of age, the ego consolidates the different part-object or object experiences that form the basis of the superego.

When superego integration does not take place, the superego remains primitive or fragmented. Internalized images that are highly idealized and perfectionistic in their demands and harsh and punitive when one does not live up to them continue to dominate the developing child's inner world. The superego then may become excessively strict, if not persecutory, or exerts itself in extreme and contradictory ways—for example, when someone acts in an impulsive or hurtful and destructive manner but then feels excessively guilty and inflicts self-punishment. The superego is a regulator of mood and self-esteem and may be involved in severe depressive states.

From a different vantage point than Jacobson, Klein, a British object relations theorist, described the development of a harsh superego that forms very early and results from the child's introjection of powerful and destructive, angry and sometimes guilt-provoking images of the parents, which are influenced by the projection of the child's own sadistic fantasies and impulses. Klein thought that the child comes to fear the retaliation of these internal representations and that guilt intensifies when the child perceives that he or she has thought or acted aggressively toward the parent, who is both good and bad. In many instances of severe psychopathology, the superego persecutes and punishes the individual and impairs his or her capacity for satisfying relationships with others.

In Fairbairn's schema, the child's response to a frustrating environment is a *moral defense,* in which he or she represses his or her perceptions of the parents as bad, continues to view the objects in the external world as good, sees himself or herself as bad, and constructs a world of inner bad objects to which the child remains related and over which the child retains the illusion of control. These internalizations have a superego function in that they sabotage any move away from the person's attachment to his or her bad objects and interfere with satisfying relationships with others. Individuals remain at the mercy of internal bad objects that persecute them and run their lives.

RELATIONAL MATRIX

In his effort to synthesize and integrate diverse object relations theories and differentiate them from classical Freudian theory, Mitchell uses the term *relational matrix* to refer to the self, the object, and transactional patterns. In his view, all human behavior occurs within an interactional field of relationships.

STRUCTURE, DEVELOPMENT, AND PSYCHOPATHOLOGY

Drawing on the basic terminology defined above, object relations theorists emphasized different aspects of early development and how they result in optimal and pathological personality structures and deficits.

BOWLBY'S PATTERNS OF ATTACHMENT AND THEIR PATHOLOGICAL OUTCOMES

Bowlby and Ainsworth described different types of attachment styles that infants display in relation to their mothers or primary caretakers. These are influenced by the caretaker's expectations, verbal and nonverbal behavior, sensitivity, and responsiveness to the infant. Once internalized, they become working affective, cognitive, and behavior models that influence the way children and adults relate to others (Biringen, 1994; McMillen, 1992; Fish, 1996; Sable, 1995).

The major attachment styles include *secure attachment,* in which the infant seems to be confident that the mother will be available and responsive, *anxious resistant attachment,* in which the infant is uncertain that the mother will be available and responsive and tends to be anxious and clinging, and *anxious avoidant attachment,* in which the infant has no confidence that the mother will be available and responsive and tends to withdraw from or avoid the love and support of others. A fourth pattern, *disorganized-disoriented attachment,* in which the infant shows signs of stess and a breakdown of goal-directed attachment behavior, also has been observed (Main & Solomon, 1990).

Although attachment styles are general, they lead to and become associated with more specific types of pathology. A secure attachment style is associated with the most adaptive behavior, but other attachment patterns (anxious resistant, anxious avoidant, and disorganized-disoriented) result in more maladaptive patterns. For example, adults with anxious resistant styles tend to be sensitive to rejection, vulnerable to separation anxiety and abandonment fears, and may show excessively clinging or distancing behavior. Those with anxious avoidant patterns are likely to be be dismissive of, indifferent to, and unconcerned about others. Disorganized-disoriented individuals are prone to more extreme states of confusion and fragmentation in the face of relationship stressors.

Bowlby's work not only contributed to our understanding of the nature of more maladaptive forms of attachment but also of the normal mourning or grief process that follows profound losses. Bowlby's observations of the sequence of protest, despair, and detachment in children who are separated from their mothers led to the formulation of similar reactions in adults who encountered major losses, including numbness, longing for the lost person, disorganization and despair, and reintegration (McMillen, 1992: 210).

MAHLER'S SEPARATION-INDIVIDUATION PROCESS AND SUBPHASE INADEQUACIES

Based on her studies of infant-mother interactions, Mahler described a chronologically ordered series of developmental phases that show the progression of the infant's initial attachment to and then gradual detachment from the mother. She stressed the mutual regulation and cuing that occurs between mother and child and the importance of maternal support and encouragement of the child's efforts at separation-individuation in facilitating optimal outcomes of this process. Although Mahler noted six sequential phases, the first two phases are precursors to separation-individuation proper.

> The *autistic phase*, which is a preattachment phase, occurs from birth until the infant is approximately one month old.

> The *symbiotic phase*, which occurs from about one to four or five months of age, marks the beginning of the infant's ability to invest in and attach to another person and to perceive the mother as a "need-satisfying object" within the infant's ego boundary. The foundation of both separation and individuation occur during the symbiotic phase as the mother begins to respond to or "mirror" the infant's individual characteristics and as the infant comes to recognize and get a "feel" for the mother, who is satisfying its needs. Optimal responsiveness during this period not only helps the child to acquire a positive core self experience but also fosters separation from the symbiotic orbit.

> The *differentiation subphase*, which occurs from about four or five to ten months, begins when the infant's attention shifts from being inwardly directed within the symbiosis to being more outwardly directed and the infant begins to separate his or her self-images from that of the mother or caretaker.

> The *practicing subphase*, which occurs from about 10 to 16 months of age, shows the acceleration of the separation-individuation process in the context of close proximity to the maternal figure, who is there to provide continuing support and encouragement. In the early practicing subphase, the child experiences the simultaneous pull of the outside world and closeness with the mother, and the child tries to keep track of the mother even when crawling away from her and attempts to relocate her if she becomes lost momentarily. Separation anxiety may increase until the child becomes reassured that mother is still there. Only

gradually do children become more able to be on their own without seeing the mother. During the second part of the practicing subphase, children enthusiastically and even joyfully explore the world around them and may appear oblivious to the mother's temporary absence. The child's sense of power and grandiosity is at its peak. Pleasure in their rapidly developing ego functions and reassurance that the mother cares and is available seem to enable children to sustain transient separations from the mother that stem from their increasing efforts at individuation.

The *rapprochement subphase,* which occurs from about 16 to 24 months of age, is characterized by the child's moves back and forth between autonomy and dependence. The child is able to be more autonomous but also exhibits increased fears of separation and loss of the object. This may stem from the increasing insecurity children experience when they begin to recognize that they are not all-powerful and the center of the universe. The child turns to the mother for help but fears being re-engulfed by her; makes increasing demands on the mother's time; wants to share everything with her; and craves constant reassurance of her love while, at times, pushing her away and showing great irritability with her. Mahler used the term "ambitendency" in describing the push-pull of the urgent and competing needs for closeness and autonomy that characterize the rapprochement period.

On the road to object constancy, which occurs from about 24 to 36 months of age and even later, reflects the child's growing ability to be on his or her own without undue concern about the mother's whereabouts. The child increasingly acquires a solid internal representation of the mother that permits the child to pursue the full expression of his or her individuality and to function independently without fearing separation or abandonment. At the same time, it is accompanied by the child's acceptance that the mother is a person in her own right with needs of her own. The child overcomes splitting and thereby internalizes and consolidates a three-dimensional view of the mother, who loves and hates, rewards and punishes, and has unique characteristics. The child is able to experience closeness without fearing engulfment. The achievement of object constancy implies the capacity to maintain a positive mental representation of the mother in her absence or in the face of frustration.

The failure of the infant-mother dyad to negotiate the different phases of the separation-individuation process may result in psychoses, borderline and narcissistic disorders, and other types of developmental arrests. Mahler herself described the likelihood of psychosis developing when severe problems in the symbiotic phase occur that impair the infant's ability to differentiate self from other and thus prevent the development of reality testing and a separate sense of self. Likewise, she thought that during the practicing period, children are very vulnerable to blows to their grandiosity and omnipotence that might result in injuries to healthy narcissism.

Numerous theorists drew on Mahler's developmental theory to explain the nature of developmental arrests associated with borderline and other types of disorders. For example, Gertrude and Rubin Blanck (1974, 1979) showed how specific separation-individuation subphase inadequacies lead to problems in the ego's structuralization and to impaired capacity for object relations. They argued that early subphase inadequacies give rise to less structuralization of the ego and to a lower level type of pathology than do later subphase inadequacies, so that the nature of borderline pathology differs depending on whether problems in caretaker-child interaction occur in the symbiotic, differentiation, practicing, rapprochement, or on the way to object constancy subphases. The Blancks used the term *borderline* to refer to a broad range of pathology that is not always clearly differentiated from the neuroses and the psychoses and that is characterized by impaired ego functioning, overwhelming affects, poor impulse control, and disturbed capacity for interpersonal relations.

Like Mahler, the Blancks emphasized the mother's contribution to developmental arrests. For example, with children who become borderline, the mother's inability to meet the infant's symbiotic needs can exacerbate the child's need for closeness and leave the child with intense symbiotic longings that compromise the separation-individuation process. As a result, some children may fear merger and ward off their intense symbiotic wishes by distancing from the mother. Likewise, the mother's inabiity to support her child's differentiation may lead to the child's tendency to merge with her and others in close relationships, tenuous ego boundaries, and psychotic regression. Intense separation anxiety may occur in the early stages of separation-individuation, and the child may equate individuation with object loss. Practicing failures may lead to severe narcissistic injury when the child confronts his or her lack of omnipotence. Alternatively, difficulties in the practicing period may leave the child joyless in the face of autonomy, unable to individuate, and dependent on dyadic interactions (Edward, Ruskin & Turrini, 1981).

Problems in the rapprochement subphase are most commonly associated with the development of the more characteristic core type of borderline disorder. Instead of encouraging and supporting the child's autonomous strivings during this period, the mother emotionally withdraws from, shows negative attitudes toward, or overtly rejects the child. Having achieved some differentiation from the mother, the child has not yet internalized a stable and integrated representation of her. The mother-child dyad's failure to master the rapprochement crisis impairs the child's attainment of both object constancy and an integrated sense of self. The child becomes preoccupied with fears of engulfment and abandonment, shows difficulty modulating angry impulses, and generally shows impaired ego and superego functioning.

If the child encounters problems in the rapprochement subphase, the child may continue to use splitting and other primitive mechanisms as major defenses, may be unable to neutralize aggression, demonstrate a lack of capacity for self-soothing, show poor affect differentiation and an absence of signal anxiety, exhibit tendencies toward action rather than verbalization, manifest deficiencies in the internalization of a stable sense of self, and fail to develop object constancy. Some higher level defenses and more neurotic-like difficulties may accompany these deficits.

Masterson (1972; 1976) and Masterson and Rinsley (1975) also built on Mahler's description of the rapprochement subphase as well as aspects of Fairbairn's theory to account for the origins of borderline disorders. In their view, mothers of children who become borderline enjoy their symbiotic phase but cannot tolerate their children's increasing efforts at individuation during rapprochement. In response to such attempts, the so-called borderline mother becomes emotionally unavailable, withdraws, or actually discourages the child's autonomous strivings while she rewards the child for his or her regressive and clinging behavior. Experiencing a terrible conflict that has two equally bad alternatives, the child may individuate at the price of experiencing depression and abandonment or remain dependent and regressed while feeling good (rewarded). Thus, the child internalizes what is termed "a split object relations unit" composed of an aggressively charged "withdrawing part-unit" and a libidinally charged "rewarding part-unit." The "withdrawing part-unit" is composed of an attacking, critical, hostile, angry, withdrawing maternal part-object in the face of the child's efforts at individuation in relation to an inadequate, bad, helpless, guilty, ugly, and empty part-self. In contrast, the "rewarding part-unit" reflects an approving and supporting maternal part-object in the face of the child's regressive and clinging behavior in relation to a good, passive, and compliant part-self. The child escapes from the abandonment depression that would result from successful individuation sought by the healthy ego through the maintenance of a pleasure-seeking or pathological ego that seeks dependency. The pathological ego helps the child to deny the reality of separation and to maintain a wish for and engage in efforts at reunion with the mother. Regressive and clinging behaviors feel good because they protect the child from the bad feelings that would ensue if he or she were to act more autonomously. If the child or adult does experience actual separation or acts of individuation at various points in life, the "withdrawing part-unit" may be activated and the person experiences a disabling abandonment depression. This development, in turn, activates the "rewarding part-unit" along with more dependent behavior. Thus, the "split object relations unit" becomes asociated with rigid defenses and interferes with healthy development and reality-based functioning.

In a different formulation that also drew, in part, on Mahlerian ideas, Adler (1985) and Adler and Buie (1979) argued that the mother's failure to provide sufficient holding experiences may produce a deficit in a child's capacity for evocative memory (the abililty to recall the memory or image of the mother in her absence). They believed that it was this deficit rather than "a split object relations unit" which leaves borderline children and adults with a terrible sense of aloneness, fears of abandonment, annihilation anxiety, and loss of self-cohesion in the face of separation. Vulnerable individuals also simultaneously long for and are threatened by intense closeness with others. Their need-fear dilemma prevents the person from entering into or sustaining close relationships or from experiencing others as holding or soothing. It also leads to a defensive patterning of interpersonal relationships that obstructs the development of a solid sense of self.

KERNBERG'S STAGES OF INTERNALIZED OBJECT RELATIONS AND BORDERLINE AND NARCISSISTIC PATHOLOGY

Describing a similar set of successive stages as Mahler, Kernberg focused less on the separation-individuation process and the impact of the caretaking environment and more on the development of an individual's internalized object relations, the progressive structuring of the psychic apparatus, and the consolidation of ego identity. Initially, his developmental timetable was earlier than Mahler's, but he later adjusted his thinking to correspond to her observations. Kernberg described the following stages.

> *Stage 1: Normal "Autism,"* or *The Primary Undifferentiated Stage,* in which the infant exists in a state of being objectless, unrelated, or undifferentiated with respect to the mother or main caretaker. Optimally, the infant starts to build up a core of pleasurable experiences.

> *Stage 2: Normal "Symbiosis"* or *The Stage of the Primary, Undifferentiated Self- and Object-Representations,* in which the infant begins to acquire a "good" internal self-object (infant-mother) image under the impact of gratification, which becomes the nucleus of the ego and a "bad" inner self-object image under the impact of frustration.

> *Stage 3: Differentiation of Self- from Object-Representations,* in which the child becomes able to differentiate between self-representations and object-representations but is not yet able to experience either the self or objects in their totality because of the child's lack of integrative capacity and his or her cognitive immaturity. The child continues to separate "good" or libidinally invested "good" self- and object-images from "bad" or aggres-

sively tinged self- and object-images that now are differentiated from aggressively infiltrated "bad" object-images. Because excessive frustration generates intense anxiety, the infant tries to expel or project rather than take in or introject the resultant "bad" self-object images. The child fears that his or her "bad" self- and object-representations will destroy the "good" self- and object-images and begins to experience severe conflict. Splitting and other primitive defenses (denial, devaluation, idealization, projective identification, and omnipotent control) come into play in order to ward off conflict and anxiety by maintaining the separation between "good" and "bad" self- and object-representations.

Stage 4: Integration of Self-Representations and Object-Representations and Development of Higher Level Intrapsychic Object Relations—Derived Structures, in which the child is able to integrate both "good" and "bad" self-images into a coherent self system and "good" and "bad" object-images into a total and three-dimensional conception of others. The child can experience bad feelings toward the self or the object without losing all the good feelings. Splitting and other related defenses gradually give way to repression as the child's major defensive operation. Thus, anxiety and guilt-arousing feelings or experiences become part of the unconscious rather than being split off or projected. The intrapsychic apparatus begins to consolidate during this stage, particularly as the superego becomes more structured. Superego development involves the transformation or "toning down" of both the extremely negative self- and object-representations and the highly positive or primitively idealized self- and object-representations. The resultant internalization of more realistic selfobject images within the superego lessen its harsh control over the child, substituting more-appropriate demands and prohibitions.

Stage 5: Consolidation of Superego and Ego Integration, in which superego integration is completed and ego identity is consolidated under the impact of real experiences with others. A harmonious inner world, which has been shaped by interactions with external objects, stabilizes the personality and affects all later interpersonal relationships.

In relating the origins of severe psychopathology to his schema regarding the development of internalized object relations (see Chapter 2), Kernberg described the formation of three stable intrapsychic structures (psychotic, borderline, and neurotic) that influence later personality development and psychopathology. In the lowest level, the psychotic structure, the child is unable to acquire the consistent ability to differentiate self-representations from object-representations and thus cannot distinguish himself or herself from others. Firm ego boundaries and the capacity for reality testing fail to develop.

Kernberg stressed the role of the overabundance of constitutionally predisposed aggression or very early frustration rather than maternal care that color the ways they experience their caretakers as resulting in the development of the intermediate level of structure, which he called borderline personality organization. Children who develop borerline personality organization are able to differentiate themselves from others so that they move beyond a psychotic structure, possess the capacity for reality testing, and display reasonably firm ego boundaries but they are unable to overcome the normal use of the splitting defense, which keeps their good (libidinally tinged) and bad (aggressively tinged) self- and object-representations separate. Splitting and other primitive defenses continue beyond their phase-appropriate emergence, and the child never acquires a realistic, three-dimensional conception of others and an integrated sense of self. Instead, identity remains diffuse and other ego functions are adversely affected—for example, the capacity to neutralize anger, impulse control, anxiety tolerance, sublimatory capacity. Thus, individuals who have a borderline personality organization show generalized ego weakness along with their pathological internalized object relations. Additionally, the resolution of the oedipal phase is compromised and the superego remains unintegrated into the rest of the intrapsychic structure and may reflect alternately extremely harsh and exacting or overly permissive internal attitudes. These structural abnormalities become a stable part of the personality and affect the individual's ways of experiencing himself or herself and of perceiving and relating to others. In some instances, even the ability to differentiate self from others is tenuous and renders the person vulnerable to brief psychotic regressions under stress.

In contrast to those who develop a psychotic or borderline structure, children who form a neurotic structure (the highest form) replace splitting as their major defense and acquire a defensive organization centering on repression and other higher-level defensive operations. They possess an integrated identity, generally good ego strength, a mature capacity for object relations, and a well-developed superego that is neither too harsh nor too lax.

According to Kernberg, it is necessary but not sufficient to know whether a patient possesses a neurotic or borderline structure in order to understand the nature of his or her psychopathology and to guide treatment. It also is essential to assess the specific type of personality—for example, dependent, obsessive-compulsive, narcisisstic, schizoid, or antisocial personality—that a person has acquired. Character type reveals the patterning of certain areas of psychosexual conflict and object relations disturbance. In Kernberg's view, both neurotic and borderline structures can be found in individuals with different types of personality disorder and other clinical syndromes, such as substance abuse and eating disorders. This perspective is at variance with the view of personality disorders embodied in the DSM-IV (APA, 1994), which sees the borderline designation as one of many personality disorders.

In addition to his delineation of borderline personality organization, Kernberg wrote extensively about individuals with narcissistic personalities, whom he regarded as having an underlying or covert borderline structure but as able to have better social functioning, impulse control, and the ability to work more effectively than other borderline individuals. Thus, higher level narcissistic personalities, unless they have a more overt borderline structure and show poor ego functioning, are able to partially fulfill their ambitions and obtain admiration from others (Kernberg, 1974: 217).

Kernberg believed that narcissistic personalities possess a grandiose self, which is a combination of the child's real self, ideal self, and ideal object. He considered the grandiose self to be a highly pathological structure, which takes the place of a normal self-concept but which nevertheless allows for somewhat better personality integration and higher functioning than is characteristic of most borderline individuals. The grandiose self is maintained by the defense of splitting and other primitive defenses and does not take in anything that contradicts it. Kernberg described narcissistic personalities as self-absorbed, deficient in their ability to love and care for others, highly ambitious, driven by a search for brilliance, wealth, beauty, and perfection, overdependent on others' admiration, easily bored, empty, lacking in empathy for others, chronically uncertain and dissatisfied with themselves, and often exploitative if not ruthless in their relationships (Kernberg, 1974: 215–216).

JACOBSON'S VIEW OF EARLY OBJECT LOSS AND DEPRESSION

Jacobson was interested in accounting for the origins and dynamics of depressive states that result from losing or becoming disillusioned with a loved one. She viewed depression as resulting from a loss of self-esteem and described how, at an early phase of development, infants begin to feel at one with their idealized and omnipotent loved objects, so much so that their self- and object-representations become merged—that is, they are unable to distinguish psychically between themselves and those they love. At this time, good (rewarding) internal images of the self and others are separated from bad (frustrating) self- and object-images. Because of the tendency toward merger with the object, when the self experiences loving feelings toward the object, the self also feels good. Self-esteem results from positive or libidinally charged feelings that are originally experienced toward others but that become directed at the self-representations. Conversely, when the self is angry at the object, the self feels bad and fears punishment. Jacobson explained that loss of self-esteem arises when there is so much anger at the object that loving feelings are eclipsed and, through the process of identification, anger is then turned against the self.

According to Jacobson, early object loss or intense feelings of anger at or disappointment in loved ones results in vulnerability to depressive reactions in later life. When traumatic experiences occur, aggression toward the object overtakes feelings of love. Consequently, the person is deprived of the ability to merge with the gratifying and all-powerful idealized image of the object and instead, devalues the object. The merger between the self- and object-images results in the self being denigrated as well, and the person feels worthless. Moreover, the superego punishes the person for the now inwardly directed anger at the object and causes the person to feel even worse.

In simple terms, one can describe the intrapsychic process that leads to depression by means of the following inner dialogue.

I love you and need you, but you are not here.

I long for you to be here to make me feel good and safe.

I am very angry with and disappointed in you for not being here.

I don't love you anymore. I don't think you're very good at all.

I don't like myself very much. What good am I?

I'm a pretty terrible and worthless person. I don't deserve to feel good. I should be punished.

KLEIN'S PARANOID/SCHIZOID AND DEPRESSIVE POSITIONS

Klein originated the concepts of the paranoid/schizoid and depressive positions. She described the paranoid/schizoid position as occurring in the first six months of life when infants' rage, envy, and greed are heightened by experiences of frustration and they vent their impulses on the object or part-object that frustrates them. Because the ego is immature and easily threatened, infants become terrified of their own primitive and over-whelming destructive impulses toward the objects or part-objects upon whom they are dependent. They are capable of using defenses to protect themselves and project their anxiety-provoking rageful impulses onto the mother. This results in their developing persecutory fears of the environ-ment. Once their impulses are projected, infants experience the outer world as being as threatening as were their original impulses, but they now can control their external enemies.

Beginning at approximately six months of age, the infant becomes more able to perceive the mother as a whole person (object) that is separate from and outside of the infant and enters the depressive position. Loving feel-ings toward the mother temper the uncomfortable and threatening aggres-sion and hatred that the infant experiences toward her. Instead of fearing retaliation, children feel guilt and anxiety about the damage they have done or can do in fantasy. In order to preserve the mother as a good object, the infant makes reparation for aggressive fantasies and impulses and experiences gratitude and guilt. The infant then introjects the more caring and guilt-ridden relationship with the mother. The depressive position strengthens the infant's ego and ability to relate to reality, but it never fully replaces the paranoid/schizoid position, with which individuals continue to struggle all through life.

Klein believed that infants experience the continuing conflict between their rageful impulses toward and persecutory fears of the mother associated with the paranoid/schizoid position and their need to love and protect her, which is related to the depressive position. Consequently, they fear that they will not be able to succeed in keeping the mother safe and that she will be destroyed. The older infant may utilize the earlier defenses of splitting, projective identification, idealization, and denial, along with more higher level *manic defenses* that are aimed at protecting the infant from feelings of valuing, depending on, losing, or mourning the object. These include the defense of omnipotence, in which infants feel that they are more powerful than and can control the object; the defense of denial, in which infants do not acknowledge their dependence on or need for the object; and manic triumph, in which infants try to defeat or are contemptuous of the object.

Klein considered the paranoid/schizoid position a normal rather than pathological development, but if early experiences are such that the infant is unable to temper his or her aggression, persecutory fears and primitive defenses may come to exert a powerful role in personality development that distorts an individual's relationships to others.

FAIRBAIRN'S ENDOPSYCHIC STRUCTURE AND THE BAD OBJECT

Fairbairn rejected Klein's notion that the infant's death instinct and destructive fantasies toward the mother would inevitably engender primitive defenses and negatively tinged internalizations. Instead, he believed that the infantile ego (or self) would remain intact and whole if relations with early caretakers were positive but that environmental failure produces splits in the ego and results in the internalization of bad objects that persecutes the individual. Moreover, he thought that there was no need for the child to internalize a good object and that internalization only occurs when the environment is frustrating. Because Fairbairn thought that it is not possible for the child who needs others to withdraw completely from objects when deprived or thwarted, he viewed the child's ego as coping with environmental failure by splitting its experiences with bad objects into the following different internal parts, the totality of which is referred to as the endopsychic structure.

> An *idealized object,* which reflects some elements of good object experiences and is satisfying and which represses the frustrating object.
>
> A *rejecting object,* which represents the mother's denial of the infant's needy self.
>
> An *exciting object,* which stimulates but frustrates the infant.
>
> A *central ego,* which adapts to the external world and relates to the parent as an idealized object.
>
> An *anti-libidinal ego,* which directs aggression towards the ego and relates to the parent as a rejecting object.
>
> A *libidinal ego,* which seeks out the exciting object and represses feelings of need and longing.

The creation of these splits in the endopsychic structure appears to alleviate but does not solve the problem of the child's frustration. They are repressed by the central ego that continues to relate to the environment. The repressed inner world becomes a closed system that exerts a powerful force on relationships with others in the real world. They operate to tempt a person into relationships that are destined to repeat the frustration of earlier connections. The child, and later the adult, cannot relinquish or escape from the control of internal bad objects that sabotage the ability to get one's needs met. The individual maintains a repressed tie to these bad objects, which substitutes for the connection to the originally frustrating external object, who often continues to be idealized. Giving up this tie would leave the person profoundly alone. The endopsychic structure impedes further personality development and prevents the individual from progressing from infantile dependence to mature dependence and from establishing loving and satisfying bonds with others. For example, a man may be attracted to a woman whom he idealizes and finds exciting but elusive and unavailable and with whom he cannot experience a mutually loving relationship while he rejects another woman who is attentive and responsive to his emotional needs. In this example, the presence of an internal idealized and exciting but frustrating object propels him to seek out a woman who is unavailable and who disappoints him, while his anti-libidinal ego acts to spurn the woman who is more loving and interested in him.

Fairbairn was quite interested in patients who exhibited a schizoid state, in which they displayed attitudes of omnipotence, isolation, and detachment and were preoccupied with fantasy and inner reality (Fairbairn, 1940). Standing apart from others, they never become truly involved, although they may learn to play a social role appropriately. At a deep level, schizoid persons fear that their love will destroy others and also hold the belief that they can control their inner bad objects (Seinfeld, 1996: 67).

GUNTRIP'S REGRESSED EGO AND THE SCHIZOID PROBLEM

Like Fairbairn, Guntrip also was intrigued with schizoid phenomena but disagreed with Fairbairn's view that schizoid individuals were dominated by their inner bad objects. Instead, he argued that the schizoid state reflected a final split in the ego (or self) in which children, and later adults, withdraw from objects altogether. Guntrip called this split the *regressed ego,* which exhibits attitudes of omnipotence, isolation, detachment, and hopelessness. The regressed ego is split off from the person's need for others, which still exists deep within the person. Guntrip thought that the regressed ego is responsible for schizoid trends in the personality, which he saw as the basis of all psychopathology. In the schizoid state, an individual may have conscious or unconscious longings to relate to others but is so fearful of the hurtful and frustrating experiences inherent in relationships that the person cannot overcome his or her isolation and feelings of emptiness.

WINNICOTT'S "GOOD-ENOUGH" MOTHER AND THE TRUE AND FALSE SELF

Winnicott used the term *facilitating environment* to reflect his view that the external environment is essential to human growth and must adapt to and respond to a child's needs in personal and unique ways. According to Winnicott, the infant's mother is the first representative of the facilitating environment, and the "good-enough" mother is one who adapts to and responds to her child's changing individualized needs and provides for the child sufficiently to help the child to grow. There is not one type of optimal mother because children exhibit a variety of needs at different times and require individualized handling or responsiveness. Although Winnicott tended to have what some might feel is an idealized view of the maternal role, he did not feel that mothers need to be perfect. Nevertheless, he thought that pregnant mothers are biologically prepared for parenting, displaying what he called *primary maternal preoccupation* with their infants' particular needs. After giving birth, they are able to establish a maternal holding environment that helps the child to feel related, safe, protected, and free from unwanted intrusions and that contains the infant's emotions and impulses. Important features of this holding environment are the mother's sensitivity to the infant, her ability to avoid too much deprivation or impingement on the infant, her skill in allowing the infant to feel that she is under the infant's control, and her consistency and reliability despite inevitable failures.

Winnicott placed considerable importance on the concept of *ego-relatedness* between the mother and infant, which sets the stage for the child's ability to develop a strong sense of self. Ego-relatedness is a type of emotional bond between two individuals who both exist as separate people but who are intimately connected. This connection begins when the good-enough mother and child interact. Winnicott observed that the growing child's *capacity to be alone* could be attributed to ego-relatedness, or in other terms, to the child's experiences in being alone in the presence of an attuned other. He also drew attention to the child's *capacity for concern,* a concept that is similar to Klein's depressive position. Winnicott thought that the capacity for concern is an outgrowth of the infant's basic sense of ego-relatedness with the mother and the infant's realization that the mother, who may at times be frustrating, is the same mother who is sustaining and holding.

A *transitional object* comes to represent the mother and at the same time can be manipulated by the child. Whatever becomes a transitional object must originally be associated with the mother in the child's experience.

Winnicott described how children use such objects to preserve the illusion of their omnipotence when they become aware that the mother is not always immediately available to meet their needs or under their direct control. Winnicott also observed that children were able to create other types of transitional experiences—for example, uttering sounds to themselves in ways that resemble how the mother might talk to or sing to the child were she present.

According to Winnicott, the *true self* represents an individual's core potentialities and develops when there is good-enough mothering. He thought that maternal failure, particularly in the form of impingements on the child, as might be reflected in overly strict expectations, leads the child to create a *false self* that adapts to the mother and the surrounding environment at the expense of the true self. As the false self, which is a facade aimed at pleasing others, becomes more rigid, it becomes split off and the person becomes alienated from his or her true self, which remains hidden. Thus, the false self is a defensive organization that both "hides and protects" the true self at the expense of its full expression. It can be more or less severe depending on the nature of early mother-child interactions, in some instances leading to psychosis.

Winnicott also described a six-stage process by which the infant evolves from dependence to independence as follows.

> *Stage 1: Extreme or Absolute Dependence,* in which the infant is unable to recognize the mother as a separate person.
>
> *Stage 2: Dependence,* in which the infant is able to begin to differentiate.
>
> *Stage 3: The Dependence-Independence Mix,* in which the child moves toward independence but has to return to dependence.
>
> *Stage 4: The Independence-Dependence Mix,* in which the child becomes increasingly autonomous but is vulnerable to being pushed too fast.
>
> *Stage 5: Toward Independence,* in which the child attains autonomy, and social sense, in which connection to the social group is possible without the person losing a sense of self.

SUMMARY

The major object relations concepts that have been described in this chapter show both overlapping and diverse views of the developmental process and the origins and nature of psychopathology. Despite their differences and the difficulty in integrating them completely, they can be used alongside one another. Longitudinal studies of early-childhood patterns and later psychopathology may help to clarify their clinical utility.

4

SELF PSYCHOLOGY: MAJOR CONCEPTS

Until Heinz Kohut's untimely death in 1981, self psychology was largely his creation. Although a close inner circle of followers contributed to the expansion and refinement of self psychological ideas, there was fundamental agreement among those who called themselves self psychologists. An emerging theory, however, self psychology was not fully worked out at the time of Kohut's death. As mentioned in Chapter 2, with Kohut's absence, the group began to explore different directions, and at present self psychology is not as unitary as it was previously. Nevertheless, there are many followers of the original Kohutian self psychological framework who find its concepts and their applications extremely meaningful. Likewise, some of the extensions and revisions of self psychology have made important contributions to this body of thought. This chapter first will consider the core developmental concepts of the Kohutian self psychology and its view of psychopathology. Then it will consider selected newer contributions.

BASIC TERMINOLOGY

Self psychology has its own terminology. What follows are some basic concepts that help to explain self psychology's view of development and the origins and nature of psychopathology.

THE SELF AND THE NARCISSISTIC LINE OF DEVELOPMENT

When Kohut first put forth self psychology, he postulated that self development existed alongside of Freud's concept of drive development. Initially, he called this line of development "narcissistic," by which he meant that all infants are born with normal and healthy self needs that require the responsiveness of the caretaking environment. Kohut described a range of such narcissistic or healthy self needs and believed that early, more archaic self needs undergo transformations during the life cycle and become more mature. Nevertheless, Kohut thought that the individual never outgrows the need for others' confirmation. He proposed that "self-selfobject relationships form the essence of psychological life from birth to death, [and] that a move from dependence (symbiosis) to independence (autonomy) in the psychological sphere is no more possible, let alone desirable, than a corresponding move from a life dependent on oxygen to a life independent of it in the biological sphere" (Kohut, 1984: 47).

Kohut regarded the self as the center of initiative of the person that organizes experience and regulates self-esteem. The content of the self is not simply determined by the nature of what infants and children take in from others because it exists in a rudimentary way from birth. It evolves, however, as a result of the interplay between the infant's innate potentialities and an empathically attuned and responsive caretaking environment.

Kohut did not view self-development as occurring according to a fixed series of stages. Instead, he described the *core nuclear self* as crystallizing as a result of mirroring (approving and confirming) responses to the child's *grandiose-exhibitionistic self* and acceptance and enjoyment of the admiration of the child's idealizing *archaic parental imago*. Gradually, the self achieves cohesiveness and stability as an enduring structure. A strong *cohesive self*, which comes about as a result of parental responsiveness and inevitable non-traumatic frustrations, gives the person a sense of vigor, inner harmony, and self-esteem. Those individuals with a cohesive sense of self are able to tolerate minor disappointments, frustrations, and blows to self-esteem without undue regression, fragmentation, or symptom formation.

SELFOBJECTS

In order for the core nuclear self to emerge, to reach its full potential, and to evolve into a cohesive structure, the self needs others. Early selfobjects are those empathic or attuned caretakers who perform vital functions for the infant that it cannot carry out itself—for example, soothing. Self psychologists believe that the infant enters the world preadapted to cue and respond to a potential selfobject milieu and relates to others in terms of their ability to meet the infant's phase-appropriate developmental needs rather than relating to others as truly separate entities.

SELFOBJECT NEEDS

Kohut identified three main types of selfobject needs: *the need for mirroring* that confirms the child's sense of vigor, greatness, and perfection; *the need for an idealization of others* whose strength and calmness soothe the child; and *the need for a twin or alter-ego* who provides the child with a sense of humanness, likeness to, and partnership with others. Other selfobject needs that have been suggested are *the need for merger experiences* with someone who is totally subject to the child's initiative and who functions as an extension of the self, *the need for an adversary* who provides a supportive but oppositional relationship in the service of autonomy, and *the need for efficacy* in having an impact on others and in being able to evoke desired responses. Although not all types of selfobject needs may be gratified in a particular child's life, rewarding experiences with at least one type of selfobject give the child a chance to develop a cohesive self (Wolf, 1988: 55).

Although Kohut thought that early selfobjects are crucial to the development of the infant's self, the need for others to provide support and sustenance continues all through life. Thus, according to Kohut, the ability to seek out gratifying selfobject experiences, in contrast to the capacity for total autonomy, is the hallmark of health. Optimally, however, the individual undergoes a transformation whereby he or she relates to others in terms of more mature rather than early or archaic selfobject needs.

THE GRANDIOSE SELF

Kohut drew attention to a normal phase in the child's development in which the grandiose self asserts itself and to the importance of the selfobject milieu's ability to respond with pleasure and enthusiasm rather than to suppress, discourage, or ignore the child's unrealistic fantasies and ambitions, need for attention, and pleasure in displaying his or her newfound talents and skills. As responsive selfobjects help the child to tolerate the inevitable reality blows to his or her omnipotence, infantile grandiosity gradually gives way to healthy ambitions and goals. Caretaking failures can lead to fixation of the grandiose self, weakening the consolidation of a healthy self-structure.

THE ARCHAIC PARENTAL IMAGO

Kohut believed that children exhibit a need to look to their parents as idealizable people who make them feel secure and soothed in relationship to parental perfection and power. In the course of life, non-traumatic experiences with the inevitable human imperfections and minor failures of these once all-powerful caretakers result in their gradual deidealization, which is necessary for optimal self-development. When this occurs, the child comes to view himself or herself and others in more realistic terms without loss of self-esteem. The absence of idealizable parents, traumatic deidealization experiences, or loss may result in weakness in the self or narcissistic vulnerability.

THE NEED FOR TWINSHIP

A third way the child can acquire a cohesive self is through experiences with someone whom the child perceives as like him or her, someone with whom one shares a common humanity or kinship. Often a grandparent, aunt or uncle, sibling, or even paid caretaker may serve this function. The sudden loss of these early twinship relationships or other types of related trauma may leave the self needful of intense twinship experiences with others in order to feel alive, connected, and affirmed.

THE BIPOLAR SELF

Kohut originally described the self as bipolar, containing three parts: one pole that embodies the child's ambitions and strivings for power and success and that flourishes in response to the mother's mirroring of the child's grandiose-exhibitionistic fantasies and behavior from approximately ages 2 to 4 years; a second pole that reflects the child's idealized goals that develop in empathic relationships with idealizable selfobjects from about ages 4 to 6; and an intermediate area of basic talents and skills that interact with the *tension arc* formed by the intersection of the two poles of ambitions and goals.

TRANSMUTING INTERNALIZATION

The self becomes strong and cohesive through a combination of attuned parenting and inevitable minor and non-traumatic *optimal frustrations,* which transform the self through the process of transmuting internalization. In this process, selfobject functions are gradually taken over by the child, rendering the actual presence of the selfobject less vital or even unnecessary. Thus, what is outside becomes internal and alters the original or archaic structures that exist. An example of transmuting internalization via optimal frustration can be seen at times when a mother who sings to her child at bedtime withdraws prior to the child's falling asleep. If this change is timed correctly and thus is not too traumatic, the child may soothe himself or herself through singing, playing, or talking, thereby identifying with and taking over the mother's function. It is important to note, however, that the child internalizes the selfobject's functions in an individualized rather than identical way, using the selfobject environment to foster its own innate potentialities.

Some self psychologists have objected to the view that frustration is essential to growth and have argued that transmuting internalizations also occur in the context of *optimal responsiveness,* a term that is more positive and inclusive than optimal frustration (Bacal, 1998: 3–34).

NARCISSISTIC RAGE AS A DISINTEGRATION PRODUCT

Rejecting classical psychoanalytic theory's conception of an innate aggressive drive, self psychologists view narcissistic rage as a reaction to or a disintegration product resulting from early selfobject failures. This rage may be remobilized later in life when a person with narcissistic vulnerability or a weak self-structure experiences disappointments, rejections, a lack of appreciation, misunderstandings, or even minor criticisms from those upon whom they depend as selfobjects. The narcissistic rage reactions that commonly result in these instances are understandable responses to a lack of selfobject attunement when the self-structure lacks sufficient cohesion and is weak.

Self psychologists also view other clinical manifestations that followers of Freudian theory would see as an individual's defensive regression to oedipal and preoedipal sexual or aggressive fantasies and behavior as disintegration products resulting from insufficiently met selfobject needs. Thus, instead of focusing on the instinctual and conflictual basis of many forms of oral, anal, and phallic preoccupations, self psychologists would view these as disintegration products resulting from selfobject failures. For example, a child's preoccupation with sexual fantasies or seemingly inappropriate demands for attention may be a consequence of parental failure to mirror the child's independence and achievements sufficiently.

COMPENSATORY STRUCTURES

In Kohut's schema, not all structural defects in the self result in pathology, since the child may be able to acquire compensatory structures that strengthen the self. These structures enable the person to make up for or repair deficits in one aspect of the self through successful development of its other facets. Thus, the child has more than one chance to achieve self-cohesion. For example, the child who is not mirrored for his intellectual abilities may cultivate his athletic prowess. In contrast to defenses, which cover over enduring defects in the self and are used to improve low self-esteem, compensatory structures actually foster self-cohesion.

PERSPECTIVES ON PSYCHOPATHOLOGY

Although self psychology initially developed to explain the problem of narcissistic personality, it gradually was used to explain a broad range of self states and self disorders. Kohut used the term *tragic man,* in contrast to Freud's *guilty man,* to express the idea that a self that is fragmented or depleted and that reflects unmirrored ambitions and is devoid of ideals is quite sad, and that this tragic state reflects the core problem of those with self disorders.

WEAKNESS IN THE SELF OR NARCISSISTIC VULNERABILITY

Self psychology sees all psychopathology as reflecting self deficits—that is, gaps, or missing or underdeveloped elements in self structure that come about as a result of unattuned or traumatic caretaking. Kohut believed that disabling self disorders occur when the child's protracted exposure to a lack of parental empathy in at least two areas of selfobject need leaves the child unable to develop the compensatory structures essential to a cohesive sense of self (Elson, 1986: 50). When there is selfobject failure of this intensity, transmuting internalizations do not occur and the self remains enfeebled. Those who remain fixated at the level of the grandiose self may develop inordinate needs for affirmation and attention, withdraw entirely from interpersonal relationships and appear cold, haughty, and self-sufficient, or dwell on unrealistic fantasies of stardom, wealth, or power sometimes in the absence of any efforts to function in the world or any real accomplishments. Difficulties in transforming the archaic parental imago may lead to later tendencies to idealize others at the expense of one's own self-regard, extreme dependence on others for the regulation of self-esteem, or an inability to depend on others due to fears of disillusionment or loss. Problems in fulfilling twinship selfobject needs may result in longings to be in close proximity to another person with whom one shares everything, difficulties tolerating separateness or difference from another person, and wishes to have one's thoughts and feelings known without having to communicate. In those who show narcissistic vulnerability, depression, shame, humiliation, rage, and even fragmentation and suicide result from even minor criticisms, lack of appreciation, disapproval, rejection, or failure to live up to one's own or others' expectations.

A CLASSIFICATION OF SELF DISORDERS

Kohut and Wolf (1978) put forth a classification of self disorders that described primary disturbances of the self, which include narcissistic personality and behavior disorders, borderline states, and psychoses; a variety of self states and character types; and secondary disturbances of the self, which include temporary reactions of a structurally undamaged self to the vicissitudes of life.

Narcissistic personality disorders involve psychological states, in contrast to *narcissistic behavior disorders,* which involve actions and interactions. Individuals with narcissistic personality disorders characteristically over-value appearances, beauty, clothes, or performance, which cover a total lack of self-regard. They are overly sensitive to slights and disappoint-ments. They may be driven in their work lives on the one hand or be unable to pursue education, training, or work on the other. Fear of failure or of not being perfect, the need for great success or repeated victories, the need to be special, and feelings of entitlement are present. They tend to idealize others, particularly those who are powerful or successful, often at their own expense, display contemptuous or insensitive attitudes toward others, isolate from others, or are unable to tolerate or accept others' differences. Individuals with narcissistic behavior disorders frequently abuse drugs, alcohol, food, and sex or engage in other compulsive, dangerous, or excit-ing activities.

Kohut viewed narcissistic personality and behavior disorders as related to but different from the more severe borderline states and psychoses. In Kohut's view, *borderline states* reflect a "permanent or protracted" breakup and enfeeblement of the self that are covered over by rigid defenses and schizoid and paranoid attitudes and behavior that ward off the selfobject attachments and protect the highly vulnerable self from fragmentation and psychosis (Tolpin, 1980). Although the self may collapse if defenses are weakened or tampered with, borderlines generally function at a higher level and remain more reality-oriented than psychotics.

Because of the realistic threat of self-fragmentation, the borderline indi-vidual cannot allow himself or herself to become attached to selfobjects or to use them for overcoming weaknesses in the self. In some instances, they desperately seek intense merger experiences with others in which they attempt to acquire necessary sustenance, but their concomitant fear of frag-mentation and inordinate sensitivity to disappointment make these attach-ments highly fragile and tumultuous. Their defects in self-structure leave them with a chronic and overwhelming sense of anxiety or dread and contribute to problems in self-regulation, self-control, self-soothing, low self-esteem, and sense of personal inadequacy. The absence of sufficient transmuting internalizations results in a search for others to perform archaic selfobject functions and to help maintain themselves against fragmentation.

SELF STATES AND CHARACTER TYPES

Among the self states that Kohut and Wolf (1978) described are the *understimulated self*, in which the person is driven to engage in exciting, distracting, and sometimes compulsive and dangerous activity in order to ward off inner deadness; the *fragmented self*, in which the person experiences chronic or recurrent loss of cohesiveness even in the face of minor rebuffs or blows to self-esteem; the *overstimulated self*, in which the person becomes easily flooded by unrealistic grandiose fantasies or anxiety when encountering even small successes or attention; and the *overburdened self*, in which the person lacks self-soothing capacity and experiences the world as unduly frightening, anxiety-producing, and dangerous.

In addition to the self states that may occur in response to the deprivations or excesses of the caretaking environment, there are some character types that develop in order to deal with circumscribed selfobject failures and resultant weakness in the self. Certain individuals become *mirror-hungry*, in which they continually search for applause and affirmation to overcome an inner sense of worthlessness and lack of self-esteem but can never be satisfied; *ideal-hungry*, in which they always seek out those they can admire for certain qualities such as beauty, power, and intelligence, in order to feel worthwhile themselves but they always wind up deidealizing others and renewing their search; *alter-ego hungry*, in which they try to find others who are just like them in certain ways in order to affirm their fragile sense of self but cannot sustain the twinship for long and look elsewhere; *merger-hungry*, in which they need to lose themselves in others who are always available and who have difficulty tolerating even the slightest frustration or separation; and *contact-shunning*, in which they avoid others out of fear that they will be swallowed up and destroyed because of their intense needs for merger.

SECONDARY DISTURBANCES OR TEMPORARY REACTIONS TO LIFE STRESS

It has been said that the most fundamental developmental tasks of adult life involve the maintenance of self-esteem and identity in the face of the biological, psychological, and social stresses and losses that occur as we grow older (Lazarus, 1991: 35). The successful achievement of these tasks is fraught even for those with relatively firm self-structures because individuals are not truly autonomous from the environment and are subject to life's vicissitudes. The impact of illness, disability, death of significant others, divorce, aging, loss of employment, diminished opportunities and status, disappointments in achieving one's goals, geographic changes, and loss of role may result in secondary disturbances of the self that lead to feelings of emptiness, depletion, grief, and rage. These reactions usually are temporary because the individual is able to recover from them through his or her own inner resources or available selfobjects and affirming activities (Elson, 1986: 40). Certain life events can be particularly troublesome and may lead to prolonged disequilibrium, when they undermine a person's compensatory self-structures or tap into underlying narcissistic vulerability.

Because there is a range of self pathology and narcissistic vulnerability, the extent to which stressful life circumstances cause a loss of self-cohesion in the individual is variable. Mild to severe symptoms develop, however, that express the person's feeling states, such as anxiety, panic, rage, or depression; that reflect defenses against the person's painful experiences; or that represent attempts to soothe or restore the self, such as substance abuse, compulsive sexual behavior, binge eating, and the like (Baker, 1991: 204–6).

EMERGING RESEARCH AND THEORY

As discussed in Chapter 2, self psychology began to move into different directions after Kohut's death in 1981. Among the many emerging views that are being promulgated, some new concepts bear special mention because of their significance.

STERN'S FOUR SENSES OF THE SELF

A psychoanalyst and researcher, Daniel Stern (1985) engaged in seminal studies of mother-infant interaction, the findings of which tended to call Mahler's account of separation-individuation phenomena into question and tended to support Kohut's views of self-development. Delineating four phases of self-development, which he preferred to call "domains of related-ness," Stern viewed each domain as codetermined by the growing infant's innate maturational capacities and the nature and degree of attunement of the caretaker environment. Constitutional or genetic factors also seemed to contribute greatly to the different ways infants interacted with the world, as did the mother's ability to fit herself to the child's temperament, needs, and behavioral patterns. The four domains are described below.

> *The Sense of Emergent Self,* which is characterized by the infant's ability from birth onward to process important information about the external and interpersonal world. The infant actively makes distinctions between people by smell and sound, identi-fies familiar objects that it has sucked, and makes connections between stimuli based on their intensity. The infant also engages in behavior that confirms its own existence as a separate being and builds up a stable picture of the physical characteristics of the interpersonal milieu.
>
> *The Sense of Core Self,* which begins as early as two to three months and continues until about seven months. It is character-ized by the infant's formation of an organized sense of a core self that has two aspects—the first in which the infant acquires a clear grasp of both its own and the significant other's separate physical presence, and the second in which it achieves a sense of the mutual influence that exists between itself and another. This view contrasts sharply with that of Mahler, who describes this period as a symbiotic one. In fact, Stern argued strongly that the infant's ability to merge with the mother is a product of its sepa-rateness rather than a reflection of a normal symbiotic phase. The infant's sense of core self in relation to the other is contin-gent upon satisfying episodes of mutual regulation that build up over time. Gratifying experiences in which the mother-infant dyad both cue and respond to one another as separate beings

who influence but do not obliterate one another are essential to the firming up of the sense of core self.

The infant's sense of a core self as separate from the other is composed of four factors that become integrated: *self-agency,* owning one's actions and not owning the actions of others; *self-coherence,* being a physical whole with boundaries and a center of action; *self-affectivity,* experiencing patterned inner qualities of feelings; and *self-history,* having a sense of continuity.

The Sense of Subjective Self, which emerges between seven and nine months when the infant moves beyond experiencing itself and others in terms of physical characteristics and discovers inner mental qualities. For example, the child not only reacts positively to the mother's overt comforting or empathic behavior but recognizes her empathic process. Likewise, the child's awareness of his or her own and others' intentions and affects permits an intersubjective relatedness to develop. This period marks the beginning of the child's capacity for true intimacy and sharing of experience. The child's attainment of a sense of subjective self builds upon, but does not supersede or replace, the sense of a core self, which continues to expand. Unlike Mahler, who describes the child's differentiation from the mother at this time, Stern drew attention to the child's growing ability to share with the mother during this period. In fact, he criticized earlier ego psychological views for their overemphasis on separation-individuation and neglect of the beginnings of intersubjective relatedness.

The Sense of Verbal Self, which occurs at about fifteen to eighteen months, when the child begins to acquire the capacity for language and symbolization. The attainment of this verbal domain of relatedness adds a different dimension to the way the child experiences himself or herself, others, and the world. The child becomes capable of viewing himself or herself objectively, performing empathic acts, engaging in symbolic play, and thinking. Language not only facilitates separation-individuation but also helps to unite two persons in a common use of symbols.

Stern's work also focused on the degree of optimal or deviant development of the child's four senses of the self, but he did not systematically address the origins and nature of adult psychopathology per se. Those deviations that were identified in the subjects he studied always reflected mismatching or unattuned transactions between children and their caretakers, rather than residing in the infant alone. It is not clear, however, which of the deviations that he observed are linked to later clinical disorders. It is likely that certain disorders arise as a consequence of misattunement in all domains of relatedness rather than being linked to one in particular. For example, the borderline individual's problems in self-cohesion described by Kohut may arise from mismatching at many levels of self-development rather than those at one stage alone.

LICHTENBERG'S FIVE MOTIVATIONAL SYSTEMS

Like Stern, Joseph Lichtenberg (1989) is a psychoanalyst and researcher who enlarged upon Kohut's view of selfobject experience but in doing so, put forth a distinctive view of development as fueled by five different motivational systems. "Lichtenberg sees the self as developing out of the experience of having needs and having these needs recognized, acknowledged, and fulfilled through affect-laden interactions with the caregiver. The self becomes, then, an independent center for initiating, organizing, and integrating motivation, and the sense of self arises from such experiences" (Shane, 1991: 224). The following five motivational systems each has its own developmental line and exists on a continuum of need- and phase-appropriate environmental responses.

> *The Motivational System Based on the Regulation of Physiological Requirements,* in which the infant is dominated by the need to have his basic bodily needs responded to, regulated, and fulfilled.

> *The Attachment-Affiliation Motivational System,* in which the infant and toddler seek connection, closeness, likeness, and intimacy.

> *The Exploratory-Assertive Motivational System,* in which the infant and child forcefully express curiosity in, and efforts to have an affect upon and be competent in, dealing with the environment.

The Aversive Motivational System, in which the infant and tod-
dler react to frustration and fear with attempts to avoid, flee, or
oppose painful situations. This system gives rise to defense formation.

The Sensual-Sexual Motivational System, in which the infant and
child express their needs for affection and soothing on the one
hand and sexual excitement and relaxation on the other.

Personality develops in relation to how the growing organism evolves the
mechanisms and coping strategies for dealing with each of these motivational systems. Particular forms of psychopathology reflect the dominance
of a particular motivational system and problems in getting the need associated with it met. The clinician must determine which motivational system is active at any given time with a patient and must also consider
whether pathological developments can be corrected through resumption
of growth model or through a reorganization of experience model, the latter of which requires more interpretation and reconstruction.

BACAL'S VIEW OF SELF PSYCHOLOGY AS A FORM OF OBJECT RELATIONS THEORY

Howard Bacal (Bacal & Newman, 1990) has tried to address what he considers to be gaps in self psychology by assimilating selected object relations
concepts into self psychology, but in so doing offers a revised version of self
psychology. In his view that self psychology is a type of object relations theory that deals with the self and its object, Bacal regards the selfobject as a
type of object relationship. He argues that one of the major gaps in self
psychology relates to its lack of attention to other uses of objects besides
the selfobject function and that this confines the theory to a more intrapsychic rather than relational focus. Instead, Bacal believes that self psychology is a more interpersonal, two-person psychology. He goes on to suggest
that self psychology would be enriched if it were to incorporate key elements from the work of object relations theorists—for example, Klein's
emphasis on fantasy, Bion's concepts of attacks on linking and the analyst

as container of the patient's unbearable feelings, Fairbairn's view of bad objects and object splitting, Guntrip's understanding of schizoid defenses, Winnicott's focus on the false self, Mahler's description of the mother's role in mediating affect containment and integration, and Stolorow's understanding of the role of conflict and defense in response to selfobject failures (Shane, 1992: 220–224). Bacal's ideas have not gained universal acceptance among the self psychologists, some of whom regard Bacal's ideas as fundamentally altering self psychology (Ornstein, 1991: 27–29; Fosshage, 1992: 234–237).

THE SHANES' TWO DIMENSIONS OF INTIMACY

Morton and Estelle Shane, along with Mary Gales (1997), also have moved beyond the original self psychological position. Concerned about self psychology's lack of attention to the range of interactions with objects beyond the selfobject experience, they have proposed that there are two dimensions of early object experiences that also emerge in the therapeutic relationship: the self with transforming other dimension—which addresses how significant others in childhood and later the therapeutic dyad are used to regulate and transform the person into coming more fully into being as a person—and the self with interpersonal sharing other dimension, which is concerned with how early and later the therapeutic relationship is used to create a capacity to be with another in mutual sharing and appreciation. In the first dimension, others, including the therapist, provide significant functions for the person's self. It is closely linked to Kohut's and Stern's work. In the second dimension, others, including the therapist, are appreciated for their own sake, and not just in relation to the patient's needs. This dimension is more closely linked to the work of the attachment and relational theorists and to newer self-psychologically informed models.

STOLOROW'S THEORY OF INTERSUBJECTIVITY

In his writings, Stolorow attacks the myth of the isolated mind and the one-person psychology, to which he argues that most psychoanalytic theories and treatment models have adhered over the years (Stolorow, 1992;

Stolorow & Atwood, 1979, 1992; Stolorow, Brandchaft & Atwood, 1987; Stolorow, Atwood & Brandchaft, 1994). Instead, he embraces a two-person psychology, which views all human behavior as codetermined by two inter- acting and mutually influencing worlds of experience, which he calls *the intersubjective field*. According to Stolorow's theory of intersubjectivity, the internalization of infant-caregiver patterns of interaction result in certain fixed principles that organize the child's subjective experiences and influ- ence further interactions with others. These structures or *organizing prin- ciples* are the essential building blocks of personality development but also are affected by the current and ongoing interactional field.

An Although Stolorow agreed that self-selfobject experiences are an impor- tant dimension of early experience, he argued that there are other organiz- ing principles that lead individuals to recreate basic conflictual relational patterns and utilize pathological defenses later in life and in treatment. A major therapeutic task is understanding the nature of a patient's organiz- ing principles and whether they reflect the selfobject or repetitive relational dimensions of behavior. Thus, intersubjectivity attempts to integrate cer- tain aspects of both classical psychoanalytic theory and ego psychology, object relations theory, and self psychology. The details of the intersubjec- tive perspective are not fully spelled out, but this framework has led to far- reaching reconceptualizations of many aspects of development, the nature of psychopathology, mistakes and impasses in treatment, and the treat- ment process itself.

An important clinical implication of the theory of intersubjectivity is that children and adults cannot be understood without reference to their interpersonal interactions, including those that occur during treatment. The observer, including the analyst or therapist, always brings his or her own organizing principles to and becomes a participant in all interactions. Consequently, in order to understand a patient, it is necessary to give up a one-sided view of what transpires in treatment, recognizing that both ther- apist and patient exert a mutual impact on one another. Therapists who practice within an intersubjective framework must always be alert to the ways in which their organizing principles—which affect their values, atti- tudes, perceptions, and theoretical and clinical stances—are influencing the way in which they perceive and interact with patients.

SUMMARY

The self psychological concepts that have been described in this chapter show a unique view of the developmental process and the origins and nature of psychopathology. Although self psychology is no longer a unitary and cohesive system of thought and there have been numerous efforts to integrate self psychological and object relations concepts, the original Kohutian formulations offer a significant perspective that has far-reaching implications for treatment.

5

TREATMENT PRINCIPLES

As noted in Chapter 2, classical Freudian psychoanalysis originally was intended to be used to treat neurotic individuals who occupied the higher end of the health-illness spectrum, had achieved a rather intact intrapsychic structure as a result of having passed through the oedipal stage of psychosexual development, and were verbal and self-reflective. Although treatment based on ego psychological principles encompassed patients who showed ego deficits stemming from preoedipal developmental stages, object relations and self psychological theories greatly expanded the range of patients and types of problems that psychoanalytically oriented treatment could address. They generated diverse treatment approaches that were aimed at modifying deep-seated pathology and repairing the developmental arrests stemming from the earliest life stages. This chapter will discuss the main principles associated with treatment based on object relations and self psychological theories.

OBJECT RELATIONS TREATMENT

Because the theories discussed in Chapter 2 envisioned somewhat distinctive perspectives on normal development and psychopathology, they gave rise to different approaches to treatment rather than one unified model. Although object relations therapies contain common elements, they reflect two major emphases with respect to their treatment goals, view of change processes, and main principles and techniques.

The first general emphasis in object relations treatment, which is evident in the writings of such theorists as Klein, Fairbairn, Kernberg, and Masterson, aims at modifying patients' pathological defenses, intrapsychic splits, and internalized self- and object-representations, including their "bad" objects. Therapists who follow this approach tend to utilize insight-oriented techniques such as confrontation and interpretation in a highly focused manner, often adopt a stance of therapeutic neutrality and abstinence (non-gratification of patients' needs), and employ a systematic focus on the here-and-now transference-countertransference dynamics, particularly the role of projective identification, in therapeutic interactions. Alternatively, the second treatment emphasis, which is described in the writings of Winnicott, Guntrip, and others, aims at creating facilitative and reparative experiences through the provision of a therapeutic holding environment and a positive relationship. Therapists who subscribe to this type of approach tend to utilize developmentally attuned interventions rather than a fixed or rigid set of technical interventions.

MODIFYING PATHOLOGICAL STRUCTURES VERSUS PROVIDING FACILITATING AND REPARATIVE EXPERIENCES

A major distinction between the two general types of object relations treatment approaches is whether they identify the goal of therapy as the modification of pathological defenses and internalized self- and object-representations or the facilitation of developmental progression and the building up of new internal structures. This distinction is related to the degree to which patients' problems are viewed as reflecting fixed, pathological internal structures that need to be torn down, so to speak, or whether they represent deficits or gaps and underdeveloped internal structures that need to be filled in or built up, or a combination of both (Goldstein, 1990: 14–29).

INSIGHT VERSUS POSITIVE RELATIONSHIP EXPERIENCES

Believing that fixed pathological object relations structures and defenses were impeding a person's development and causing serious difficulties, Klein, Fairbairn, Kernberg, and Masterson favored a modifying approach and stressed the role of insight in producing change. Fairbairn did recognize the role of the therapeutic relationship as a force in enabling the therapist to enter the patient's closed inner world in order to start a process of natural growth, but he was inclined to favor his interpretive rather than good object function in his actual work. Nevertheless, he bridged the more interpretive emphasis of Freud and Klein with the holding and relational emphasis of Winnicott, Guntrip, and others (Seinfeld, 1993: 53–82). Likewise, in addition to stressing the importance of confrontative and interpretive techniques in the early phases of treatment, Masterson (1976) wrote of the importance of providing good object experiences in therapy in order to promote separation-individuation after the patient had made considerable progress.

In contrast to those who stressed the goal of modification and the role of insight, Winnicott, Guntrip, and others believed that treatment always should be facilitative and reparative and thought that the experience of the therapeutic relationship was more important than insight and the content of interpretations. "At the deepest level, psychotherapy is replacement therapy, providing for the patient what the mother failed to provide at the beginning of life" (Guntrip, 1973: 191). They pointed out the importance of the therapist enabling the patient to feel safe and secure, to seek refuge in the therapeutic relationship and just be, to find and use the therapist, and to support the development of the patient's true self. Both thought that patients would use such an environment to seek what they needed in order to resume their development.

Guntrip also drew attention to the need for the therapist to reach for patients sufficiently so that they would reemerge from their withdrawal. He described a patient as facing a dilemma in therapy in which he or she may feel, "I can't reach you. If you can't reach me I'm lost . . . I haven't got a real self to relate with. I'm not a real person. I need you to find me in some way that enables me to find you" (Guntrip, 1973: 185). In the period of reemergence, the fragile patient may try to retreat, and the analyst must remain steadfast in his or her ability to stay with the patient.

NEUTRALITY AND ABSTINENCE VERSUS MEETING PATIENTS' NEEDS

Some object relations theorists, such as Kernberg and Masterson, have recommended that therapists adhere to a technically neutral and abstinent position in which they refrain from offering direct support or meeting patients' needs. A technically neutral response to a female patient who arrives at a session and enthusiastically tells the therapist of a triumph and waits expectantly for some positive reaction, would be: "Let us try to understand why it is so important that I tell you I am pleased with your success." Or, to a male patient who is threatening to break off yet another romantic relationship with a loving woman out of seemingly increasing boredom, the therapist might say: "It seems important to consider why you always become disinterested in and want to end relationships with women who care about you." A violation of technical neutrality in the first example would be reflected in the therapist gratifying the patient's need for a positive response. Likewise, in the second example, a non-neutral therapist might have encouraged the patient to stay in the relationship rather than impulsively ending it.

Other theorists hold the view that remaining neutral and refraining from the selective gratification of patients' needs for additional time, advice, direct questions, or requests for personal information about the therapist are not always useful and often can be detrimental, reexposing many patients to what feels like the neglect, indifference, frustration, and lack of caring of their early lives. They point out that many individuals who come to treatment show deficits—that is, gaps or undeveloped areas of their internal structure—are emotionally labile and unable to regulate or manage their intense feelings and impulses, yearn for closeness but fear and distance from relationships, and are suspicious of but sometimes try to provoke revictimization. Consequently, therapists need to be more human, genuine, self-disclosing, and gratifying. It is essential that the therapist establish a therapeutic holding environment that stabilizes them, helps them feel safe so that they can regress, enables them to contain and verbalize their feelings, and facilitates their cooperation and trust. "The behaviour of the analyst ... by being good enough in the matter of adaptation to need, is gradually perceived by the patient as something that raises a hope that the true self may at last be able to take the risks involved in its starting to experience living. Eventually the false self hands over to the analyst" (Khan, 1975: xxix).

In order to create the proper therapeutic holding environment, therapists need to be flexible and creative in the ways in which they use themselves in treatment. Some patients may require structure and limits to help them maintain control of their behavior, and others may need the therapist to be accessible and to be more active in reaching out to them and in offering concrete evidence of the therapist's understanding, caring, and consistency. Winnicott believed that treatment failed more from the therapist's inability to meet the patients' needs than from their so-called resistances (Khan,1975: xxvi). In this connection, he often accommodated his patients' needs for extra time and contact between sessions, was more tentative in the way he framed interpretations, readily provided validation, verbalized the patients' feelings, gave explanations to help them understand the difficulties of their lives, and even engaged in limited non-sexual physical contact, such as holding hands (Seinfeld, 1993: 114).

CONFRONTATION AND INTERPRETATION VERSUS THE USE OF MORE DEVELOPMENTALLY ATTUNED TECHNIQUES

Some object relations approaches rely heavily on confrontation and interpretation of pathological internalized object relations, whereas others use a greater range of developmentally attuned techniques. For example, Klein was known for her interpretations of the deepest layers of the patient's cannibalistic, murderous, and devouring impulses and fears and the primitive defenses used to deal with them. Her interpretations, which seem quite extreme and bizarre to others, used language that reflected the patient's primitive inner states (Solomon, 1995). One of Klein's explanations for utilizing deep interpretations was that these would actually show patients that their deepest anxieties were understood and thus would have a calming effect.

Fairbairn (1952, 1954) also used interpretations extensively to make patients aware of their internal splits, the reasons for them, and the ways in which they operated in the patients' lives. He focused particularly on patients' attachment to "bad" internal objects that prevented them from embracing life or "good" object experiences along with interpretation of the patient's search for "exciting" objects that nevertheless disappoint or are unavailable to the patient. In some respects, Fairbairn tried to perform a kind of psychological exorcism of these bad objects.

Despite their emphasis on using the therapeutic relationship as a major force for change, Winnicott offered interpretations about the protective role of the false-self organization, which is often manifested in the therapeutic relationship by patients' efforts to adapt to the therapist's expectations at the expense of their own needs, and Guntrip interpreted patients' schizoid withdrawal and its function in safeguarding them from fantasized injury.

In delineating his object relations approach to the treatment of borderline personality organization, Kernberg (1975, 1976, 1984) stressed the confrontation and interpretation of the patient's primitive defenses, particularly splitting, denial, idealization, devaluation, projective identification, and omnipotent control. He argued that these defenses not only distort patients' functioning and obstruct identity integration but they also endanger the treatment. Consequently, Kernberg advised therapists to point out and actively oppose these defenses. He drew attention to the fact that what might appear to be a therapeutic alliance, positive transference reaction, or idealization actually served to ward off and defend against a patient's intense rage. If this defense was to go unnoticed and untouched, impulsive acting-out or destruction of the therapeutic relationship might ensue. Thus, Kernberg urged therapists to identify what he called the patient's *latent negative transference reactions* that might threaten the treatment. For example, in treating a male patient who had a history of angry, sudden terminations of treatment after first idealizing and then finding fault with and dismissing his therapists, the current therapist might draw attention to the patient's initial idealization of him and its defensive function. He might ask, "Is it possible that your feelings of admiration are covering other more devaluing feelings you have toward me? Perhaps you are protecting both of us from your anger by seeming to look up to me, but if I do something that displeases you, you may turn your anger against me as you have done with your other therapists and leave me too."

Once the therapist understands the ways in which primitive defenses distort the treatment relationship, the therapist can interpret the link between patients' behavior in the treatment to their current difficulties with others. In the example above, the patient also had reported having lost numerous jobs because of his angry outbursts at his co-workers and similarly, often grew impatient with and critical of women he was dating. In a session in which the patient began to verbally attack the therapist for his "lame comments," the therapist said, "I wonder if you are aware that you have changed from admiring me to thinking I'm totally useless and stupid. This type of reaction also seems to get you into trouble in your work and personal relationships."

Kernberg also outlined three sometimes overlapping steps to helping patients to identify and integrate their often split-off internalized images of themselves and others. In the first step, the therapist reflects on how the patient is coming across and describing others in the session and how this compares to other ways the patient has portrayed himself or herself and others. The therapist then points out these differences and asks the patient to explain them. Second, the therapist focuses on the self- and object-representations that are expressed in the transference and attempts to evaluate "who is doing what to whom" or "who is experiencing what from whom" (Kernberg, 1984: 107). In the third step, the therapist helps the patient to connect his or her reactions to others. This process goes on repetitively, and it is a difficult process because the very defenses that the therapist confronts serve to prevent such integration.

Also applying object relations thinking to their work with borderline patients, Masterson (1972, 1976) and Masterson and Rinsely (1975) used a confrontative treatment that aimed at altering the patient's defenses and split object relations structures. Because their pathological defenses ward off bad feelings, upon entering treatment, patients feel good even when acting in self-destructive and dysfunctional ways. This stems from the patient's internalization of a split object relations unit in which individuation is associated with withdrawal, object loss, and punishment, and dependence is associated with love and reward. The patient's individuation makes the patient feel bad and his or her dependence makes the patient feel good but at the expense of healthy functioning. Masterson and Rinsely urged therapists to draw attention to the split that exists and to the patient's efforts at remaining dependent in order to avoid feelings of abandonment. The patient tries to resist this awareness, and the therapist, in turn, continues to point out this defensive reaction. The patient becomes fearful that therapy will lead to individuation, and thus abandonment, and seeks dependency as a resistance. There are repeated cycles of the activation of both the rewarding and withdrawing part-object relations units during the treatment. Eventually, when the patient is able to engage in more autonomous efforts, the therapist may need to actively support patients' efforts at separation-individuation.

In addition to or instead of this use of confrontative and interpretive techniques, other more developmentally attuned interventions can be used. An important technique in the advanced stages of treatment of borderline patients, following Masterson's thinking, involves "communicative matching." Since borderline patients usually have had little support for their early attempts at individuation, the therapist should actively encourage and approve of the patient's independent wishes and efforts in ways that are similar to a mother's provision of "supplies" to the growing child. As the patient shows signs of a newly emerging self in the treatment, the therapist conveys interest, enthusiasm, and even a similar type of mood and manner of expression as does the patient. These qualities provide the patient with a new experience with a "good" object that the patient can internalize to take the place of the "bad" object that rewards regressive, clinging behavior.

Gertrude and Rubin Blanck (1974, 1979) thought the entire treatment should be based on the therapist's evaluation of a patient's needs and difficulties that stem from their separation-individuation subphases' inadequacies rather than on the basis of an arbitrary and inflexible set of guidelines. They envisioned the therapeutic relationship as being used to selectively replicate the growth-enhancing aspects of the parent-child relationship. The main rule of thumb that guided their choice of techniques was that the less intact the patient, the more the treatment will need to vary from classical techniques and provide "measured gratifications." With patients who show severe deficits in internal structure, the therapist not only provides a benign and caring atmosphere but deliberately uses his or her relationship with the patient to facilitate development through separation-individuation subphases.

Determining what the patient has missed and how to repair the developmental lesions that exist requires sophisticated and sensitive assessment skills and creative yet disciplined responses. The Blancks caution that the therapist must possess an attitude that "guards the autonomy" of the patient, avoiding directing the patient's life, using himself or herself as a model of how to live, imposing his or her own values, or encouraging too much dependency. Whatever identifications take place in the treatment as a result of the impact of the therapeutic relationship should be consistent with the patient's innate and developing potentialities. Dependency occurs, of necessity, but is a temporary way station on the road to the patient's eventual independence.

Winnicott (1965) and Guntrip (1973) also held the view that " . . . one cannot practice a stereotyped technique on patients: one can only be a real person for and with the patient" (Guntrip, 1973: 185). Winnicott was concerned that interpretations could be too intrusive and impinging on patients and interfere with their ability to feel safe (Khan, 1975: xxvi). In describing the nature of therapy, he wrote of the need for *management,* a term that is interchangeable with the therapeutic holding environment, along with interpretation. "Management, in fact, is the provision of that environment adaptation, in the clinical situation and outside it, which the patient had lacked in his developmental process. . . . It is only when management has been effective for the patient that interpretive work can have clinical value" (Khan, 1975: xxvii).

Winnicott's concept of management included not only the therapist's use of himself or herself with the patient but also the nature of the physical aspects of the treatment setting and the mobilization of environmental supports outside of the treatment surrounding. He delineated three types, the first of which pertains to the quality of the treatment setting and its freedom from impingement, the second of which involves the meeting of the patient's developmental needs and the provision of a space in which the patient can move around and just be, and the third of which necessitates the use of family, friends, and external environmental structures for support.

FOCUSING ON TRANSFERENCE-COUNTERTRANSFERENCE DYNAMICS

All object relations therapies use the here-and-now interaction in the treatment relationship as a major source of understanding patients' inner worlds, psychopathological internalized object relations, or areas of developmental need and deficit. The various treatment approaches differ some-

what in their specific focus, the degree to which they confront and interpret the transference-countertransference dynamics that manifest themselves in the therapeutic relationship, and the extent to which they view
these dynamics as influenced by the patient or by a complex system of
mutual influence between therapist and patient.

A major tenet of object relations theory is that patients bring their past
internalized relationship patterns and ways of viewing the self and others
into the therapeutic relationship. They may not be able to discuss these
patterns or their origins verbally but they are reflected in their behavior in
treatment. Moreover, such behavior engenders or "induces" reactions in
therapists, which may be merely experienced or acted upon. This fundamental idea has been expressed by the use of various terms, such as interaction, object replication, enactment, actualization, and projective identification (Aron, 1996: 189–220). Whatever its name, this process has diagnostic
and therapeutic significance. An object relations therapist must pay attention to not only what patients say but to how they act and also to what the
therapist is feeling (and doing). The therapist tries to understand, often
with the collaboration of the patient, how this interactional pattern reflects
the patient's past experiences with significant others as well as his or her
main problems.

Because of the occurrence of this type of interaction in treatment, object
relations theory has reconceptualized the concept of countertransference,
which traditionally referred to feelings that arise in therapists during treatment that stem from their own past experiences and areas of conflict and
pathology. The totalistic conception of countertransference that arises as a
result of object relations thinking includes all of the therapist's conscious
and unconscious reactions to the patient, including those that are induced
by the patient's personality, psychopathology, and life situation (Hanna,
1993a & b).

The totalistic view of countertransference encompasses what Winnicott
(1949) termed "objective countertransference," which refers to natural or
quite justifiable reactions of the therapist to extreme aspects of the
patient's behavior and both "concordant" and "complementary" identification (Racker, 1957). In concordant identification, the therapist identifies
with the main emotion that the patient is feeling at a given time or with the

feeling that the patient has put into the therapist by means of projective identification. For example, the therapist's empathic immersion in the patient's experience may lead him or her to experience the patient's rage, or the therapist's feelings of anger may stem from the patient's use of projective identification, in which the patient projects his or her aggressive, often disavowed, impulses into the therapist, who then is experienced as a hostile enemy who can be justifiably hated and controlled. In complementary identification, the therapist takes on a role in response to the patient's behavior. He or she may begin to feel like a harsh and controlling figure while the patient experiences fear of the therapist who is perceived as being like the patient's authoritarian parent.

The main treatment implication of the totalistic conception of countertransference involves the therapist's ability *to contain*—that is, to hold in his or her mind the patient's projective identifications without acting upon them, to use his or her containment function to understand the nature of the patient's internalized object relations as they appear in or are enacted in the transference-countertransference dynamics, to confront and interpret these dynamics to the patient, to connect these patterns to difficulties in the patient's current life, and to link them to the patient's early experiences with others. For example, in feeling increasingly overwhelmed, inadequate, and frustrated in the face of a woman patient's persistent complaints of her chronic physical symptoms and emotional suffering and her annoyance at the therapist's efforts to be of help, the male therapist might take note of and question his reactions and ask himself if there might be an important relational pattern being enacted in the treatment. He might comment to the patient, "You and I seem to be engaged in an interaction in which you feel yourself to be in pain and discomfort and experience me as totally inept and uncaring when I try to offer suggestions. I wonder if you could be trying to communicate to me how blamed, inadequate, and powerless you felt when you were a child and were unable to help your father overcome his back pain and depression?" Later, after having confirmed that the patient had in fact often tried to reach her father but could not penetrate his misery, the therapist asked, "Is it possible that some of the problems you have been having in maintaining relationships with men come from your expectation and anger that they will not be there for you, and you're driving them away with your many complaints about their treatment of you?" This example, as well as the therapeutic principle technique that it illustrates, assumes that the therapist's feelings in the interaction are resulting from what the patient is inducing rather than coming from the therapist's own personal and idiosyncratic reactions to the patient.

Although Klein and Kernberg stressed the regularity with which aggressive impulses are projected into the therapist, there is a broad range of feelings, ways of perceiving the self and others, and relational patterns that find their way into the transference-countertransference dynamics. For example, dependent and caretaker, victim and abuser, victim and rescuer, and weak and powerful roles may be enacted (Cashdan, 1988).

Recently, numerous authors who adhere to a relational framework (Ehrenberg, 1995; Hoffman, 1983; Maroda, 1999; Renik, 1995) have advocated the use of countertransference disclosure—that is, the revealing of feelings that the therapist has about the patient or in interaction with the patient. They argue that such disclosure opens up the discussion of potentially frightening and disruptive feelings, clarifies the nature of projective identification and enactments, shows the patient that the therapist has gotten the message about the strong disavowed affects that the patient is inducing in the therapist, and enables the patient to experience the therapist as genuine and truthful. Thus, therapists might express their feelings of being overwhelmed, inadequate, defensive, frustrated, or of wanting to protect the patient in response to the patient's comments and behavior in the session and ask the patient what he or she thinks might be going on between them. Or if the therapist feels confused about the therapist-patient interaction and what it means, the therapist might say this and ask the patient to clarify what is going on.

Because of the intense nature of patients' tendencies to engage in projective identification and to enact their earlier relational patterns in treatment, therapists may be tempted to act on rather than to contain what has been projected into them, and this can lead to serious impediments to successful treatment, to prolonged stalemates and power struggles, and to premature termination. Likewise, there may be a tendency to retaliate against what are experienced as patients' assaults on the therapist by making inappropriate confrontations, interpretations, and self-disclosures. Maroda

(1999) distinguishes between what the therapist feels and how the therapist behaves, since the goal is to provide new kinds of experiences for the patient. Feeling and disclosing are okay, but behaving in keeping with what is being projected and enacted is not. She further cautions therapists not to disclose strong feelings at times when they feel on the verge of being out of control and expresses caution about revealing erotic countertransference because of its being too stimulating and threatening generally.

Even when countertransference self-disclosure and confrontation and interpretation of projective identification are carried out in a sensitive and tactful manner, there is a risk that many patients may experience these techniques as too blaming and assaultive, particularly at early points in treatment. Moreover, some object relations theorists, such as Winnicott and Guntrip, would be focused on the degree to which patients are seeking new types of relational experiences and better responses to long-standing needs rather than always replaying their past pathological interactions. They would be more likely to rely on the containment function rather than to use confrontation and interpretation as techniques of first choice.

The recent emphasis in relational theory on the mutual impact of therapist and patient, rather than on the impact of the patient's pathology alone in causing the patient's and therapist's behavior in treatment, suggests strongly that it is erroneous to view so-called enactments as stemming only from the therapist's participation in what is being induced in him or her by the patient (Aron, 1996: 221–253). It is difficult to know which member of the interaction started the enactment or when it began. A therapist's strong feelings that arise in working with a patient may stem from his or her own issues, which are stimulated but not induced by the patient. As Maroda notes (1999: 121–140), a therapist's own personality and past can get together with the patient's need for pathological forms of enactment and that this is a serious therapeutic problem that also makes it difficult to know who is doing what to whom. The therapist may be at risk for participating in a repetition or enactment of both the patient's and therapist's earlier experiences without recognizing and understanding this. Consequently, it may often be better and safer to contain such feelings until one has a better grasp of what is going on or to verbalize to the patient one's uncertainty about how to understand what is happening between patient

and therapist and to invite the patient to participate in the process of clari-
fying the therapist-patient interaction.

SELF PSYCHOLOGICAL TREATMENT

Kohutian self psychology has a relatively clear set of treatment principles in
contrast to object relations theory, although some greater variation has
been introduced as self psychology has expanded beyond its Kohutian
base. Because it sees all psychopathology as reflecting self deficits—that is,
gaps, missing, or underdeveloped elements in self-structure that come
about as a result of unattuned or traumatic caretaking, treatment based on
self psychological principles provides patients with a second chance to
complete their development. It aims at building and strengthening the personality. Self psychologists believe that individuals with self deficits, or
what is termed narcissistic vulnerability, require a treatment relationship
that is more empathic, human, experiential, and reparative than is characteristic of traditional psychotherapy. In this respect, self psychological
treatment resembles those British object relations approaches that are
more facilitative and reparative. Because it directs itself to ameliorating self
deficits and to helping patients to restore their self-cohesiveness at times of
life stress and crisis, self psychological treatment has a broad application.

ATTITUDE ABOUT MENTAL HEALTH

The self psychological therapist prizes non-destructive self-expression in
all its forms rather than a "maturity morality" in which the patient is
encouraged to live his or her life in accordance with society's or the therapist's values and expectations regarding what is normal and appropriate.
Being different is not equated with being pathological. This attitude is particularly important in helping patients to find sustaining selfobjects and in
expressing their creativity. Enabling the patient to develop "a sense of inner
freedom, of joyful search, and the courageous ability to go one's own way"
(Kohut, 1984:169) takes precedence over helping them to conform to reality.

GOALS

Kohut saw the goal of self psychological treatment as helping patients to develop new self-structures and a greater degree of self-cohesion. Viewing self-actualization in all its forms as an important result of treatment, he had a less normative and prescriptive view of the criteria for good mental health than is characteristic of more Freudian, ego psychological, and object relations formulations. Conforming to society's expectations and being totally autonomous are not equated with healthy functioning, and being different is not seen as necessarily pathological (Elson, 1986). Successful self psychological treatment leads to more stable or restored self-esteem regulation and cohesiveness, increased creativity, freer self-expression, the capacity for pleasure and joy, the enjoyment of one's uniqueness, and the ability to seek out more mature and responsive selfobjects.

EXPERIENCE-NEAR EMPATHY

In contrast to those psychotherapeutic approaches that have advocated that therapists function as an objective, neutral, and detached observer who makes interpretations from an "experience-distant" position, the self psychological therapist engages in "experience-near empathy," which involves the therapist's abiity to engage in "vicarious introspection" (Kohut, 1957). Kohut thought that the traditional stance exposed highly vulnerable patients to the traumatic or non-responsive conditions of their early life and did not create the safety and responsiveness that are essential to the treatment process. Experience-near empathy involves trying to understand what it is like to be the client. The therapist needs to immerse himself or herself in the patient's experience and to relinquish the role of expert judge of what the patient thinks and feels. The therapist must try to put aside his or her own ideas about what the patient needs in order to hear what the patient wants and to understand the patient's subjective truth. Moreover, the therapist gives up a one-sided view of what transpires in treatment, recognizing that both therapist and patient exist in an intersubjective context in which they exert a mutual impact on one another. The therapist must be willing to examine his or her possible contributions to the patient's reactions and to accept the validity of the patient's experience of the therapist.

THE SELFOBJECT TRANSFERENCES

In his efforts at treating patients with narcissistic personality disorders, Kohut discovered what he called the "selfobject transferences," which reflect the revival of frustrated early mirroring, idealization, and alter-ego, or twinship, needs in the new, more empathic and non-judgmental context of treatment. Wolf (1988: 124–135), a close collaborator and loyal follower of Kohut, expanded the types of selfobject transferences to include the transference of creativity and the adversarial transference.

All of the selfobject transferences contain elements of *merger*, or defenses against them. In merger, the patient experiences the therapist as an extension of himself or herself who does not have an independent center of initiative. Instead, the therapist is subject to the patient's wishes and needs and must be totally in tune with them. When patients defend against such merger experiences, they may maintain distance from the therapist in order to protect themselves from reexperiencing trauma at the hands of a disappointing or frustrating selfobject.

> The *mirror transference* is one in which the patient seeks acceptance and confirmation of the self. This often takes the form of wanting the therapist's validation, admiration, applause, approval, and enthusiastic participation in the patient's affect states.

> The *alter-ego*, or *twinship*, *transference* is one in which the patient experiences the therapist as a carbon copy of or someone like himself or herself. Patients who exhibit this type of transference often assume that the therapist thinks, feels, and behaves as they do and are derailed if they become aware of the therapist's difference from the patient.

> The *idealizing transference* shows itself in the patient's admiring or looking up to the therapist as a soothing, strong, wise, and good selfobject.

> The *transference of creativity* involves an experience of merger with a selfobject while engaged in a demanding creative task, such as an artistic endeavor.

> The *adversarial transference* involves the need for a supportive relationship that the patient can oppose in order to grow.

Despite the fact that selfobject transferences may take exaggerated and extreme forms of the patient's frustrated developmental needs, they must be recognized as understandable, albeit dysfunctional, outcomes of the client's early caretaking experiences. Usually, one dominant form of self-object transference will emerge, although there can be shifts over time. The appearance of a selfobject transference in treatment provides narcissistically vulnerable individuals a significant opportunity to ameliorate the effects of their past development and to move forward. Thus, any signs of such a reaction should be allowed to flourish and be welcomed rather than be discouraged, confronted, or intentionally disrupted. This principle is diametrically opposed to the object relations emphasis on pointing out and interpreting primitive defenses and so-called enactments.

OVERCOMING RESISTANCE TO THE EMERGENCE OF SELFOBJECT TRANSFERENCES

In the beginning of treatment, an atmosphere of acceptance and empathy usually mobilizes many individuals' early frustrated selfobject needs and mobilizes the development of a selfobject transference without the therapist having to do anything special. Because entering into a selfobject transference provides patients with opportunities to complete their development but also puts them at risk to be re-traumatized, those patients who have had experiences of severe frustrations or disruptions in their earliest selfobject relationships may have difficulty exposing themselves to disappointment or injury once again. They may erect defenses that keep them from becoming involved in treatment. Self psychology reinterpreted the concept of resistance as patients' efforts to maintain self-cohesion and to avoid disappointment and injury. Overcoming a patient's fear of being re-traumatized (Wolf, 1988: 111) is the main therapeutic task in the initial stage of treatment. This is accomplished by the therapist conveying empathic understanding of the patient's anxiety about being let down or hurt and by moving at the patient's pace.

Some patients will require more than empathic understanding in order for them to establish a meaningful bond with the therapist. They will require concrete evidence that their needs are understood, demonstrations of the therapist's active caring, genuineness, and responsiveness, or the actual experience of having their needs met selectively. Whether or not they seek it out directly or inspire the therapist to provide it, selective therapist self-disclosure may play an important role in enabling some patients to feel that their needs are understood, to risk relating, to diminish their feelings of shame and aloneness, to remember and explore traumatic experiences, and to feel validated in their very existence (Goldstein, 1994, 1997a). Additionally, some individuals experience chronic feelings of rage due to the severe and repeated assaults they experienced in early childhood. They can be very provocative and assaultive, taxing the therapist's empathic abilities. Continuing to relate to their feelings as understandable outcomes of the emotional injuries they have experienced is indicated and will eventually modulate their behavior.

UNDERSTANDING AND EXPLAINING

Self psychology does rely on the use of interpretations, but their foci differ substantially from those in classical Freudian psychoanalysis, ego psychological treatment, or many object relations approaches. Interpretation or explanation within self psychology emphasizes the linkages between patients' selfobject needs or the defenses against them and early parental empathic failures and their impact. The self psychological therapist may need to refrain from explaining or using interpretation for a prolonged period with certain patients, who may experience even seemingly empathic comments as unwanted intrusions. For such patients, the therapist may need to be content with his or her understanding and mirroring functions.

OPTIMAL FRUSTRATION OR OPTIMAL RESPONSIVENESS

Originally, Kohut did not advocate that the analyst actually try to meet the patient's selfobject needs nor that he or she deliberately try to frustrate the patient. Instead, he viewed the analyst's role as one of empathically understanding those needs and explaining their origins in the patient's early caretaking experiences. In this context, he thought that certain frustrations and therapist mistakes that would disrupt the treatment were inevitable.

What was important was the analyst's ability to respond to the patient with sufficient empathy and to repair any disruptions in the treatment relationship so that they would be non-traumatic or "optimal" and would thereby be growth-enhancing.

Some self psychologists interpreted some of Kohut's interventions in analysis as well as his writings as suggesting that gratification of some of the patient's selfobject needs was indicated. Wolf (1988: 131–135) cautioned, however, that the emphasis on gratification in some segments of the self psychological community stemmed from a misconception about Kohut's intent and held to the view that the therapeutic task is to understand and explain but not to gratify selfobject transference needs. In contrast, Bacal (1985: 225) argued that Kohut's emphasis on frustration as a prerequisite for the development of psychic structure was an unfortunate carryover of the instinctual emphasis in classical psychoanalysis and recommended that this outmoded concept be replaced by an emphasis on *optimal responsiveness*. He also suggested that the therapist engage in "regulatory interactions with the patient that facilitate the patient's development (Bacal, 1998: 127). This might involve providing affirmation and helping patients see that they have an impact on the therapist. In providing optimal responsiveness, the therapist might selectively provide actual "mirroring" as well as respond in soothing or other need-fulfilling ways (Asbury, 1990).

Although many writers in the treatment community warn of the problems inherent in the meeting of patients' needs, it is important to recognize that there are potential dangers in the use of any technique and there are risks in refraining from being responsive. The therapist's attempts to empathically relate to why the patient feels he or she needs the therapist to actually respond and what it means to the patient to be frustrated may not be sufficient.

DISRUPTION AND REPAIR OF SELFOBJECT TRANSFERENCES

Once the selfobject transference is on a firmer footing, patients experience a greater sense of well-being and often are able to contain their feelings to a greater degree. Inevitable disruptions occur, however, and derail the treatment until they are overcome. These reactions commonly result from the therapist's lack of attunement to the patient's needs, failure to live up to the patient's expectations, or inevitable constraints of the treatment. Patients may experience turbulent emotions and setbacks or may react quite negatively to the therapist, sometimes without recognizing the triggers for their responses. It is crucial for the therapist to attempt to repair the rupture so that the selfobject transference can be restored as soon as it is noticed.

The necessary repair of the relationship results from the therapist's recognition that something has gone wrong in the therapist-patient interaction and his or her exploration of the patient's perception of the therapist's possible insensitivity, mistakes, or failures that have led to the disruption. The therapist must try to understand and accept the validity of the patient's subjective experience and point of view, even if it is at variance with the therapist's view of his or her own behavior and intentions. Usually, it is advisable for therapists to give some type of explanation for their lapse, to acknowledge the kernel of truth that is present in the patient's perceptions, and in some instances, an apology might be indicated.

It is not always easy to accomplish these tasks, particularly for those unaccustomed to using this approach. Well-meaning and empathic therapists may nevertheless make what are experienced by the patient as inadvertent and unintentional lapses or errors even while thinking they are doing the right thing or staunchly defending their point of view and actions. "There is a ubiquitous resistance to the acknowledgement that the truth we believe about ourselves is no more (though no less) real than the patient's view of us . . ." (Schwaber, 1983: 389). Sometimes therapists are shocked at what appears to be a patient's distortion, hypersensitivity, or extreme reaction to what are seemingly minor incidents or they fear that empathizing with the patient will be taken as approval of dysfunctional behavior. Although this risk exists, particularly with patients whose reality testing may be shaky, it is usually a misplaced concern. There is a difference between trying to understand patients from their point of view and approving of their behavior. Additionally, empathizing with patients' subjective experience does not prohibit therapists from sharing their own perceptions of the situation or their reasons for certain actions.

The repair of the selfobject transference disruption has both immediate and long-term benefits. It gets the treatment back on track in the short run but repeated disruption-restoration sequences over the course of treatment strengthen selfobject connections and are the major pathway for change. The therapist's willingness to acknowledge and even apologize for his or her lack of empathic attunement and to validate the patient's perceptions of reality in a non-defensive manner provide a new type of experience in the patient's life that leads to transmuting internalizations of the patient's archaic needs and self structures.

In working with disruptions in the selfobject transferences, the therapist also might explore and explain how the current derailment resembles incidents in the patient's past when his significant selfobjects were disappointing and frustrating and how these early experiences have led to certain characteristic expectations of and responses to others in the patient's current life. It is important, however, for the therapist not to move too quickly into this type of approach, before having sufficiently acknowledged the patient's perception of the therapist's actual role in precipitating the disruption.

ENCOURAGING HEALTHY NARCISSISM AND RELATIONSHIPS WITH APPROPRIATE SELFOBJECTS

As patients develop or regain greater self-cohesion and firmer self-structures as a part of self psychological treatment involves, it often is important for them to find ways of expressing their healthy narcissistic needs and to find new and more appropriate selfobjects. Although this may occur spontaneously, some patients may require that the therapist support and validate such efforts. For example, the therapist might encourage patients to locate a new job, return to school, develop new interests, find outlets for their creative urges, ambitious strivings, and social values, make new friends, or join social or professional organizations.

Does the self-psychological therapist consciously try to reparent the patient? Kohut advised against the therapist deliberately attempting to play roles that are opposite to those of the parents and did not believe that treatment makes up for the psychological traumas of the past. Further, even an empathic therapist is not perfect and disappoints and frustrates patients at times (Wolf, 1988: l04). Nevertheless, Kohut acknowledged the curative impact of empathy in its own right. Likewise, by emphasizing the importance of the empathic climate and interactive process of the treatment, rather than the content of interpretations per se, Kohut recognized the power of reparative experiences as well as insight. Previously reluctant to use the term "corrective emotional experience," because of its association with Alexander's seemingly more manipulative approach that fell into disrepute in psychoanalytic circles, in his last book, Kohut (1984) embraced his more circumscribed view of this valuable concept.

THE ROLE OF CONFRONTATION, LIMITS, AND STRUCTURE

Self psychologists generally argue against the use of confrontations and limits in treatment, but it is not always possible to contain impulsiveness and tendencies toward destructive behavior through empathic understanding and responsiveness alone. More active interventions may be necessary with some patients in order to safeguard the treatment and the patient's life. Kohut himself reported a case in which he responded to an analysand's unrepentant, angry account of his reckless driving and angry encounter with a police officer by telling him, "You are a complete idiot" (1984: 74) and then went on to convey concern about his potentially destructive behavior in numerous situations. Kohut never explained why he resorted to this seemingly spontaneous intervention rather than trying another approach. He clearly was not advocating his tactic, but he was suggesting that even self psychologists cannot sit back and allow patients to hurt themselves or others in certain dire situations.

In keeping with self psychological principles, it is possible to use limits and structure and to show concern about the patient's behavior as long as the therapist maintains empathy with the patient's urgent needs. The therapist's ability to integrate "empathic confrontations" and a problem-solving approach about what might help the patient to contain his or her behavior may enable treatment to be successful with impulsive or potentially destructive individuals. "While some patients may experience even the most gentle confrontation of their defenses or their potentially self-defeating patterns as an attack, the therapist can take responsibility for communicating concern in non-assaultive and respectful ways. There is a subtle but important difference between telling a patient of one's worries about the extent of his or her drinking and informing the patient that he or she is showing denial in the face of alcohol abuse (Goldstein, 1990: 196). Likewise, a distinction can be made between telling a patient that the time has come for both therapist and patient to think together about how they can help the patient to refrain from drinking excessively and instructing the patient that he or she must stop abusing alcohol or treatment will end.

COUNTERTRANSFERENCE ISSUES

Because Kohut viewed the therapist's empathic failures as causing transference disruptions, he thought that therapists needed to be self-scrutinizing with respect to the reasons for their lack of attunement to patients and in helping therapists to overcome the countertransference feelings that were interfering with the treatment. Sometimes therapists become aware of their countertransference only when disruptions occur.

In understanding and countertransference, self psychology tends to focus on the therapists' vulnerabilities that stem from their own selfobject needs and developmental difficulties and that may be exacerbated by working with a particular patient or at a special time in the therapist's life. Self psychologists tend to minimize the concepts of projective identification, induced countertransference, and enactment in treatment because they reflect a one-sided a view of the nature of the patient-therapist interaction and fail to recognize the patient's hope for a new kind of selfobject experience that helps them complete his or her development. Moreover, saying that a client is "inducing" a particular response in the therapist runs the risk of blaming the client and shifting the responsibility for the therapist's lack of attunement to the patient. This is a complex issue that some self psychological writers who have moved beyond Kohut's original framework have begun to address.

A common countertransference pitfall involves the therapist's need for the patient to fulfill selfobject functions. For example, the therapist may need the patient's applause, idealization, validation, and affirmation. This may result in interventions that meet the therapist's rather than the patient's needs or that replay the patient's problematic past. There also is a risk that the therapist's current life situation makes him or her vulnerable to using the patient to fulfill intimacy needs.

There always is a danger for vulnerable therapists who work with particularly withdrawn, self-absorbed, or devaluing patients who have difficulty relating and deny the therapist's separate existence or value to sometimes feel resentful that they do not exist as separate or are not appreciated for who they are. This can lead to unattuned responses that invade the patient's space, interfere with the process of idealization, or demand too much closeness.

Another pitfall that often is neglected in many segments of the psychotherapy community may occur when a therapist's ethnic, racial, class, cultural, or religious background, gender and sexual orientation, or experience with oppression is very different from that of the patient. There is a risk of misinterpretation of the patient's life experiences and communications that result in unattuned interventions or what has been termed a cultural countertransference (Perez Foster, 1999). It is important to note, however, that although instances of serious misattunement often arise when the therapist cannot empathize with a patient who is so different from the therapist, a more subtle but often just as problematic countertransference problem arises when the therapist is too much like the patient (Stolorow & Atwood, 1992: 103–122).

THE INTERSUBJECTIVE FIELD

Those who have tried to articulate a "two-person" rather than one-person psychology have argued that Kohutian self psychology has a too one-sided view of patient-therapist interaction that does not sufficiently address the impact of the therapist's personality on the patient. They suggest that therapists, instead of ridding themselves of non-empathic attitudes and reactions and denying themselves a subjective existence as is recommended according to self psychological principles, should actively consider the ongoing impact of the personalities of both the patient and the therapist on the treatment process and help the patient to think about both participants as separate people. A related criticism by the two-psychology advocates is that the original self psychological model, in focusing on the patient's selfobject needs and the therapist's empathic understanding and optimal responsiveness to those needs, fails to recognize other organizing principles that govern patients' behavior and cause them to repeat patho-logical relational patterns in the treatment as well as to seek more positive forms of other forms of subject-to-subject rather than only self-selfobject relating in treatment.

Stolorow and his colleagues (Stolorow & Atwood, 1992) have drawn attention to the impact of the different organizing principles that both patients and therapists bring to their work and recognize other forms of relating besides the selfobject dimension in development and in the treat-ment situation. Stolorow argues that the therapist needs to determine which organizing principles are dominant in creating the patient's difficul-ties and how these are manifested in the treatment relationship. Because therapist and patient may have different or similar organizing principles, collusions may occur in which both participants in treatment share a simi-lar but not necessarily helpful stance or disjunctions may arise in which the organizing principles of therapist and patient are quite disparate. Under-standing the intersubjective nature of the patient-therapist interaction in which both participants exert a mutual impact on one another becomes an important treatment focus.

ACCOMMODATIONS TO OBJECT RELATIONS THEORY

Moving beyond the original self psychological position in order to accom-modate object relations concepts, Bacal & Newman (1990) and Bacal (1991) have suggested expanding self psychological treatment to address other types of earlier experiences with objects—for example, "bad" inter-nal objects—and the patient's tendency to repeat earlier pathological rela-tional patterns. Likewise, the implications of Lichtenberg's (1989) view of motivational systems has implications for reworking and expanding the major transference paradigms that occur in treatment and their relation-ship to the patient's current difficulties. Finally, Shane, Shane, and Gales (1997) have reconceptualized what occurs in the therapeutic relationship as encompassing two dimensions of intimacy: the self with transforming other dimension which addressed how the therapeutic dyad is used to regulate and transform the patient toward coming more fully into being as a person in his or her own right and the self with interpersonal sharing other dimension, concerned with how the relationship is used to create a capacity to be with an other in mutual sharing and appreciation. In the first dimension, the therapist provides significant functions for the patient's self, and in the second dimension, in contrast, the therapist is experienced by the patient as an other whose self, motives, intentions, emotions, and subjectivity are appreciated for their own sake, and not just in relation to the patient's needs. The authors do not consider this second dimension to be transference but reflective of a new self with new other experience as compared to either an old self with old other or old self with new other relational configurations. This may require supplying the patient with an affectively attuned response that matches that of the patient or that meets the patient's need for "a positive new experience of shared humanity, a heightened mutuality, affection, liking, and even love exchanged between the two participants in the analytic dyad, not always equally, and above all, not ever without the patient's development maintained as central to the interaction between them" (p. 54).

SUMMARY

This chapter has described the main treatment principles that stem from object relations theory and self psychology. It has shown that despite some overlapping techniques, object relations therapies tend to group around two different emphases, the modifying and the facilitative-reparative, the latter of which is somewhat closer to the self psychological model. Both of these aim at achieving fundamental personality change, but the modifying approach relies more extensively on insight-oriented techniques, including a prominent focus on transference-countertransference dynamics, whereas the facilitative-reparative model places significance on positive relationship experiences in treatment. The self psychological treatment model is more unified than the object relations approaches and is characterized by a strong reliance on the therapist's capacity for empathic attunement and responsiveness to the patient at every step of the treatment process and on the therapist's ability to overcome any countertransference reactions that might interfere with this capacity. Although there have been some efforts to integrate object relations and self psychological thinking, there is not a consensus about a unified treatment approach at present. Each major approach has its own strengths and limitations and makes an important contribution to working with a range of patients and human problems. Based on a careful assessment of the patient's developmental needs and major problems, the clinician may decide that one approach may lend itself more than the other in working with different patients.

PART II

SOCIAL WORK TREATMENT

PRINCIPLES AND APPLICATIONS

6

ASSESSMENT AND TREATMENT PLANNING

As described in the preceding chapters, both object relations theory and self psychology view early relationships as playing a major role in the development of personality structures that are essential to optimal functioning, mature and satisfying interpersonal relationships, and a cohesive and positive sense of self. Environmental frustration or insufficiency causes these structures to become malformed or to show gaps or weakness and lead to pathological outcomes and lifetime vulnerability. Such malformations, deficits, and vulnerabilities are rather fixed and usually do not spontaneously correct themselves. They influence the ways in which individuals deal with stressful life transitions and events, are at the root of many clinical syndromes following the DSM-IV (APA, 1994), and contribute to academic, work-related, couple, family, and other types of interpersonal problems, traumatic reactions, child maltreatment, and domestic and other forms of violence.

Object relations theory and self psychology have significant implications for assessment and intervention in social work practice. Because they embody distinctive perspectives on the developmental process and the origins and nature of human problems spanning the entire health-illness spectrum, they offer social workers special lenses from which to view their clients' capacities, strengths, and difficulties. They have enlarged our understanding of change processes, expanded our repertoire of interventions, shed new light on the role of the treatment relationship, and focused attention on the mutual impact of therapist and client. In order to be useful to social work practitioners, object relations and self psychological treatment principles, which are an outgrowth of psychoanalysis, need to be adapted to the special and varied nature of social work practice, which, in contrast to psychoanalysis, generally has greater constraints and serves clients with a more complex mix of person-environmental difficulties.

THE NATURE OF ASSESSMENT

There usually is not a separate diagnostic phase in most social work treatment today, so that assessment and intervention often go hand in hand from the beginning of the work. Although there continue to be clinicians who believe that assessment should emerge gradually as the client reveals important information at his or her own pace, the common practice in social work as well as in psychotherapy, in the current climate of managed care, is to arrive at an early assessment in order to establish appropriate goals and select an appropriate method of intervention. Nevertheless, assessment is always a continuous activity as new data become available or as the client's situation changes.

The worker focuses on five interrelated facets of the client's situation: the presenting problem—that is, the reasons for which the client is seeking help; the factors in the client's present biopsychosocial situation that are involved in the problem; the degree to which there are underlying problems that are related to the presenting problem; the client's motivation and expectations; and the client's internal capacities and external resources (Goldstein & Noonan, 1999: 65–91). As part of a broader and more inclusive psychosocial assessment (Goldstein & Noonan, 1999: 80–83), object relations and self psychological concepts contribute important foci to the overall evaluation of the client and in determining the goals and nature of treatment.

In assessing the client, the worker should seek an answer to four general questions.

① Do the client's presenting symptoms or problems reflect reactions to current life stressors or are they evidence of long-standing personality difficulties? The answer to this first question helps the worker to evaluate how amenable the client's problem is to intervention. Usually, it is easier to address difficulties that are responses to here-and-now life events rather than related to past and ongoing maladaptive personality traits and patterns. It also helps the worker to decide whether the goals of treatment should be based mainly on alleviating the client's present situation or should also encompass trying to bring about more fundamental personality change.

② To what degree do the client's presenting symptoms and problems reflect object relations or self pathology? The answer to this second question informs whether the worker focuses on the client's attachment styles, separation-individuation issues, internalized self- and object-representations, bad objects and schizoid traits, relationship patterns, self-esteem regulation, self-concept, or self-cohesion.

(3) Do the client's presenting symptoms and problems reflect malformed intrapsychic structures, conflict, and primitive defenses or developmental deficits? The answer to this third question contributes to the worker's decision about how to go about helping the client—that is, whether to engage in interventions that attempt to modify a client's pathological structures or to employ those that are more facilitative-reparative in nature.

(4) What are the client's inner capacities, motivation to work on his or her problems, and environmental supports and resources? The answer to this fourth question helps the worker in understanding what clients want and expect, what they need from the external environment, and what environmental resources may be relied on or used to support treatment efforts.

It is unlikely that there are simple either-or answers to the four general questions listed above. In many instances, factors in both the client's past and current life circumstances are contributing to his or her difficulties. Moreover, the client may have both object relations and self pathology, exhibit both malformed and entrenched structures and areas of deficit, and require an approach that combines modifying and facilitative-reparative techniques. The worker will need to decide whether current problems can be resolved without attending to underlying issues, what aspects of the client's problem should take priority, and which method to use to best reach the client and create the conditions for improvement and change. Even in cases in which the worker believes that it may be necessary to address underlying issues and to modify or repair certain features of the client's personality, it may not always be possible to embark upon these goals because of the constraints of time or as a result of the client's lack of motivation or environmental supports.

GUIDELINES FOR ASSESSMENT

In order to answer the four questions listed above, workers should use the following ten guidelines.

1 The worker should explore the meaningful relationships and supports in a client's current life situation and determine whether there are any positive or negative changes, disruptions, disappointments, rejections, humiliations, conflicts, or losses that might have triggered or contributed to the client's presenting problems. For example, the death of a life partner may result not only in grief but also in feelings of worthlessness, inner badness, and guilt. The breakup of a relationship may lead not only to feelings of loss but also to a sense of shame, feelings of being unattractive and unlovable, and to social withdrawal. Or having to deal with the disapproval of a friend who provided validation and affirmation may leave a person feeling insecure, inadequate, and depleted.

2 The worker should explore whether the client is undergoing life transitions or events that are stimulating separation-individuation issues, depriving them of significant selfobjects and supports, activating feelings of guilt and a need for self-punishment, threatening or assaulting their self-concept and compensatory structures, or inflicting blows to self-esteem. For example, a highly intelligent and capable student who separates from an admiring and supportive family, friends, and teachers in order to attend college away from home may become depressed and anxious and worry about failing because of feeling less intelligent and competent than the other students. Getting a promotion to a position of greater responsibility and status may lead to severe anxiety, fear of failure, and dependent behavior. A new mother who eagerly anticipates the birth of her infant and who endured a depriving and traumatic childhood may develop feelings of hatred and murderous impulses after her baby girl is born when the infant cries and seems inconsolable. A man who celebrates his fiftieth birthday begins to fear that he has lost his physical and mental edge and may start to ruminate about losing his job, the limitations of time, lost opportunities, and illness and death. Or a woman who reaches a long-sought-after goal, such as getting a Ph.D., may become despairing about ever pleasing a demanding and critical parent and mildly suicidal.

3 The worker should consider whether clients' current problems are linked to their characteristic ways of seeing and relating to themselves and others and the world. Does the client always experience himself as an independent loner who expects little from others

who are seen as uncaring and insignificant? Does the client see herself as dependent, fearful, and powerless and in need of being rescued by someone who seems independent, courageous, and strong? Does the client view himself or herself as an innocent bystander or victim of others' insensitivity and cruelty? Does the client view herself as wanting to be close to others who always seem to maintain distance from her? Is the client a caretaker who finds others who appear needy and dependent? Does the client pride himself or herself on his or her autonomy and become involved with others who also are seen as independent?

4 The worker should determine the degree to which the clients' current problems are connected to the ways in which they characteristically submerge or subordinate their self needs to the needs of others, look to others to provide them with a sense of self, or rely on others to fulfill certain selfobject needs. For example, does a woman who uses alcohol to ease her inner anxiety and who feels at a loss as to who she really is describe herself as always compliant, eager to please, unassuming, and as always giving preference to others' needs over her own? Does a professional woman drive herself occupationally to the point of exhaustion in order to get approval and attention from others? Does an ambitious but insecure man always try to seek out older, more successful men at work to mentor him while feeling anxious and inadequate when he has to work independently? Does a woman tend to lose herself in relationships with men and feel totally depleted and empty if they reject her?

5 The worker should understand the nature of a client's self-concept, what helps the client to maintain it, whether it is realistic, and whether the client accepts or rejects "undesirable" aspects of his or her behavior. For example, a married woman may see herself as always kind and loving and require her husband to validate her view of herself, becoming defensive and angry if he complains that she does not listen to him and is controlling without considering that he may be right. An unsuccessful and financially insecure male actor may view himself as highly talented and deserving of a great part while he holds back from auditioning, rejects his acting coach's advice, and refuses to seek other employment because he rationalizes that working will interfere with his acting career. A woman client who experiences herself as "always a bridesmaid and never a bride" because of her feelings of not being attractive and

lack of confidence may devalue herself when she meets a man who might be a romantic possibility, thereby contributing to his lack of interest. Or a woman whose self-concept centers on her appearance and independence may undergo a severe depression after breast cancer treatment that necessitates a mastectomy and cosmetic surgery.

6 The worker should identify whether clients possess a stable, integrated, and three-dimensional conception of themselves and others or tend to see themselves and others in unidimensional or contradictory ways. Does the client appear, speak, and act very differently from session to session or have a history of abrupt reversals in appearance, behavior, or interests? Does the client portray significant people in "black-and-white" ways that make them seem all "good" or all "bad"? Does the client shift in his or her attitudes toward others so that someone who is admired is soon devalued? Is it possible to get a feeling for the human characteristics of the people in a client's life or to get a sense of who the client really is?

7 The worker should evaluate the nature of the client's attachment style, separation-individuation achievements, usual repertoire of defenses, internal capacities, and compensatory structures. Is the client someone who approaches others easily, insecure and anxious in the ways in which he or she reaches out to others, or avoidant of relationships? To what extent has the client mastered the separation-individuation process, or does he or she show behavior that reflects subphase deficits? Does a client have the ability to see himself or herself as separate from others, to be alone, to be self-soothing, to pursue autonomous activities, or to retain a sense of connection to others when separated from them? Does a client tend to use splitting, denial, and projective identification, for example, as major defenses? Does a client seem dependent on a particular capacity, personality trait, interest, or activity for his or her self-concept, self-esteem, and sense of well-being?

8 The worker should investigate the client's significant early relationships and experiences in order to understand where and how the client's development progressed or became derailed. What were the common relationship configurations in the family? Who interacted with whom and in what characteristic ways? How did the client seem to approach relationships in early childhood and later in life? Were the client's significant caretakers basically

attuned to the client and were they idealizable figures? Did they provide sufficient mirroring of the client's capacities, talents, and interests? Did they encourage separation-individuation? Did they use the client to meet their needs and expectations? Was there subtle or outright neglect and abuse? Were there early losses, major disruptions, or other traumatic events?

9 The worker should appraise the impact of clients' cultural background, gender, sexual orientation, and other types of diversity and unusual life experiences on their usual ways of seeing and relating to themselves and others and the world. Seeing life through the eyes of clients who come from diverse backgrounds requires that workers transcend their own cultural training. This is hard to do because there is a tendency to take for granted what is deeply embedded in us and to experience one's own view of the world and patterns of behavior as "right." It is important to consider how the client's self-concept, identity, relational patterns, values, attitudes toward life, and expectations have been influenced by his or her particular cultural background. To what degree does the client identify with and accept his or her cultural background, gender, or sexual orientation? How have the clients' experiences with disapproval, rejection, stigma, discrimination, and oppression from an early age shaped their internalizations, opportunities, and supports?

10 The worker should ascertain the nature of the relational and other types of environmental supports that are available to and that can be mobilized on behalf of the client. Are the client's family and friends supportive of his or her efforts to get help? Does the environment contain constraints on and/or opportunities for self development? Does the client need to have some type of environmental provision?

SOURCES OF DATA

There are two main sources of data upon which to base an assessment: what clients say about themselves and their current and past experiences, and how they interact with the worker in treatment. Although information about the client that comes from others—such as referral sources, other professionals, or family members—may be instructive, it should not constitute the final word. Such information needs to be clarified with the help and participation of the client.

What Clients Say About Themselves

There are several different methods of exploring what clients say about themselves, the first of which involves taking a highly focused survey of the client's current life and history. This method may provide considerable factual information but does not shed much light on a client's feelings and subjective experience or on the nuances of relationships with others. Because it is highly structured, it is not particularly responsive to where the client is or to engagement issues.

A second method of gathering relevant information requires that the worker invite the client to share his or her story or personal narrative and talk about what is on his or her mind while the worker engages in empathic listening and sensitive exploration and efforts at clarification. The worker tries to understand the client from his or her subjective experience and to balance the act of seeking crucial information with the need to be attuned to a client's pace and style of relating. It is possible for the worker to question the client about areas that the client doesn't mention spontaneously or to go into greater depth so long as the worker bridges his or her interest in certain areas of the client's life and experience with where the client is and maintains a collaborative and attuned stance. For example, in working with a woman who is contemplating separating from her husband and who uses sessions to focus on his undesirable qualities, the worker might say, "I know your life with your husband is very difficult right now, and it helps you to talk about it. It would help me to understand your relationship with your husband better if you could tell me about how you met and what your early years together were like." If the client then describes a very idyllic relationship with her husband in their early years and speaks as if he still has the very same positive qualities that she always admired, the worker might respond, "It must be very hard for you to experience the changes in him. What do you think has happened?" Because this approach is not challenging, it helps clients to feel understood and accepted.

A third method of exploration entails the worker's close attention to what the client chooses to discuss and then pointedly probing or challenging the client to explain any areas of confusion, inconsistencies, or contradictions that show themselves in the client's communications. The worker may also confront and interpret what appear to be the client's defensive operations or seeming resistances in order to see how the client responds to such interventions—for example, whether the client becomes more or less realistic, defensive, or integrated. After the client in the preceding example described her earlier relationship with her husband without commenting on the changes in him, the worker might say, "When you describe your husband, it's as if you are talking about two different people. Sometimes he seems wonderful, and at other times he seems awful. What do you think accounts for the change in your view of him?" The intent of this question is to clarify whether the client is open to discussing her different views of her husband and can explain the changes in their relationship or instead becomes defensive and unable to reconcile her contradictory perceptions of him. If the latter possibility proved to be true, this might indicate that the client's use of splitting was influencing her experience of her husband. Of course, drawing such a conclusion would be premature without further corroboration. The risk of the worker's using this method is that the client may feel attacked, and his or her understandable reactions to the worker's comments might be misinterpreted as evidence of maladaptive defenses.

How Clients and Workers Interact
Both object relations theory and self psychology rely extensively on what transpires in the client-worker interaction as a major source of data for assessment because clients bring their characteristic defenses, views of relating to others, and selfobject needs into the treatment relationship. Although psychoanalytically oriented treatment tries to foster the conditions that encourage this process, it occurs nonetheless in all forms of therapeutic contact but may go unnoticed for a time in some cognitive-behavioral or task-oriented treatments that are highly structured and minimize the relational component of the treatment. Even in these approaches, clients who bring a tendency to rebel against authority, for example, and oppose the efforts of a well-meaning but highly directive worker, or those who are exceedingly compliant and willing to submerge their own needs in order to get approval from others, may seem to do well so long as they

experience the worker as a source of support and encouragement. They regress when the relationship is interrupted or disappoints them. Recognizing these tendencies early in the contact might allow the worker to anticipate and address them either before or at the point at which they interfere with treatment.

The object relations emphasis on identifying and understanding clients' characteristic defenses, needs, attitudes, and behavior as they appear in the client-worker relationship rests on the assumption that how clients act in the treatment situation is an accurate reflection of their usual attributes and behavior and thus are important clues to how clients contribute to their difficulties outside of the treatment relationship. Although this view has merit, it is important to bear in mind that the worker's personality, theoretical biases, and interventions influence what the worker perceives, his or her interpretation of what is observed, and how the client behaves. Thus, workers must be self-scrutinizing about the impact of their attitudes, belief systems, and actions on the assessment process and cautious in forming conclusions about the client without sufficient evidence. For example, before concluding that a client has deficits or pathological defenses and relational patterns based on his or her interactions in treatment, the worker should consider whether his or her demeanor, tone of voice, and comments are sufficiently engaging or whether the worker is coming across in a judgmental fashion or inadvertently making it hard for the client to be open and involved in the treatment. Likewise, a worker's negative labeling, lack of appreciation, or misinterpretation of certain aspects of a client's cultural background or lifestyle may lead to his or her defining client characteristics that are merely different as pathological and to making insensitive, if not assaultive, interventions. In order to clarify whether the worker is interpreting the client correctly or influencing the client, it is useful to check out certain perceptions with the client.

PLANNING TREATMENT

Assessment should be related to the process of setting realistic goals and establishing appropriate interventions. It is likely that many clients will have more than one type of difficulty. The worker will need to decide, often with the help of the client, what seems doable in the time allotted, which area of the client's functioning should take priority, and which approach is best suited to achieve the treatment goals. The worker may use his or her understanding of the client to address the client's current problems while leaving underlying difficulties untouched or to ameliorate more long-standing pathology. A focus on improving the client's current situation might be a necessary tactic in situations in which there are time or financial constraints or when the client is not motivated to address more chronic difficulties in their functioning. If the worker believes that more ongoing treatment is indicated and would be optimal in a particular instance, it may be necessary to help the client to identify, and educate the client about, the underlying issues that are playing a role in his or her current problems and to help the client consider how treatment can improve the quality of the client's life.

CASE EXAMPLES

The following case examples show how the worker arrived at an assessment of the client based on current and historical information and on the client's interactions with the worker and how the worker used the assessment to guide treatment planning.

AN ANXIOUS-RESISTANT ATTACHMENT STYLE

In the example below, the client's pattern of relating to others became evident through her descriptions of herself and her early behavior in treatment.

THE MILLS CASE EXCERPT 1 Ms. Mills was a legal secretary who sought treatment right after she celebrated her fiftieth birthday because she was deeply unhappy with her life, her job, her apartment, her lack of friends, and unmarried state. She told the female worker that she had trouble being alone but had difficulty reaching out to friends, whom she felt were insensitive, self-involved, and unavailable when she needed them. She said she had given up on dating because she hated waiting for men to call her and felt too upset when a man whom she liked and was pursuing would distance from her. She had sought help previously from a male worker whom she liked initially, but she felt that he spoke to her reluctantly and couldn't wait to end their conversation when she began to telephone him when she felt anxious. Thinking he would eventually get tired of her, she left treatment after a month.

In their first meeting, Ms. Mills asked the worker if she were open to accepting telephone calls in between regularly scheduled meetings if the client became anxious. Although the worker said that she would, the client canceled her next appointment. When the worker called her to reschedule, the client spoke of her ambivalence about being in treatment. The worker asked if she had done anything to discourage the client. The client said that the worker seemed both sensitive and competent but she nevertheless feared that her demands would be too great for the worker to handle. When the worker empathically related to the client's fears of being rejected and abandoned, the client scheduled another meeting. In the following weeks, there were frequent, if not continual, tests of the worker's willingness to be available and responsive to the client, who was alert to any possible lapse of attention on the worker's part. Because the worker understood these behaviors as part of the client's "anxious-resistant attachment style," she was able to communicate her understanding and acceptance of the client's hypervigilance and to be responsive to her.

SEPARATION-INDIVIDUATION SUBPHASE INADEQUACIES

In the following excerpt from the Mills case, the client's problems seemed to reflect various separation-individuation subphase inadequacies.

THE MILLS CASE EXCERPT 2   In exploring Ms. Mills's anxiety states, the worker learned that they tended to occur when Ms. Mills was by herself in her apartment, after returning from seeing friends or if she had no plans for a weekend. When feeling anxious, she felt that no one cared about whether she lived or died, that she was an unlovable person, and that she would always be alone. She was unable to soothe herself with the knowledge that she had experiences with others, both past and present, that were loving and close because she had a paucity of such relationships and she had no emotional memory of those that were good. Even if she enjoyed herself with a friend, she forgot the experience after she separated from her companion. Although she usually felt that there was no one to whom she could reach out when she became anxious, when she did call a friend, she was sensitive to any signs of her displeasure or lack of enthusiasm.

In a similar fashion, Ms. Mills often complained of how alone she felt even after having a session with the worker in which she shared her feelings and seemed to feel understood. She appeared to lose her sense of connection to the worker immediately upon leaving her office and did not think about what had been discussed in the session. The worker understood all of these experiences as stemming from Ms. Mills's lack of object constancy and recognized that it would be a positive development in their relationship if Ms. Mills did think about and actually try to contact the worker when she became unduly anxious but that it would also be important for the worker and client to discuss how such calls made Ms. Mills feel because of her tendency to perceive others as rejecting.

Another problem that troubled Ms. Mills was her job. She felt unappreciated by her office manager and often abused by the attorneys. Yet, she felt dependent on her place of employment, and this feeling along with her sense of inadequacy and apprehensiveness prevented her from seeking a different position. In responding to the worker's questions, Ms. Mills acknowledged that she feared becoming dependent on the worker, who might take advantage of her dependency and mistreat her while the client would be unable to leave. Although there were several possible ways to interpret her fear of taking independent action, the worker thought that it might be linked to practicing subphase issues. In this connection, the worker learned that although Ms. Mills's parents had not been particularly nurturing and loving, her mother, in particular, discouraged her autonomous strivings and reinforced her dependence.

NEGATIVE SELF- AND OBJECT-REPRESENTATIONS

In trying to assess the self- and object-representations that were evident in the ways in which Ms. Mills spoke about both herself and others and also behaved in treatment, the worker arrived at the following description.

THE MILLS CASE EXCERPT 3 Ms. Mills experienced herself at times as an insecure, unworthy, unlovable, anxious, and needy person who longed for the acceptance, love, and encouragement of others but who had to protect herself from others because of their insensitivity, indifference, lack of appreciation, unavailability, and tendencies toward exploitation. There seemed to be considerable bases for the origins of these self- and object-representations in Ms. Mills's relationships with her parents. It also appeared that Ms. Mills's view of herself and others were rather fixed and led her to engage in behaviors that reinforced rather than corrected them. Additionally, she tended to dismiss aspects of herself, others, and her relationships that did not fit her more characteristic views of herself and others—for example, experiences in which she was praised for her competence, sought after by others, or rewarded for showing initiative.

Discussion

In establishing goals and planning treatment, the worker thought that although Ms. Mills's fiftieth birthday had triggered her attempt to get help for herself, she had long-standing feelings of dependency, low self-esteem, distrust, difficulties in holding on to positive experiences with others, and deficits in her capacity for self-soothing. It seemed important and appropriate to focus on helping Ms. Mills to feel better and take more constructive actions in the short run while trying to strengthen her overall functioning in the long run.

Ms. Mills herself recognized the long-standing nature of her problems and was amenable and able to engage in ongoing treatment. The worker thought it would be beneficial to enable Ms. Mills to feel secure and appreciated in her relationship with the worker and to find ways of helping her to maintain a sense of connection with the worker between sessions. She believed that this would lessen Ms. Mills's feelings of anxiety and aloneness and improve her ability to soothe herself. Then it might be possible for the client to use the relationship with the worker as a secure base from which she could "practice" venturing forth occupationally and in her interpersonal relationships. The worker was uncertain whether Ms. Mills would be able to let go of her fixed and negative self- and object-representations if the worker became a new kind of object and helped Ms. Mills see herself more positively or instead would insist on the presence of, or even try to bring about, the attitudes and behavior that she anticipated and feared in the worker and others. It seemed likely that the worker would need to provide a new kind of object experience in the treatment and to point out and interpret the ways in which the client held on to negative views of herself and ways of relating to others.

SPLITTING AND PROJECTIVE IDENTIFICATION

Having prepared herself for the possibility that Ms. Mills might have difficulty perceiving the worker as positive in her attitudes and feelings toward her and might even try to provoke rejection, she was alert to any feelings she might have that the client might be provoking her to act in ways that would confirm her negative expectations.

THE MILLS CASE EXCERPT 4 After a month of treatment, Ms. Mills began to telephone the worker once a week and the worker would speak to the client for a few minutes or call her back and engage in a brief interchange. Later, she would ask Ms. Mills how she experienced their conversations. Treatment proceeded smoothly until the client called several times in a few days at unusual hours, so that it was difficult for the worker to return her calls. Becoming frustrated by not being able to reach Ms. Mills, the worker realized that were she to show her feelings in some way, this might provide the client with evidence of the worker's negative reaction to her. Yet, the worker did not want to ignore the client's provocative behavior. The worker responded to the calls as best she could and in the next face-to-face session, after exploring what was making the client feel so desperate, the following interchange took place.

Worker: I know this has been a very hard week for you, but I need to share a concern. I want to be there for you, but I am not sure if you believe that and whether you are waiting for me to show that I don't really care, just like everyone else in your life.

Ms. Mills: Why are you saying that?

Worker: I was worried that my inability to reach you quickly after you called would show you that I really can't be trusted, but I also wondered if you were inadvertently making it difficult for me to get back to you?

Ms. Mills: It made me feel good that you tried to call back and left messages when you couldn't reach me and didn't seem angry. I didn't think you would call back. Maybe I do expect the worst and make it hard for people to respond to me in the way that I want.

Worker: That's an important observation. I guess I also wonder what will happen in the future if I'm not always able to respond to you in the way you want. Will I become like everyone else despite the fact that today you see me as caring?

Ms. Mills: Probably. That's how I am. You're either for me or against me.

Worker: Well, I'll have to be careful then.

"BAD" INTERNAL OBJECTS

The next example shows how a client's persistent difficulties in achieving satisfying relationships were related to her attachment to "bad" exciting and rejecting internal objects and how this issue infiltrated the client-worker relationship.

THE WRIGHT CASE Ms. Wright, a 40-year-old single woman who worked as a nursing administrator, sought treatment because of her deteriorating relationship with Jack, an unemployed alcoholic man who was prone to abusive outbursts. She knew she had to end her relationship with Jack but she felt guilty about leaving him. She was filled with feelings of hopelessness about her future. She wanted to marry and have children but her "biological clock" was running out. She often felt that it was her fate to be alone, but she couldn't explain why. "I know I pick the wrong men and I ruin my chances with those who care about me."

Prior to meeting Jack, Ms. Wright had many romantic relationships that did not work out. Either she was attracted to men who were exciting, energetic, and successful but unreliable and unavailable for commitment or she broke off with those who were stable and wanted to marry her because they were not interesting enough. More recently, she had wondered if she was being too hard on them. There was one man in particular whom she thought she loved, but she pushed him away. She recently learned that he had married one of her old friends and felt a great sense of loss and regret. When she met Jack, he seemed to be fun-loving and adventuresome, but Ms. Wright soon realized he had a drinking problem. Although he was verbally abusive to her at times, he always was apologetic and filled with remorse. She felt he needed her and she had trouble extricating herself from their relationship.

A salient aspect of Ms. Wright's background was her unhappy childhood, in which there was considerable marital discord. Her mother was needy and depressed and drank excessively while her father, a dynamic and successful businessman, traveled frequently and engaged in numerous extramarital affairs. Ms. Wright admired her father and sought his approval despite his unavailability and rejection of her. She experienced her mother as a burden but felt she could not abandon her.

Ms. Wright's behavior in the treatment seemed to fluctuate and was quite puzzling. At times she experienced the worker as a "fantastic find" whom she was eager to please but fearful of alienating. On other occasions, Ms. Wright became critical of the worker and accused her of being insensitive, weak, and incompetent. A third perception that Ms. Wright seemed to have of the worker at times was that of a lonely person who needed Ms. Wright.

Discussion

The worker thought that Ms. Wright's problematic relationships reflected her attachment to "bad" internal objects that prohibited her from becoming involved with men who cared for her and propelled her to seek out those with whom she could repeat her frustrating but longed-for relationship with her father. Alternatively, she found and stayed with a depressed and emotionally disturbed man who resembled her unhappy and guilt-ridden relationship with her depressed mother.

In planning treatment, the worker thought that helping Ms. Wright to leave her relationship with Jack too early in the treatment would increase her guilt and that encouraging her to seek out new and more satisfying relationships would likely lead to a repetition of her characteristic patterns. It appeared that Ms. Wright needed to understand the reasons underlying her difficulties and to use this knowledge to free herself from her pathological attachment to her "bad" internal objects.

SCHIZOID TENDENCIES

The following example shows how a client's schizoid tendencies became more evident in the client-worker interaction despite his externally friendly and cooperative demeanor.

THE ANDREWS CASE Mr. Andrews, a tall, attractive, and overtly friendly 49-year-old, highly intelligent computer programmer, sought help after being told by Rita, his female partner of two years, that she would end their relationship if he did not seek treatment after she became aware of his sexual acting-out and intermittent substance abuse. He discussed the rather sad events of his early life somewhat matter of factly, recounting how his mother was an intermittently warm but depressed alcoholic; how his father was distant and cold; how his parents suddenly divorced when he was 10; having been separated from his mother, who abused drugs and died prematurely; having to deal with the remarriage of his father to his mother's sister, whom he never accepted; and never being able to please or get a "pat on the back" from his father. Mr. Andrews was a loner who totally relied on himself.

Worker: I understand what you are telling me, but it is hard for me to get a sense of what all these events were like for you.

Mr. Andrews: I don't really know. I'll have to give it some thought.

Worker: Perhaps it's difficult for you to be in touch with your feelings about these events? Do you think I am pushing you too hard?

Mr. Andrews: No, your question is quite reasonable. I should be able to answer you. I don't always know what I'm feeling. This is how I get into trouble with Rita sometimes. She thinks I'm holding out on her, but I'm not. I mean, sometimes I do because I don't want her to know what I'm feeling, but that's not always true.

Worker: What worries you about opening up to Rita at times?

Mr. Andrews: What comes to mind is that I don't want her to know me. I don't want to be controlled. I think she will want more and more.

Worker: It would be understandable if you were concerned about what might happen if you open up here.

Mr. Andrews: I don't think you have an agenda in the same way Rita does. Well, I'm not sure she has an agenda. Maybe it's just my natural suspiciousness.

Worker: When we speak, are you aware of holding back feelings or are you not feeling much of anything?

Mr. Andrews: Rita asked me the same question in a more pointed and less tactful way. I guess she felt frustrated with my response or, to be more accurate, lack of response to her. It's as if my emotions are in cold storage. I know I must have them but I can't seem to get to them, but I can tell you exactly what happened to me thirty years ago.

Worker: Do you think that your sexual acting-out and addictive behavior are ways of numbing or soothing yourself?

Mr. Andrews: I don't think so. I just want to get high and have a great sexual experience.

Worker: What's motivating you to give that up?

Mr. Andrews: I don't really want to, but I will. I recognize that I have to if I want to keep my relationship with Rita. She is the first person that I have ever let myself care about. It's not easy. I don't always like it. Sex and drugs seem a lot safer.

Discussion

The worker recognized that helping Mr. Andrews gain sobriety was important but only "the tip of the iceberg," and that it might be easier to help him to refrain from sexual acting-out and drugs in the short run while leaving him vulnerable to a relapse in the long run. Nevertheless, she thought that connecting Mr. Andrews to a substance abuse program was a first step and a less threatening one than trying to help him get in touch with the inner needs and feelings that he was warding off. She realized it would be necessary to proceed at a pace that was non-threatening to the client because it seemed clear that any move toward being more open and able to experience his feelings, while essential to his recovery and well-being, would likely be frightening.

A FALSE SELF ORGANIZATION

The next case illustrates the worker's gradual awareness that she was dealing with a client whose tendency to comply with others' expectations and wishes led her to develop some features of a false self organization. There may be different degrees of this condition, and clients often are not able to tell the worker directly about this problem because they are not always aware of how much they have become alienated from their true selves and submerged their own needs.

THE SAMUELS CASE Ms. Samuels, a 22-year-old Jewish woman, came for help at her family's urging because of a recurrence of bulimia following her return to her family's home in a suburb of New York after graduating from college. She planned to find employment and to live at home for a year until she had enough money to be on her own. She had originally planned to find an apartment in the city with her college roommate, but her parents persuaded her to move back home so that she could save money. She described her family as close and was grateful to her parents for helping her choose the right school and for paying all her expenses. She said she would have taken loans and worked part-time but her parents wanted her to focus on her course work. Ms. Samuels reported that she had enjoyed college but now felt ready to move on. Many of her friends lived in the New York area, so she felt she could maintain contact with them. She said that she had studied drama in college and had originally wanted to pursue a career in theater but her parents had convinced her that it would be better for her to work as a teacher and attend graduate school. She said she did not know why she was binge-eating and vomiting again, as she was relieved to have given up this behavior when she was away from home.

In her interaction with the worker, Ms. Samuels was pleasant, had a good sense of humor, was eager to please, seemed compliant with the rules of the treatment, was alert to clues about what she thought the worker wanted to hear, and spoke of her family in somewhat superficial but glowing terms.

Worker: Everything seems so perfect that it is difficult to understand what is wrong.

Ms. Samuels: My friends tease me about my "perfect" family.

Worker: Can you say more about that?

Ms. Samuels: They think that I have this need to see my family as totally loving and wonderful and that I need to please them and don't see how they control me.

Worker: Why do you think your friends are concerned?

Ms. Samuels: Well, they think I talk about Mom and Dad too much and can't make a move without their advice and consent. They have seen me worry about my grades and about what my parents will think about the guys I'm dating.

Worker: What's your reaction to what your friends say?

Ms. Samuels: Mom and Dad are usually right. They have had a lot of life experience. Besides, I don't want to lose them by becoming too different from them.

Worker: Why is losing them an issue?

Ms. Samuels: Well, I've seen how they practically disowned my older sister when she married a man they did not approve of. It was scary to see how my father acted. He wouldn't talk to her. Then there's my brother. They're still not talking to him because he moved to California.

Worker: Are you saying that you have to give up what you want or even who you are if it's different from what your parents want for you?

Ms. Samuels: That's what my friends say, but I'm not sure.

Worker: It seems like that idea makes you a little uncomfortable.

Ms. Samuels: I don't want to think that it's true.

Worker: I guess that feels unsafe. Is the fact that you have given up your dream of going into the theater related to your parents in some way?

Ms. Samuels: In a way. They think it's not for me. I've listened to their opinion. They definitely have a point. Sometimes, I feel like it's okay even if I fail. At least I will have tried. I'm not sure what I should do. It is difficult to break into the theater but my teachers have told me I have talent and I love it when I'm on the stage or even reading a part. Then, I can be anyone I want to be.

Worker: It seems difficult for you to feel that you can be who you want to be in your real life if it clashes with others' expectations. Is it possible that your bulimia has something to do with that?

Ms. Samuels: What's the connection?

Worker: Sometimes we can feel two ways about something. On the one hand, we can feel we are doing the right thing, and then somewhere deep inside we feel we are giving up what we want and that we don't have any control. Your bulimia might be your way of expressing that feeling. What do you think?

Ms. Samuels: Sometimes I do feel like I'm living someone else's life rather than my own and that I have to be perfect at it, but I don't know why I feel this way. I don't like it when I vomit but I don't want to gain weight. My mother says I'm worse because I just left college and am going through a transition. That's why she wants me to get help. I told her I was glad to leave school but would talk to someone if it made her feel better. You seem to be understanding.

Worker: I would like to try to help you in your transition.

Discussion

Based on her brief interaction with this client, which information in subsequent meetings confirmed, the worker thought that the recurrence of Ms. Wright's eating disorder was not related simply to her graduating from college or to expectable life stage separation-individuation issues. She thought that Ms. Wright was having difficulty being her own person to the extent that she was alienated from what her true needs and wishes were. Leaving college and returning to her family's home and their more direct control seemed to be triggering her symptoms even though she did not make this connection herself. Being compliant, needing to be perfect, and having accepted the subordination of her needs to her family, Ms. Samuels seemed to be only dimly aware that she was living out her parents' rather than her own life. The worker concluded that she would need to proceed slowly and focus on helping Ms. Samuels in her "life transition." Ms. Samuels accepted her family's control, and it would likely threaten the treatment if the family felt that the worker was trying to enable Ms. Samuels become more of her own person and to separate from them. The worker also anticipated that Ms. Samuels's parents would want to have contact with the worker and she discussed how to manage this with the client should the need arise. Ms. Samuels did not mind if the worker spoke to her parents, and worker and client agreed that the worker would discuss what she would say to the parents with Ms. Samuels.

FRUSTRATED SELFOBJECT NEEDS

The following example shows how a client's selfobject needs were being frustrated in his job and causing him to experience increasing stress and how those same needs manifested themselves in the treatment situation.

THE MORRIS CASE Mr. Morris, age 42, sought help at the urging of his primary care physician, who was concerned about his headaches and high blood pressure and learned that he was quite stressed in his position as an art director in an advertising firm. Mr. Morris had recently been hired to manage a chaotic department of fifteen people. There was an inside candidate for the position who was passed over but who stayed with the group. He was resentful of Mr. Morris and was barely cooperative with him. The other employees, while more accepting of Mr. Morris, were caught in a loyalty conflict and were reserved in the way they related to him. Mr. Morris had come from a very supportive work environment in which he was well-liked and viewed as highly competent. In his new position, he felt overwhelmed by the increasing demands on his time, the projects that seemed beyond his direct control, and the lack of overt enthusiasm for his leadership. He worked long hours and felt depressed and irritable. He worried that his immediate superior would become critical of his performance and experienced considerable anger at the people under his charge, which he concealed. Another stress on Mr. Morris was the fact that he and his wife had purchased an expensive country house and he grew fearful that he would lose his job, his house, and his wife. He thought of looking for another position but thought it would not look good for him to leave his position so soon.

Mr. Morris said that he had always been able to get affirmation and validation of his intelligence and talent in his work life despite not having received such support from his parents. The youngest of four much older children, he grew up quite isolated from his siblings. His mother was 44 and his father was 53 when he was born, and both parents seemed to lack the energy and motivation to be too involved with him. The parents were financially secure until his father lost all of his money, became ill, and died of a heart attack during Mr. Morris's adolescence. He admired his father, although they were not close.

Mr. Morris was an excellent student but always feared he would fail. He drove himself in his academic work and had very high standards. He used to become ill before examinations in high school and college and would study all the time to the point of exhaustion. Getting less than superior grades would throw him into a tailspin in which he became depressed, reproached himself, and experienced a loss of self-esteem. As an adult, he maintained somewhat distant and strained relationships with his mother and siblings. Mr. Morris married when he was 37 and he described his wife as having helped him to relax to a greater degree than previously, although more recently he had succeeded in making her more anxious about the future.

In their first meeting, Mr. Morris seemed ashamed of his work difficulties and expressed fear that the worker would judge him and think he was a failure. He was visibly relieved by the worker's empathy with what it was like for him to have left a very supportive work environment to enter one that was quite stressful. When the worker validated that Mr. Morris was doing the best he could in a very difficult situation, he soon became less panicky and felt less alone. He began to relate to the worker as someone like him who could share his experiences at work and whom he could use as a sounding board in his efforts to problem-solve about how to deal with his staff.

Discussion

In experiencing Mr. Morris's rather immediate response to her and in learning of his history, the worker recognized that in the past, Mr. Morris had maintained his self-esteem by being able to control his environment, to perform in keeping with his perfectionism, to obtain affirmation and validation from others, and to be financially successful. Yet he seemed to suffer from underlying feelings of inadequacy and insecurity. The worker thought that Mr. Morris's new position and promotion had led to a drastic change in his selfobject environment that was causing problems in self-esteem regulation, severe anxiety, and a loss of self-cohesion and reflected major weakness in his sense of self. Consequently, the worker believed that the greater responsibilities and particular problems of his new position along with the increased financial burden of a country house also were contributing to his fear that he would fail and become like his father.

Mr. Morris's selfobject needs became immediately apparent in the client-worker interaction. The worker's recognition of and ability to convey empathic understanding of these needs and what was thwarting them helped the client to engage in treatment and better deal with his work problems. She thought that engaging in "optimal responsiveness" to these needs would play a role in helping the client feel better in the short run and in strengthening the client's self in the long run.

CULTURE, DISCRIMINATION, AND A NEGATIVE SELF-CONCEPT

The final case example portrays a client whose cultural background differed from that of the worker and how the worker began to understand and relate to the client.

THE D'AGOSTINO CASE Mr. D'Agostino, a Sicilian-American gay 48-year-old unemployed man, sought treatment because of his increasing feelings of worthlessness and hopelessness after having been let go from a company where he had worked for many years. He described his work life as a failure and feared that his male partner of twelve years would tire of and leave him. He supported himself financially through unemployment insurance and his partner's help and worried that he would not find another job. He recounted that he was fired because his work was not up to par and that his performance had started to wane when his immediate superior placed increasing pressure on Mr. D'Agostino to produce. Instead of working harder, he began to doubt his abilities and procrastinated in meeting his responsibilities.

In sharing his history, Mr. D'Agostino said that from an early age, he always felt he was a disappointment to his parents. He recalled being intense and moody and feeling like "an oddball" in comparison to his brothers. He felt a sense of alienation from his father, who was emotionally removed and critical and whom he regarded as weak. He described his parents as "good people" basically but "old country" and limited in their awareness of the outside world. His mother was more accessible emotionally but was often depressed herself. His father worked for his older brothers as a mechanic and expected Mr. D'Agostino to work in the garage, which he hated because his peers called him a "grease monkey" and taunted him for being Sicilian. He was a studious student but described his parents as uninterested in his academic and other interests and his Irish Catholic teachers as favoring the Irish over the Italian students. Although he was proud of his heritage as an adult, he was bitter about having been demeaned for being a Sicilian-American from an early age and for being made to feel worse than a second-class citizen. He used to feel deeply ashamed of his ethnicity and of being poor. He thought it was ironic that he then had to deal with the second stigma of being gay, which he tried to hide from his family and even from himself.

Mr. D'Agostino had some superficial friendships and dated women occasionally in high school in order to "fit in," but he tended to keep to himself. He attended a city college but did not pursue graduate studies because he did not feel smart enough and had no funds. He worked in a series of unfulfilling jobs in journalism after graduation but had trouble supporting himself financially. He took a job in the insurance field that paid better but he hated the work. He lacked the confidence and money to go back to school, which he thought would help him advance. He worked for different companies but mismanaged his finances and accumulated considerable debt, requiring him to declare bankruptcy. He had just begun to get himself on a better financial footing when he lost his job.

Closeted as a gay man until he was in his twenties, Mr. D'Agostino had some short-lived relationships until he met his current partner. He viewed their relationship as the "best thing" in his life and he felt frightened of ruining it. The partner was very encouraging of Mr. D'Agostino's participation in Italian and gay organizations and also urged him to get help.

Mr. D'Agostino filled his early sessions with his depressive ruminations and spoke of his sense of alienation from others and his feelings of shame. Because of the emphasis that Mr. D'Agostino placed on his ethnicity and sensing his caution in opening up to the female worker, she asked him if he felt that the worker could understand and appreciate him even if she did not share his Sicilian-American background. Mr. D'Agostino replied that the worker seemed to be accepting of him and he had always thought that Jews and Italians got along pretty well. He continued to be guarded in sessions, however, and when the worker questioned him about this, Mr. D'Agostino replied, "I'm not aware of holding back, but I may be so used to not sharing what I think and feel that I don't even notice when I'm doing it. It took me a long time to be open with Dan, my partner. He had to work hard to draw me out."

The worker began to feel that the client needed some concrete evidence of her ability to enter his world, and she soon had the opportunity.

Mr. D'Agostino: I got really bent out of shape last night after I watched an episode of *The Sopranos* on television. Ordinarily, I love the show and think it's great, but last night it really bothered me. Do you ever watch it?

Worker: Yes. In fact, I saw it last night too. What particularly upset you?

Mr. D'Agostino: I'm glad you saw it. It makes it easier to talk about it. I'm not sure what triggered my reaction, but I began to feel angry at myself for liking the program because it perpetuates the perceptions of Italians as mafiosi and does nothing to show their positive contributions.

Worker: I can understand your feeling that way. It's a sensitive subject for you in the light of your own struggles. You don't want people to think of you as being like Tony [the main character].

Mr. D'Agostino: People have looked down at me and I have some of the same mannerisms and beliefs as the characters on TV.

Worker: It's hard to feel comfortable with who you are, as if being Italian or Sicilian is a bad thing. Do you think that I see the "bad" rather than the "good" side of you?

Mr. D'Agostino: I guess I always expect that. I'd like to go back to Sicily for another visit. I really enjoyed seeing what it was like.

Worker: When I was there recently, I was amazed by the temples and other ruins. Sicily's history is so interesting.

Mr. D'Agostino: I think it is too. You have actually been to Sicily? Where did you go?

Discussion

This interchange marked a turning point in the client-worker relationship as Mr. D'Agostino began to share more positive parts of himself with the worker. He began to use Italian phrases and translated them when the worker showed interest. He commented humorously on his own personality characteristics, such as his sense of doom and gloom and fatalism, which he identified as culturally syntonic.

It seemed clear to the worker that Mr. D'Agostino's current problems were connected to past issues and that both had to be the focus of treatment. He had received negative messages about his ethnicity and sexual orientation from his family and the surrounding social environment that he internalized and that contributed to his negative self-concept. Moreover, he had identified with many aspects of his parents' cultural background and social class, which also influenced his view of himself. Additionally, he lacked mirroring and encouragement from his parents and teachers, idealizable and positive role models whom he could look up to, and those with whom he shared a sense of likeness. He had difficulty feeling good about his own talents and capacities and pursuing his ambitions. He had to suppress his sexuality and protect himself from others getting to know him. As an adult, Mr. D'Agostino was highly dependent on the approval of others to feel good about himself but felt pressured and anxious if anything was expected of him. He was vulnerable to assaults to his self-esteem and bouts of depression when he received minor criticisms or did not get the recognition he wanted. When depressed, he engaged in self-sabotaging behavior, the results of which reinforced his negative views of himself. A major positive aspect of his life was his relationship with his partner, a caring and supportive man.

SUMMARY

This chapter has considered and illustrated some of the implications of object relations theory and self psychology for assessment and planning treatment. It viewed assessment as a necessary and continuous activity that relies both on what the client tells the worker directly and on how the client interacts with the worker in the treatment situation. The chapter stressed the importance of evaluating the degree to which a client's presenting problems are being triggered by his or her current situation and/or whether they are part of chronic object relations and self pathology. The chapter described ten guidelines for assessment of object relations and self-

development and illustrated the assessment and treatment planning
process by means of numerous case examples that show how the worker
utilized current and historical information about the client and the client's
interaction in treatment to arrive at an assessment and to plan treatment.

7

THE BEGINNING PHASE

A time-honored and still valuable social work practice principle is for the worker "to be where the client is." This requires that workers are sensitive to and show their understanding of the client's concerns, expectations, personality characteristics, life situation, and cultural background and that they employ attuned interventions. Familiarity with object relations theory and self psychology expands workers' ability to be empathic with and to engage a wide range of clients, particularly those who often are termed "difficult."

ESTABLISHING A THERAPEUTIC HOLDING ENVIRONMENT

In the beginning phase of social work treatment, it has been customary to admonish the worker to be non-judgmental and accepting in his or her attitudes and to underscore the importance of establishing a therapeutic alliance, an ego psychological concept that refers to the client's rational capacity to perceive the worker as a reasonable, helping person and to cooperate in achieving the treatment goals that have been jointly identified (Goldstein, 1995a: 203). Many clients may not be able to form a therapeutic alliance easily at an early point, however, because they are distrustful, frightened, and hopeless or show developmental arrests that result in their being anxiety-ridden, prone to anger and volatility, impulsive, and lacking in self-soothing capacities or object constancy. Other measures are necessary. It is essential for the worker to create a therapeutic holding environment that helps to stabilize clients, enables them to feel safe, assists them in containing and verbalizing their feelings, mobilizes their motivation, and facilitates their cooperation with and trust of the worker.

GENERAL CONSIDERATIONS

Although there are some general features of an optimal therapeutic holding environment, such as consistency, clarity about expectations, empathy, genuineness, acceptance, interest, clear boundaries, and respect for cultural and other kinds of diversity, its components should be individualized and flexible based on an assessment of the client. It is important to consider the type of treatment structure and physical conditions that may help the client, the client's developmental needs and how to best respond to them, and the kind of environmental supports outside of the treatment that may be necessary. For example, clients who are sensitive to noise, distracted by visual stimuli, and the like may require a space that is free from such impingements; those who are frightened of small and closed spaces may need to meet in a more open setting, one with windows, or in an office with the door ajar; individuals who are demanding of time, erratic in their session attendance, disorganized, or impulsive may benefit from the establishment of clear guidelines and limits to help them maintain control of their behavior; clients who need to feel reassured of the worker's availability, realness, and interest may need to have freer access to and selective personal information about the worker and extra time; those who become anxious and are unable to maintain a sense of connection to the worker outside of sessions may need to have more frequent sessions or greater accessibility to the worker; individuals who have difficulty sharing their thoughts and feelings may require the worker to be active in reaching for and verbalizing what the client might be experiencing; clients who are especially sensitive to having their thoughts intruded upon may need the worker to wait for the client to speak and to initiate a request for feedback; and those who are impulsive, who display addictive behavior, or who are self-destructive and suicidal may need active and protective interventions, such as day treatment, twelve-step programs, family involvement, or other types of external structure.

While maintaining therapeutic and ethical boundaries so as not to threaten or overstimulate patients, workers may need to be more real and responsive to some of their clients' requests and needs for selected personal information, additional time, more frequent contact, or concrete evidence of their caring. If workers do not think it is advisable or are not able to be responsive to the client's requests, it is important to convey understanding of the reasons behind them without implying that the client is being too demanding or needy.

It can be seen from the preceding discussion that workers should be willing to adapt to their clients to the extent possible and appropriate rather than always insisting that the client comply with the worker's usual or preferred ways of doing things. Following this principle may be difficult when the treatment setting adheres to rigid procedures, imposes inflexible rules and policies, or shows insensitivity to the clients' needs for evening appointments, consistent office assignments, easy access, and the like.

CONTAINMENT AND TRANSITIONAL PHENOMENA

Another important characteristic of a therapeutic holding environment is the worker's ability to contain the client's turbulent feelings and impulses. In order to do this, the worker must be able to help clients to get in touch with and verbalize their feelings, to understand the client's symbolic communications or his or her attempts to put his or her feelings into actions, to refrain from counter-reacting to the client, and to set reasonable limits on disruptive, inappropriate, or extreme behavior.

For those clients who experience severe anxiety and feelings of aloneness outside of sessions and who are unable to maintain a sense of connection to the worker due to insufficient self-soothing capacities and lack of object constancy, the use of transitional objects or phenomena may be an indispensable component of a therapeutic holding environment (Wells & Glickauf-Hughes, 1986). Clients can be instructed to write down their thoughts and feelings or to visualize being with the worker or others who are supportive figures when they are by themselves. The worker may actually give the client an object such as a book, paperweight, or photograph that can serve as a reminder of the worker or the worker may arrange to talk to clients briefly by telephone at designated times or send them postcards during vacation periods. Sometimes telephone answering devices serve as transitional objects and clients are reassured by hearing the worker's voice without having to speak to the worker personally. E-mail can be another means by which the client and worker communicate with one another, but its use may require some guidelines and limits so that it does not become intrusive.

THE ROLE OF EXPERIENCE-NEAR EMPATHY

A crucial ingredient to the provision of a therapeutic holding environment is the worker's ability to engage in "experience-near-empathy" rather than "experience-distant" interventions. The worker tries to put himself or herself in the client's shoes, so to speak, and to see the world in the ways that the client experiences it. He or she tries to understand what it is like to be the client even if the worker has perceptions, attitudes, values, life experiences, and background different from those of the client. The worker appreciates that what the client thinks and feels has its own truth. In contrast, experience-distant interventions are those that are imposed upon clients from the outside without sufficient regard for their point of view or feelings. The worker believes that his or her view of the client is correct—for example, with a dependent client who experiences severe anxiety upon leaving sessions and fears that something bad will happen, the worker asserts his or her view that the client is really angry at the worker despite the fact that he or she does not experience this feeling. Although it is possible that the client is not aware of or may deny the presence of anger that may be contributing to his or her separation anxiety, the worker's insistence on his or her point of view may result in the client not feeling heard or understood. Sometimes, however, the worker's interpretation stems from his or her theoretical beliefs rather than his or her actual experience of the client and may not accurately reflect what is behind the client's fear.

Because clients have different needs and ways of viewing themselves and others, being empathic takes many forms and does not always look the same. For example, showing empathy for a schizoid man's disconnection requires that the worker understand the function of his or her isolation rather than try to force more closeness. Empathy with a mother who is frightened of hurting her children in a fit of temper and frustration necessitates that the worker convey understanding of how violent and out of control she feels at times rather than reassuring her that she will not act out.

Although most, if not all, practitioners are likely to see themselves as reasonably empathic people, this does not mean that it is easy to engage in experience-near empathy. Constraints on the worker's ability to be empathic stem from several sources—including the worker's own attitudes, values, beliefs, personality characteristics, and background—that may make it difficult to understand or accept a client who is different from the worker; the worker's theoretical biases or his or her range of knowledge about human development and psychopathology that cause the worker to interpret the client's feelings and behavior in keeping with the worker's limited or preferred views and to ignore other possibilities; clients can be "difficult" and provoke or make inordinate demands on the worker; clients attempt to enact their earlier relational patterns in the client-worker interaction and induce the worker to experience certain feelings and to play certain roles in relation to the client; and the worker may have been taught to act in certain ways rather than others in the treatment situation and may not be able to be flexible and responsive in addressing certain client needs.

Additionally, a frequent problem that arises when workers try to be empathic with a client who is highly contradictory, uses primitive defenses, and may not be aware of or recognize aspects of their personality or behavior that are contributing to their problems is the worker's concern that being empathic implies going along or colluding with the client. The worker may not realize that the client's experience of the worker's attunement and willingness to enter his or her world has therapeutic benefit and is more important at times than helping the client identify his or her problematic behavior. It also bears mentioning that trying to understand a client from his or her vantage point and accepting the client's feelings should not be equated with agreeing with the client. It is possible for a worker to show that he or she understands the client but has a different perspective on what is occurring without pushing the correctness of his or her point of view. In this manner, the worker can stretch the client's thinking about himself or herself without the worker imposing on the client's reality in an authoritarian and single-minded way.

THE USE OF LIMITS AND STRUCTURE

The worker's ability to convey that he or she understands the client and his or her efforts to contain the client's feelings and impulses may not be sufficient to "hold" certain clients, who exhibit behaviors that are potentially self-sabotaging, dangerous, or destructive. It may be useful for workers to engage clients in a collaborative problem-solving effort about what will enable them to manage their anxiety, impulsiveness, or erratic and self-destructive behavior. In addition to helping patients to control impulses that are harmful to themselves and others, the worker's setting of limits "can be a new experience for the patient with a person who appropriately cares and protects . . ." (Adler, 1985: 212). This is particularly important with clients who have backgrounds of deprivation and neglect. The worker's passivity in the face of a client's out-of-control or otherwise destructive behavior can signal a repetition of the inadequacies of his or her early caretakers. At the same time, workers must be sensitive to the fact that setting limits also interferes with the autonomy of clients, who may feel that the worker is trying to control them. This issue is confounded when the worker sets limits, in part, because he or she is unable to tolerate the client's behavior. Yet, the failure to set appropriate limits in a timely way makes the worker more vulnerable to becoming angry at the client when his or her behavior taxes the worker's patience.

Optimally, limits should be established thoughtfully rather than as a consequence of the worker's anger or because of his or her own anxiety or preferences. The unilateral establishment of strict rules should be avoided. Although it might be helpful at times to employ the practice, recommended by Kernberg and his colleagues (1989) and Linehan (1993), of utilizing written contracts with clear consequences if clients fail to live up to the agreement, this is a rather extreme approach. Moreover, there should be sufficient flexibility in the treatment structure to maintain clients in treatment when they are unable to adhere to agreed-upon rules or procedures without their being viewed as "non-compliant" or terminated from treatment. For example, some clients who abuse drugs, alcohol, or food or who engage in self-mutilation and other forms of destructive behavior may not be able to maintain total abstinence or refrain from their usual behavior as a prerequisite for treatment. Such a requirement assumes that such clients are healthier than is usually the case. In most instances, the worker's timing in placing expectations on clients for ceasing such actions is important. Waiting or accepting inevitable slips does not imply that the worker is ignoring, minimizing, or condoning a client's actions. Rather the worker continues to address the behavior by keeping it in focus, exploring its current triggers or underlying causes, identifying the gratification obtained from it and resistance to giving it up, and helping clients find other ways of managing their urgent feeling states.

It may be tempting to employ a confrontative approach to address client behaviors that are interfering with the treatment—such as missing sessions, coming late, drinking or smoking marijuana before sessions, or not paying fees in a timely fashion—or that are likely to disrupt the treatment, such as a history of repeated sudden terminations. It generally is preferable to comment on the more immediately problematic aspects of the clients' behavior in nonjudgmental ways that show an understanding of their inner states, fears, and difficulties while also problem-solving with them about how to manage themselves better. In order to do this, it is necessary for workers to see beyond their clients' often rageful, provocative, grandiose, and seemingly manipulative behavior to their underlying anxiety, fears of being victimized, injured self-esteem, anticipation of rejection and abandonment, and attempts to distance and preserve autonomy.

For many individuals, particularly those who face highly stressful life situations or who are socially isolated and without environmental and material supports, developing a therapeutic holding environment must include the client's life space. The worker can help the client to develop daily routines that will provide them with more structure, refer them to twelve-step programs for help with addictive behavior, or engage in collaborative contacts with others who can be of assistance.

OVERCOMING OBSTACLES TO FORMING A POSITIVE RELATIONSHIP

Despite the worker's efforts, there will be those clients who will have difficulty forming a positive connection to the worker early in treatment because of their fear of being re-traumatized as they were as children or their need to replicate pathological interactions. It also is possible, however, that the worker contributes to this state of affairs as a result of factors in his or her own personality and background that impinge on the treatment or because the worker is unable to restrain his or her tendency to become provoked by the client's efforts to "induce" the worker to act in negative ways toward the client. Moreover, the client's environment may contain impediments to his or her positive involvement in the helping process.

EMPATHIZING WITH THE CLIENT'S FEARS OF RE-TRAUMATIZATION

Many clients may ward off the formation of a positive relationship that they desperately need in order to protect themselves from being disappointed, rejected, controlled, betrayed, or damaged in ways they experienced early in life. They may seem indifferent, distant, critical, or provocative or they may test the worker repeatedly. In order to overcome these resistances to using the worker as a sustaining selfobject, the worker provides a consistently supportive and empathic environment as described earlier but also acknowledges and shows understanding of the obstacles to the client's development of a beginning selfobject transference. In some cases, it may be necessary for the worker to set limits on the dangerous or destructive behavior that clients engage in as part of their resistance.

In the Mills and Andrews cases described in Chapter 6, both clients displayed defenses against their need for a positive relationship with the worker out of fear. It took the worker's steadiness, accessibility, reaching-out, understanding of her fears of involvement, and ability to pass Ms. Mills's testing for her to gradually let the worker in. Likewise, the worker had to show her recognition of how fearful Mr. Andrews was of being known, which he equated with being controlled, and to allow him his autonomy in order for Mr. Andrews to begin to let the worker be important to him. The following example also portrays a client's efforts to ward off an attachment to the worker lest the client be let down, hurt, and frustrated, as she had been all through her life.

THE SIMON CASE Ms. Simon, a 38-year-old woman, a head nurse in a hospital specializing in the treatment of cancer, sought help when she felt so emotionally depleted and depressed that she was forced to take a brief vacation by her immediate administrator. In addition to supervising a large staff and interacting with patients, Ms. Simon spent a considerable amount of her non-work time with her aging but still active parents, who viewed her as their lifeline and expected her to be attentive to their needs. She felt alone in this responsibility because her two older siblings were not particularly interested in or capable of being helpful to them. Ms. Simon lived alone with her two cats and tended to isolate herself from many friends, saying that she treasured the time she spent alone without anyone making any demands on her. She experienced relationships as a burden in that people expected her to be "up" and to listen to them while no one really was there for her. She readily acknowledged that she did not tell anyone what she needed because "What's the point? If you have to tell people what you need, it's not the same as their sensing it themselves." Ms. Simon described having had many unhappy relationships with men whom she also found to be totally unreliable and insensitive, so she had given up on dating temporarily. "Besides, I don't have time anyway."

Ms. Simon prided herself on her self-reliance, stating that she would not have survived if she had not taken care of herself from an early age. She had desperately wanted to be able to count on others but couldn't except for one aunt, who died when Ms. Simon was about 13. She described her parents as infantile, self-centered, withholding, critical, demanding, and irresponsible. They expected her to be available to them at a moment's notice and made her feel guilty if she ever took any time for herself. A chilling incident occurred when she was 17 and was raped at knifepoint. Instead of offering comfort, her parents blamed her and made her leave the house and barely spoke to her for six months. She was taken in by a friend's parents. On another occasion, when Ms. Simon was 25, the man whom she had been dating for a year and loved left her for another woman. She was devastated, but when she told her parents, they went into a tirade about her bad judgment in men and hung up on her when she began to cry.

Ms. Simon had a drive to be financially independent and attended college and later a nursing M.S. program, both at great financial cost because of her having to take out loans, some of which she was still paying off. Ms. Simon took pride in being a very hardworking and highly competent nurse on whom others counted. She worked long hours and was meticulous in completing her projects and meeting deadlines and rarely took any time off.

In her meetings with the worker, Ms. Simon told her story in a matter-of-fact manner and frequently laughed nervously after describing upsetting events and interactions. She was friendly but tried to be light and superficial about herself. She acknowledged with a laugh that she had trouble letting people in because she did not want anything she said to be used against her. She spontaneously linked this feeling to her past experiences with her parents, who accused her of selfishness if she said or did anything about which they did not approve. It seemed difficult for Ms. Simon to allow herself to take in the worker's sympathetic comments or suggestions but responded more positively to the worker's empathy with how hard her life was. If the worker remarked on how difficult it must have been for Ms. Simon to feel that no one was there for her, she would brush this statement aside, saying, "Well, what's past is past and there's nothing going to change it. I just have to deal with it." If the worker suggested that it might be good for her to work less or to involve her siblings in helping her parents or to engage in some pleasurable activities, Ms. Simon would explain why it was impossible for her to do so. If the worker commented on how hard Ms. Simon worked, on how much she juggled, and how relieved she must feel when she was home alone and no one was asking her do to something, she would acknowledge the truth in what the worker said.

Ms. Simon seemed to like to come for sessions and shared more easily but continued to keep her distance. Sometimes she would call to say that she could not attend a particular session because of having to work or to tend to an errand for her parents. When the worker said that she could reschedule the meeting or speak by phone, Ms. Simon quickly agreed to this arrangement and would apologize for inconveniencing the worker and thank her for being flexible. The worker thought that Ms. Simon often struggled between wanting to share more of herself with, and to count on, the worker to a greater degree and her feeling that she must continue to be self-reliant and self-protective in order to avoid exposing herself to disappointment. When the worker commented on this, Ms. Simon responded that perhaps that was true. As a result of the worker's persistent efforts to be empathic with her understandable fears of being vulnerable in the light of her past experiences, Ms. Simon slowly was able to begin to look to her for support in dealing with her life.

Discussion

The worker was struck by the degree to which Ms. Simon's selfobject needs as a child and adolescent had been neglected by her family, how overburdened she had been when younger and continued to be as an adult, and by her "pseudo" self-sufficiency in the sense that she felt that she had to rely on herself while concurrently yearning to have someone who would be sensitive to her and fulfill her needs completely. Another problem was that the mainstays of her self-concept were overwork, self-sacrifice, and self-denial, all of which were contributing to her depleted and depressed state but were necessary to bolster her self-esteem and kept her from feeling guilty.

Although Ms. Simon's current life situation was stressful, she had longstanding difficulties that were trapping her but from which she did not know how to free herself. She also feared disappointment and was quite adamant in her feeling that her way of dealing with her life was the only way. The worker did not feel that it would be advantageous to challenge the client to look at what was keeping her stuck. Instead, she recognized the need to move slowly in order to gain Ms. Simon's trust and to help her become involved in the treatment as beginning steps.

CONFRONTING SPLITTING AND PROJECTIVE IDENTIFICATION

There are those object relations theorists who view the difficulties that some clients have in forming a positive relationship with the worker as stemming from their tendencies to use the defenses of splitting and projective identification and to replicate internalized interpersonal interactions in their relationship with the worker. Such clients may not be able to take in the worker's genuine wish to be helpful and efforts to be empathic. It is hard for them to experience the worker as a "good" object on a consistent basis or at all. They often display unwarranted anger at the worker, whom they see as a potentially dangerous or "bad" depriving or frustrating object. This anger may result from feeling that no one will ever be able to assuage their sense of aloneness or give them what they need, from the projection of their own negative feelings, from their envy of and fear of the worker upon whom they are dependent, or from their belief that they are undeserving of the worker's help because of their sense of being bad (Adler, 1985: 50–51). Sometimes they fluctuate in their feelings about and perception of the worker, seeing him or her as all "good" or all "bad," or they maintain a suspicious attitude toward the worker despite their surface compliance. Other clients who are impulsive may become management problems because they tend to act-out their intense feeling states or attempt to deal with their inner turmoil by means of substance abuse or other forms of addictive and destructive behavior. Because these behaviors often threaten the treatment and may also place clients in dangerous situations in their daily lives, it may be necessary to point out the client's defenses, distortions, and problematic behavior. The worker tries to help clients to acknowledge and to diminish their use of such mechanisms, to correct their misperceptions, to own their own feelings, and to restrain their acting-out.

The term "confrontation" is unfortunate because it often is associated with an angry showdown or fight. Confrontation may be experienced by the client as an attack because it generally draws attention to uncomfortable or disturbing contradictions in or aspects of the client's feelings and behavior that he or she may not fully recognize but which others experience. The main purpose of confrontation is to overcome the client's resistance to such recognition (Adler, 1985: 121–122). Confrontation should not be used when the worker is angry at the client. Although it is utilized generally when the therapeutic relationship has been firmly established, there are instances in which it is necessary to use confrontation in the beginning phase in order to address and overcome obstacles to the client's engaging in treatment.

It is important to note that some self psychological clinicians have argued that it is a mistake to view the reactions described above as caused by pathological defenses. Recognizing that it is difficult to maintain an empathic stance in the face of clients' extreme responses, they argue that it is important for the worker to see beyond the client's "difficult" attributes and relate empathically to their underlying anxiety, desperation, low self-esteem, fears of abandonment, and hopelessness rather than employ confrontations and interpretations that provoke rather than diffuse more flagrant behavior (Brandchaft & Stolorow, 1984a & b; Magid, 1984; Dublin, 1992).

Those clinicians who favor the use of confrontation at times in the treatment process would look to several indicators, including the presence of splitting defenses, evidenced by contradictory attitudes, feeling states, and behaviors that the client does not integrate and that contribute to his or her difficulties; the use of projective identification in the relationship with the worker and others in the client's life; the threat of dangerous or destructive behaviors that are not in the best interests of the client or others in the client's life; and the presence of enactments of pathological internalized self- and object-representations and relational patterns in the client-worker relationship, which will be discussed more fully in Chapter 8. In employing confrontation, a nonjudgmental attitude is needed. When addressing primitive defenses or self-defeating and self-destructive behavior, it is important to do so in ways that show an understanding of the client's intense and seemingly urgent needs and feeling states and that acknowledge how the client may have adopted certain attitudes and behavior in order to survive difficult life circumstances.

In the following example, the worker attempted to confront the client when she became concerned that the client was going to sabotage her job, as she had done with other situations in her life.

THE LITTLE CASE When Ms. Little, a 45-year-old word processor, sought help, she was very distraught. She had had a severe attack of irritable bowel syndrome and had been experiencing increasing stress at work. She was depressed, hopeless, irritable, and feared that she would make herself so ill that she would not want to go on living. She was not overtly suicidal but felt that she did not want to live if she was going to have ongoing medical problems and physical pain. Her medical doctor seemed to be losing patience with Ms. Little, whom he found to be demanding and resistant to his advice. He felt that she needed treatment for her emotional problems, which he felt were contributing to her physical symptoms.

Ms. Little had recently left another therapist in a rage after participating in a research study on depression at a local hospital, where she received a brief course of cognitive/behavioral treatment and antidepressant medication. She experienced some slight improvement but relapsed quickly. Although she had consented to being in the study and thought her participation would be a way of not having to pay for treatment, she felt that she had been treated insensitively and was used as a "guinea pig." She had not expected to be terminated upon completing the study and was angry that the hospital felt no responsibility to continue her treatment. She was furious at her therapist, a psychologist, whom she had idealized initially but who turned out to be "a robot" who had no feelings about her. The psychologist had suggested that she see a psychiatrist for medication, but Ms. Little was resistant to this idea because she feared its side effects and because she did not get much help from the drugs she had been given previously and was apprehensive about their side effects.

Ms. Little originally entered the depression study because she was upset about her frequent physical symptoms and about the course of her life. She was quite distrustful of treatment and had difficulty complying with the treatment regimen. An extremely perfectionistic and anxious person, Ms. Little tried to control her environment and was constantly frustrated when people did not behave in the ways that she wanted or events occurred that she had not anticipated. Consequently, she was frequently angry and upset about the assaults of everyday life, such as the subway being delayed, getting an incorrect telephone bill, or having to deal with a slow salesperson or supermarket clerk. She was preoccupied with her health and had numerous physical problems. Additionally, a major problem was her anger and rage, which she had difficulty containing in the work situation and elsewhere. On one occasion, she was threatened physically by a man in the subway whom she cursed at for stepping on her foot. Prior to seeking help, Ms. Little was told that she might be let go by her supervisor at work if she did not stop getting into confrontations and difficult interpersonal conflicts. Although she had restrained some of her more provocative behavior with her coworkers for a time, Ms. Little's patience with them was growing thin. She complained bitterly about their incompetence, bad attitudes, and irresponsibility and felt that she was not going to work hard and look the other way when they did not do their share and gossiped with one another all the time.

Ms. Little's parents lived on Long Island. From an early age and continuing to the present, Ms. Little struggled with complying with their wishes and demands on her and fighting off their need for control. Ms.

Little's only other relatives were her brother, sister-in-law, and two nieces, whom she visited infrequently because she was rarely invited to stay at their home and "I'm not going to put myself out to go there and come home in one day." She had few friends as she tended to break off relationships because her friends were basically "selfish and insensitive." She did not appear to be aware that she projected her own feelings onto almost everyone in her environment, treated them badly, and then reacted to their justifiable responses to her as if they were enemies.

Ms. Little filled her early meetings with the worker with her anger against her previous therapist, the hospital, her coworkers, and her supervisor. She watched the worker's reactions intently. Although she said she liked the worker, who seemed sensitive to and understanding of her, she was alert to anything the worker said or did not say that indicated that she was not in total agreement with the client's viewpoint. While saying she was lucky to have been assigned to the worker, she expressed considerable distrust of her and the treatment process. She attacked most therapists as being interested in controlling their clients and using them to meet their own needs. For the most part, the worker listened and empathized with the client's feelings, but her rage seemed to escalate and she appeared to be on the verge of confronting a coworker and engaging in a work slowdown that would have unfortunate consequences. The worker's anxiety about Ms. Little sabotaging her job mounted and she wanted to share this with the client. She was concerned, however, that any attempts she would make to help Ms. Little to curtail her provocative behavior and to own her own role in creating her work problems would result in her turning against the worker and leaving treatment. The worker sensed that her wanting to confront Ms. Little might also reflect Ms. Little's having "induced" her to play the role of an unfeeling and critical person, which could then justify Ms. Little's perception of her as being like everyone else in her life. At one point, the following interchange took place.

Worker: I find myself in a dilemma. I am concerned that what I am going to say will cause you to feel that I am not on your side, but if I do not tell you what I am thinking, I am not doing my best to help you.

Ms. Little: You can tell me what you think. Why do you think you can't?

Worker: Because you often seem to develop negative feelings toward people whom you feel do not understand you or who do not share your views.

Ms. Little: Most people don't understand me but you have so far.

Worker: Well, that's the point. You feel good toward me when I agree with you, but what if I express a view that is different from yours? Will you feel that I'm the enemy too?

Ms. Little: Probably. But you can try. Just don't expect me to agree with you.

Worker: Although your coworkers may not live up to your standards and are often unpleasant, I'm concerned about your letting your anger at them get out of control in a way that winds up hurting you.

Ms. Little: I don't want them to take advantage of me and to get away with how they treat me.

Worker: Is it possible that they are not against you to begin with but that they sense your anger at and negative judgments of them and then react badly to you?

Ms. Little: So what? I still don't have to take it from them. Do you expect me to be a doormat?

Worker: So now you are feeling that I am on their side and against you because I am asking you to consider how you might be contributing to your work problems.

Ms. Little: What do you want me to do? I am who I am. No one is going to control me.

Worker: I understand that you feel very angry at how your coworkers act and that you want to get back at them. No one wants to be controlled. In your life you have had to fight to be your own person and to control your own life.

Ms. Little: That's true. I'm glad you see that.

Worker: Maybe it is hard for you to see that not everyone wants to control you and that sometimes your way of dealing with others may cause them to feel that you are trying to control them? When I say this to you, you feel that I am trying to control you.

Ms. Little: Aren't you?

Worker: I can understand that you might feel that way, but I am concerned about you doing something that will wind up hurting you. I thought it might be useful for us to consider other ways you could deal with your anger at your coworkers so that you don't lose your job.

Ms. Little: Well, maybe your motives are good, but I don't even care about whether or not I lose my job. I want to get back at them.

Worker: That is an understandable feeling and what you do is up to you, but I was under the impression from what you have told me that you also do not want to lose your job now. It is hard to have it both ways, to have the satisfaction of getting back at your coworkers without hurting yourself in the process.

Ms. Little: When I feel angry, I don't think about other feelings I have. It's what I'm feeling at the moment that counts. Maybe that does hurt me at times. I don't really want to talk about this anymore. I want to change the subject.

Worker: We can change the subject now if it's too hard to continue, but we may need to come back to it soon.

Discussion

Because of the non-punitive manner in which the worker managed this interaction, the client was able to tolerate the worker's move away from her empathic stance without completely turning against her. Although fighting off the worker's comments, she briefly acknowledged her "black-and-white" or unintegrated responses to situations. To the degree that primitive defenses are rigid and pervasive, repeated confrontations and interpretations may have to be used. A balance between this type of intervention and those that are more sustaining is necessary, however, in order to maintain the client-worker relationship.

INTERSUBJECTIVITY IN THE CLIENT-WORKER RELATIONSHIP

There is general consensus that those who work with clients who suffer from developmental arrests are especially vulnerable to problematic reactions that can obstruct their work because of the impact of their urgent needs, primitive defenses, angry, demanding and provocative behavior, and intense transference reactions. This point of view tends to hold clients responsible for all obstacles to engagement, but sometimes it is workers rather than clients who are "difficult" because of their lack of attunement, unintentional insensitivity, overly harsh comments, failure to respond to clients' needs, or cultural countertransference (Perez Foster, 1999). Even when a client is "inducing" a reaction in the worker, it is important for the worker to contain rather than act-out his or her feelings.

Workers and clients exert a mutual impact on one another all through treatment. Consequently, workers must be open to the possibility and to examining how their attitudes, belief systems, personality, background, life experiences, and interventions may be affecting the client. Labeling clients as difficult can be inaccurate because of the intersubjective nature of the interventive process. For example, the worker's insistence on a rigid treatment structure and his or her inflexibility can have detrimental effects. Many clients are unable to tolerate or comply with strict rules, not because they are resistant or non-cooperative but because such demands are threatening or do not fit their needs and expectations. Likewise, interpretive techniques may be experienced as unempathic with the client's need to have a sympathetic listener or may go beyond what clients are able to assimilate. Additionally, when a worker's ethnic, racial, class, cultural, or religious background, gender and sexual orientation, or experience with oppression is very different from that of the patient, there is a risk of misinterpretation of the patient's life experiences and communications that result in unattuned interventions.

In whatever ways that clients present themselves, the worker's ability to be empathic with clients, to be flexible in their use of themselves, and to recognize and bridge differences that exist can transform a seemingly difficult client into one who can benefit from the helping process. It is important to bear in mind, however, that problems occur not only when workers differ from their clients in major ways but also when workers are too much like them (Stolorow & Atwood, 1992: 103–122).

THE WORKER'S PERSONAL COUNTERTRANSFERENCE

The emphasis on the client's contribution to the worker's countertransference and to the creation of enactments of early pathological relational patterns in the treatment does not replace the traditional view that a worker's countertransference can stem from his or her own personal developmental difficulties and result in negative consequences for the treatment. Moreover, even if a client is inducing a reaction in the worker, it is important for the worker to contain rather than act-out his or her feelings. Moreover, as will be discussed further in Chapter 8, there are many instances in which the worker's ability to take responsibility for having caused a disruption in the therapeutic relationship will repair whatever rift has occurred and also can have a positive effect on the client and the treatment process.

Some of the most common countertransference pitfalls stem from the worker's need for and pathological use of the client. For example, the worker may need the client's applause, idealization, validation, or affirmation or may look to the client for intimacy or to bolster his or her sense of omnipotence, grandiosity, or need for power and control. These needs may result in the worker's unintentional but sometimes conscious use or exploitation of the client and to a repetition of earlier pathological interactions in both the worker's and the client's life. For example, the worker may communicate that the worker expects the client to provide mirroring, to depend on the worker for support and guidance, or to keep the worker on a pedestal, or the worker may exert control over a client or seduce the client emotionally only to frustrate and reject the client.

There is always a danger for narcissistically vulnerable workers who work with particularly withdrawn or self-absorbed clients who deny the worker's separate existence, devaluing clients who attack the worker's ability to be helpful, or entitled clients who make enormous demands. Workers may respond with resentment and intrusive interventions in order to be seen by the client, helplessness and hopelessness about the client's ability to get better, a loss of a sense of competence, guilt for not being able to rescue the client or live up to his or her expectations of the therapist's omnipotence, anger at the client's sense of entitlement and demands for unconditional care and nurture, envy of the client for having such an empathic, nurturing, and dedicated worker, or heroic efforts to reach the client. Sometimes workers become fatigued and begin to have excessive self-doubts about the value of treatment and their career choice.

There is also a risk that the worker's current life situation rather than his or her developmental issues makes it more tempting to use a client to fulfill selfobject and intimacy needs. As the losses and stresses of life itself as well as the vagaries of managed care create their own assaults and deprivations for workers, who work long hours with often so-called difficult clients and who may not always have sufficient supports in their own lives, it is not difficult to imagine that workers' frustrated needs to be seen, heard, appreciated, and to be close may creep into the therapeutic relationship, making it more difficult to be disciplined in the treatment.

In the following case example, the worker developed very strong feelings of wanting to share her own personal experiences with her client, who formed a twinship transference in the treatment.

THE WALKER CASE Ms. Walker, a woman in her late thirties, was employed as a social worker. She sought help because she was having serious conflicts about her relationship with a man ten years her senior. She related to the worker as her contemporary and as a professional peer and looked to her for a certain amount of mirroring and twinship. Both the worker and client had grown up in the same midwestern city, came from similar working-class backgrounds, and struggled financially to attend college. The worker was quite conscious of the need to monitor her feelings toward the client because of her feelings of kinship toward her. In a session just after the recent death of an aunt with whom she had a very close relationship, Ms. Walker nostalgically and emotionally recalled her shopping trips with her aunt to a department store and described in detail scenes that she remembered. Her sadness about the loss of her aunt and her positive feelings for her were both palpable. The worker began to feel stirred by her own childhood memories of having done the same things in the very same place, but by herself rather than with a loved and loving companion. She felt an intense urge to tell the client that she knew exactly what she was talking about, that she had been there too, and to ask her if she remembered such and such about the place. She restrained herself with difficultly and commented on how much the client's relationship with her aunt had meant to her and had given her and that she could understand her sense of loss but also her continuing feelings of connection.

Discussion

In this example, the worker recognized that her powerful feelings had little to do with what Ms. Walker was feeling in the session and that they stemmed from her own personal issues. She understood that the client was grieving in the reassuring presence of someone whom she felt understood her and that the worker's life experience did not seem relevant and would have been intrusive. In reflecting on this incident, the worker realized that she was somewhat envious of the client's positive memories because her own were tinged with some sadness and that it would have been comforting for her to have shared them with the client. In the moment, the worker needed a selfobject.

The Walker example also points out that although instances of serious misattunement often arise when the worker cannot empathize with a client who is different from the worker, a more subtle but often just as problematic countertransference problem arises when the worker and client are similar.

ENVIRONMENTAL IMPEDIMENTS

There are occasions when the conditions of the client's interpersonal or environmental milieu actively work against the client's involvement in treatment, impede progress, or cause the client to withdraw from treatment prematurely. For example, when a woman who seeks treatment because of her unhappiness with her dominating husband begins to be more assertive and noncompliant, her husband may become even more controlling, blame the worker for destroying their relationship, and demand that she end the treatment. This state of affairs may induce intense conflict in the client, who may not be ready to take a firm stand or cause a serious rift with her husband. Likewise, a young adult who is struggling to free herself from the control of her family may encounter the family's escalating disapproval and threats of abandonment or rejection and thwart the still-vulnerable client's efforts to be her own person.

Because helping clients obtain certain types of resources may be an indispensable or major part of the interventive process, their lack of availability may stand in the way of achieving treatment goals. Often workers and clients experience considerable frustration in their attempts to locate and access services such as substance abuse programs, vocational training programs, after-school programs, shelters for battered women, inpatient psychiatric treatment, and supervised living situations. Moreover, helping clients to secure entitlements and other types of concrete services may involve continued delays.

SELECTIVE TECHNIQUES

Although the full range of therapeutic techniques is available to the practitioner, object relations and self psychology reflect different views about how these interventions are used than do traditional treatment models.

BEING A NEW AND REAL OBJECT

Therapeutic change results from the client's identification with and internalization of the worker as a new kind of object who "holds" the client, supports and encourages his or her separation-individuation, provides selective experiences of interpersonal intimacy, and allows his or her real personality to be evident. The worker does not deliberately set out to reparent the client but does interact with the client in growth-promoting ways that the client may not have experienced previously. The worker's realness becomes apparent through not always being perfectly attuned to the client, by displaying certain limits with respect to his or her availability and responsiveness, and through self-disclosing aspects of his or her real personality, interests, attitudes, and background. It must be noted, however, that many clients have difficulty perceiving and relating to the objective qualities of the worker and in their ability to use the worker to forward their development. Their need for archaic forms of selfobject relatedness is too great and must be gratified. Being real may need to wait until later stages of the treatment.

The worker's ability to be a new kind of object also shows the client that there is a world of potentially more gratifying relationships than the client had experienced previously. This helps the client to take risks in developing relationships outside of the treatment that can serve to reinforce new ways of relating to others and perceiving the self.

PROVIDING SELFOBJECT FUNCTIONS

The provision of support and encouragement has certainly been a part of most treatment methods at times, but self psychology introduced the importance of the worker serving as an actual selfobject in a variety of ways that enable clients to strengthen their self structures through the process of transmuting internalization. Because so many clients who come for help have not experienced validation of their feelings and experiences, have not had idealizable adults in their lives, or have not been able to share a sense of likeness with significant others, it often is important for the worker to provide a range of selfobject functions.

In addition to providing acknowledgment and affirmation of, as well as resonance with, the client's feelings, it also is especially important for the worker to search out, identify, validate, and work with clients' strengths and talents. It is not always easy to do this when clients are beleaguered by severe personality pathology. At the very least, however, the fact that they have sought help is a strength upon which to build. Likewise, it is useful to acknowledge the fact that even those who display long-standing and severe problems may have shown remarkable resiliency in surviving difficult circumstances and that many of their problematic attitudes and behavior may have helped them to survive.

The worker's willingness to self-disclose aspects of his or her own personality, interests, attitudes, background, life experiences, and thoughts and feelings during the course of treatment is an important therapeutic tool.

There are clients who or situations that require the worker to be more real, and certain types of responsiveness may be necessary to help clients develop selfobject transferences, to reveal themselves, to remember and explore traumatic experiences, to feel validated in their very existence, or to own disavowed aspects of their own feelings and behavior. In this respect, the thoughtful and sometimes spontaneous use of self-disclosure can be considered to be a form of empathic attunement and selfobject responsiveness that does not preclude exploration or interpretation. In fact, it may enable the client to become more self-disclosing, more able to explore emotionally significant areas, and more able to discover walled-off areas of experience. Worker self-disclosure also can help clients to establish a meaningful connection, to feel less alone, to bear shame and humiliation, grief, fear, and other painful emotions, to discover and validate their own selfhood, to have a positive role model or exposure to alternative ways of thinking and acting, and to bridge actual differences that exist between worker and client, to discover the differences between and separateness of the client and worker, and to foster experiences of intimacy and sharing.

It also is beneficial for the worker to encourage clients in their quest for more mature selfobjects in the world outside of treatment. Likewise, the worker should support the client's efforts in seeking out opportunities to express their selfobject needs through developing their interests, expanding their activities, or finding new employment.

THE D'AGOSTINO CASE CONTINUES In the case of Mr. D'Agostino, who was discussed in Chapter 6, the worker tried to connect to Mr. D'Agostino's life experience and Sicilian-American background by being more open about herself. After acknowledging being a fan of his favorite television show, *The Sopranos,* she disclosed that she had visited Sicily and was interested in Sicilian culture. Mr. D'Agostino began to develop a selfobject transference in which he experienced the worker as someone like him. The worker showed interest in the articles that Mr. D'Agostino brought in about Italian culture, and they exchanged views of movies and plays and later discussed all of the minute details of his employment search. The worker also tried to help him to explore the origins of and modify his negative views of himself, validated his talents and capacities, and encouraged the expression of his creativity and literary interests. A major thrust of the work was helping the client to identify the negative messages that he had received as a child about his ethnicity and sexual orientation and how these had affected his views of himself. Although Mr. D'Agostino's difficulty in moving beyond his depressive self-concept and pessimism were quite pronounced, he gradually began to feel better about himself and to more seriously seek employment. He returned to his pessimistic outlook and feelings of failure at times when he encountered obstacles or experienced slights from others or when he did not feel that the worker was completely in tune with him. He recovered quickly from these relapses and began to have longer periods of feeling good about himself. He eventually found a reasonably good job in another area of insurance that was somewhat more interesting and challenging than his previous position and enrolled in a writing course.

THE NATURE OF EXPLANATION AND/OR INTERPRETATION

The worker employs explanations and/or interpretations to help clients understand their inner experiences, defenses, and reactions. These techniques, however, need to be used carefully and as part of the worker's efforts to help the client sustain, and in some instances to restore, a positive therapeutic relationship and to move the treatment forward.

The term *explanation* has two different meanings, in that it sometimes refers to an educative technique that precedes interpretation and is designed to help the client understand the presence and origin of developmental arrests, particularly related to separation-individuation subphase difficulties (Goldstein, 1990: 148–149). *Explanation* also is used interchangeably with the term *interpretation,* particularly by self psychologists, in order to differentiate interpretations around selfobject needs from more classical interpretations of unconscious wishes, instinctual impulses, and superego conflicts.

Using explanation as an educative tool is useful in appealing to the client's observing ego and in making the client an ally in the process of understanding the nature of his or her deficits, extreme reactions, and relational patterns. For example, the worker might tell a client that the reason he or she is having trouble maintaining a connection to the worker between sessions is that when the client was a child and was separated from or frustrated by his or her mother, he or she was never helped to feel that the mother would return or that she would continue to be loving and gratifying. Similarly, a worker may explain to a client who tends to use splitting as a defense that the client tends to see people as all "good" when they are being supportive, and that he or she then idealizes them, or as all "bad" when they disappoint the client and then the client becomes devaluing of them. The worker may go on to educate the client about the early origins of this reaction. Likewise, the worker may tell a client who is very depressed as a result of being criticized by an employer that the client has experienced a blow to his self-esteem because of the criticism and is feeling like a bad person because he or she is very dependent on others' approval in order to feel good about himself or herself. The worker may add that the client's excessive need for approval and his or her extreme reaction to criticism stem from never having been helped to feel good about his or her own abilities early in life.

In addition to using self psychological explanations or interpretations, the focus of interpretation varies greatly depending on the nature of the pathology that is deemed to be present in a particular case.

Interpretations of Separation-Individuation Subphase Issues

In the course of treatment, clients demonstrate needs and behavior that are linked to early separation-individuation subphase issues. It is important for the worker to distinguish between those client behaviors that are phase-appropriate and in the service of growth, given the client's developmental level, from those that are maladaptive and in the service of resistance or regression. The worker should support adaptive behavior and selectively gratify phase-appropriate needs, such as the client's efforts to practice making independent decisions or to what may be his or her legitimate need for the worker to read his or her thoughts and feelings. The worker should reserve interpretations for more problematic reactions, such as the client's efforts to cling to the worker or to compel the worker to give advice and guidance when the client is capable of being autonomous and making his or her own decisions. In such instances, the worker might say, "I know that you are acting as if you need me to be present all the time and want me to tell you what to do, but this may be your way of avoiding being independent because it scares you." When there is a mix of adaptive and maladaptive features in the same behavior, the worker should offer interpretations that are attuned to the most advanced level of what is being expressed. For example, a client's announcement that he or she plans to take a vacation from treatment may reflect his or her positive although uncomfortable efforts to individuate. Interpreting this attempt at individuation as resistance may be experienced by the patient as a lack of attunement and may have a countertherapeutic effect. Instead, the worker can acknowledge the positive aspects of the client's readiness to test out being on his or her own while at the same time questioning whether it is necessary to do this in such an "all or nothing" manner to prove that the client can be independent of the worker. Alternatively, if the worker observes that the client is becoming distraught and dependent because he or she is experiencing a sense of loss or abandonment depression related to increasingly autonomous behavior or achievements, withdrawing from the worker because of feelings of dependence in order to reassure himself or herself of his or her separateness, or missing sessions in order to avoid facing painful feelings, the worker might interpret these actions accordingly.

Interpretation of Resistance to a Selfobject Transference
As discussed earlier, clients bring fears of varying intensity to treatment and may defend against the emergence of their frustrated childhood needs in the therapeutic relationship. The greater their earlier trauma, the more likely it is that they will be frightened of exposing themselves to being disappointed or mistreated once more. Moreover, maintaining distance may be the only way the client can maintain his or her sense of self. Rather than interpreting such fears and needs, it may be necessary for the worker to remain in an understanding phase for a period of time until the client feels safer or is able to accept the worker's comments rather than see them as unwanted intrusions. When the worker does decide to offer interpretations to the client, he or she should convey that the client's "resistance" is an understandable outcome of his earlier life experiences, which the client fears will be repeated.

Interpretation of Selfobject Needs and Empathic Failures

The worker also offers empathic explanations or interpretations that link clients' problems to frustrations of their selfobject needs by others in their current environment and that connect the presence of their archaic longings to empathic failures on the part of their parents and significant others in their early lives. Thus, with a perfectionistic man whose self-esteem hinges on others' admiration of him and who angrily sends out resumés and becomes demoralized if he does not get the praise he seeks, the worker might say, "You drive yourself very hard, and it is very difficult for you to feel that you are valued if people are not enthusiastic about your work. Perhaps this is because you felt so little acknowledgment from your father when you were younger, no matter how hard you tried." With a woman client whose view of a good marriage is that couples never fight and who becomes enraged at her husband and threatens to leave him when he has an occasional burst of anger, the worker might say, "It feels intolerable to you when your husband does not live up to your ideal. It makes you feel like you have failed. Perhaps your strong feelings about this are related to your having felt like you were to blame when your father would yell at you and your mother when you were a child and to your understandable need to believe that if you were good enough or really lovable, no one would ever get angry at you." Likewise, with a woman client, such as Ms. Samuels in Chapter 6, who had adopted a false self in the face of her parents' needs for her to be what they wanted and who did not know or develop her true self, the worker might say, "You are experiencing an internal conflict between your need to be what you think you parents want you to be and your desire to be your own person. This is very difficult for you because you learned as a child that it was necessary for you to live out your parents' expectations of you in order to keep them happy and to get their love. It is likely that you were not helped to get to know and value your own needs, wants, and abilities." The purpose of these interpretations is to help the client see that his or her reactions, although understandable, stem from earlier frustrating interactions that have left the client feeling particularly needy of certain types of responses from others to maintain his or her self-esteem and self-cohesion. Repeated interpretations as well as the repair of disruptions in the client-worker relationship, which will be discussed in

Chapter 8, result in strengthening clients' self-structures and enabling them to be less vulnerable to extreme reactions.

Interpretation of the Presence of "Bad" Internal Objects

There are many clients who are chronically or repeatedly depressed, who have trouble feeling good for very long, if at all, who exhibit self-defeating and self-destructive behavior, who are unable to make good choices in their relationships and work life, who display entrenched negative attitudes about themselves, and who have difficulty experiencing others as good objects. It appears as if they are stuck or are clinging to their negative views of themselves and others or to their penchant for entering into frustrating interactions and difficult situations no matter how much empathy or support they receive or how much success or achievement they obtain.

It often is necessary for the worker to draw attention to clients' difficulties in freeing themselves from their attachment to "bad" internal objects that dominate their behavior. Clients may not be aware of this dynamic or may accept its presence but be unable to extricate themselves from these powerful introjects because were they to do so, they would feel totally alone or extremely guilty. The client acts as if he or she would rather stay attached to their internal bad objects than form more satisfying relationships with others or adopt a more positive view of themselves. Interpretations of this dynamic often are resisted by the client because they are attacking the client's tie to internal objects that he or she needs consciously or unconsciously. Such interpretations should be offered in ways that do not blame the client for his or her pathology. Moreover, the client needs to feel that the worker understands his or her needs not to risk any change. For example, with a male client like Mr. D'Agostino in Chapter 6, who felt he could never please his critical father and who persists in viewing himself as a total failure despite evidence to the contrary, the worker might say, "You seem to have adopted your father's view of you and listen to his voice internally and cannot see yourself as capable of success despite your achievements and others' positive opinions of you. In this way, you stay connected to him. I guess it would make you feel too alone to risk feeling differently about yourself. It would mean losing him in some way. In a strange way, you can't prove him wrong. You keep him as the idealized parent whose praise and love you wanted so desperately." Likewise, with a client like Ms. Wright in Chapter 6, who had a history of a disappointing relationship with her charming but rejecting father and who drove men who cared for her away and instead was attracted to exciting but emotionally unavailable and unreliable men, the worker might say, "This pattern you have is being driven by your internal attachment to your father, whom you adored but who made you feel unlovable and was never there for you. You keep trying to get a man like him to care for you but end up feeling rejected once more. When a different type of man who could really be there for you shows up, something inside of you pushes him away and you remain attached to your charming but frustrating father."

In order to be effective, the interpretations of the presence of so-called "bad" objects should come after the worker has pointed out the ways in which they are operating in his or her life. The worker also must help the client to understand the link between his or her current feelings and behavior to the ways in which he or she was responded to and to the people with whom the client identified in his or her early life. This interpretive emphasis must be accompanied by the worker's provision of sufficient "holding," help in clients' developing more positive internalizations, and encouragement in risking new behaviors that can lead to reinforcement of different ways of experiencing themselves and others.

SUMMARY

This chapter has described and illustrated some major components of the beginning phase of social work treatment, focusing on how to establish and overcome obstacles to developing a positive client-worker relationship and the use of selective techniques. It stressed the importance of creating an individualized holding environment and described its general characteristics, the role of experience-near-empathy, containment and transitional phenomena, and limits and structure. It considered obstacles to the development of a positive treatment relationship that stem from the client's fears of retraumatization, their tendency to distort the relationship through their use of primitive defenses and tendency to replicate earlier relational patterns, the mutual impact of worker and client, and the worker's personal countertransference reactions. In discussing selected treatment techniques, the chapter emphasized the worker's use of self in providing real object experiences and selfobject functions on the one hand and use of confrontation and a range of interpretations on the other.

8

MIDDLE PHASE ISSUES

In the beginning of treatment, interventions tend to be geared to engaging and sustaining the client, whereas in the middle phase, they are aimed at ameliorating the problems for which the client has sought help. Even in the best of situations, however, treatment does not proceed smoothly as disruptions, obstacles, and impasses occur. Self psychology and object relations theory reflect two fundamentally different ways of addressing issues that arise in the client-worker relationship, particularly during the middle phase of treatment. Self psychologists emphasize the importance of the worker's role in repairing disruptions of the client-worker relationship, while object relations followers tend to focus on how the worker addresses the client's tendency to "enact" earlier pathological interactions in the treatment. Additionally, current relational and intersubjective theorists stress the benefit of the worker and client actively considering the ongoing impact of the similarities and differences in their personalities on the treatment process. They also underscore the importance of the worker's recognition of and responsiveness to other forms of object relating that the client exhibits besides using the worker as a selfobject.

REPAIRING DISRUPTIONS OF THE SELFOBJECT TRANSFERENCE

Self psychologists believe that the way in which workers address clients' selfobject needs that are expressed in the client-worker relationship is the most important factor contributing to client improvement. The formation of a selfobject transference provides many clients with a second chance to complete their development. In those cases in which the clients' presenting problems are related to the frustration of their selfobject needs, the worker's attuned interventions can restore their equilibrium and help them to regain a sense of well-being.

During the course of treatment, when the selfobject transferences operate smoothly, clients usually feel positively toward the worker and experience a sense of cohesiveness. When there is a disruption in the client-worker relationship, the client may show a range of acute reactions, including anger, disappointment, loss, feelings of injury, deidealization, depletion, and fragmentation. Continuing tension and lack of harmony in the client-worker relationship as a result of unresolved disruptions may derail the therapeutic work and result in a stalemate. Consequently, the worker must quickly recognize and repair the inevitable disruptions that occur as part of the treatment process. These commonly result from the worker's failure to live up to the client's expectations and from his or her unavailability, inadvertent lapses in empathy, mistakes, or unattuned responses. When such disruptions are repaired and the selfobject transference is restored, the client regains his or her feeling of well-being and the treatment resumes its proper course.

There is another reason why disturbances in the selfobject transference and their repair are important. Repeated disruption-restoration sequences are part of the work of the treatment. They present clients with instances in which they experience and come to accept human limitations, disappointments, and failures that are non-traumatic because of the worker's non-defensive and empathic attitudes and interventions. For clients who have had few, if any, interactions with significant others of this nature, the client-worker relationship can serve as a powerful new opportunity that enables them to solidify their selfobject connections and, over time, to strengthen their self-structures through the process of transmuting internalization.

The worker does not deliberately set out to create disruptions of the selfobject transference. The potential for such disturbances are built into the therapeutic process and cannot be completely avoided because the treatment has certain constraints that potentially frustrate the client. For example, the worker is not always available, each session is time-limited, vacations and illness occur, and interruptions, such as emergency telephone calls, take place. Likewise, the worker is only human and sometimes gets tired, sick, has difficulty concentrating, fails to understand the client at times, or does not always respond sensitively. Moreover, the worker is not able to embody all the ideal or perfect characteristics that clients seek.

It is crucial that the atmosphere of the treatment and the worker's overall ability to be empathic and responsive be "good enough" to provide a stable backdrop in which temporary and non-traumatic disruptions can be overcome. If the disappointments in or frustrations by the worker are too profound or perpetual—that is, if they lead to severe regressions of overwhelming rage and aloneness or to irreparable injuries—or the worker is not sufficiently understanding and responsive most of the time, it is likely that disruptions will not be worked through.

The restoration of the worker as a good selfobject results from open acknowledgment by both participants in the treatment that the client-worker relationship has been derailed. The worker engages in empathic exploration of the triggers for the disruption, conveys understanding of the client's feelings and perceptions, and assumes responsibility and sometimes expresses regret for his or her role in contributing to the disturbance.

Indicators that the client-worker relationship has become disrupted include the client's angry, critical, and hurt reactions, missed sessions, non-communicativeness, and increased depression, anxiety, suspiciousness, withdrawal, acting-out, or disorganization. In drawing attention to and exploring the significance of these signs, it is important for the worker to be non-accusatory and, in some instances, to actively verbalize that the worker may have let the client down in some way, failed to understand him or her, made an insensitive comment, or was insufficiently responsive.

Indispensable features of the worker's ability to repair the disruption are his or her efforts to try to understand the client's reactions, even if they seem extreme and unwarranted, and to accept the validity of the client's subjective experience even if it is at variance with the worker's intentions or perceptions. The worker refrains from confronting the client with the seemingly distorted or overly intense nature of the client's responses. This does not mean that workers cannot share their own perceptions of the situation or their reasons for their behavior. The purpose of such explanations, however, is to clarify where and how misunderstandings and misinterpretations may have taken place rather than to convince the client that the worker is "right" and the client is "wrong."

In addition to acknowledging his or her role in contributing to disruptions in the selfobject transference, the worker also may make empathic interpretations that link such disturbances to earlier frustrations and disappointments in the client's life, particularly with respect to the client's parents or early caretakers. Such interpretations enable clients to explore and understand the origins of their archaic selfobject needs. Thus, both the worker's repair of disruptions and the interpretive process enable the client to undergo a maturational and strengthening process. It is important to note that when clients recognize their past deprivations and relinquish some of their archaic yearnings, they may experience a painful grief process that must be worked through.

The emphasis on the worker's exploration of and acknowledgment of his or her role in contributing to the disruptions that occur in the client-worker relationship places responsibility on workers to understand and overcome any theoretical leanings and personal or cultural countertransference reactions that might interfere with their empathic abilities and lead to unattuned responses. This thrust does not imply that the client is free from so-called "infantile" needs and pathological traits, but it does mean that the worker's correct empathy with the client will enable them to maintain even archaic selfobject connections.

CASE EXAMPLES

The following examples illustrate some common types of disruptions of the client's selfobject transference and how the worker managed them.

A LACK OF SUFFICIENT MIRRORING

In the D'Agostino case described previously, once a selfobject transference that combined twinship and mirroring elements was established, seemingly minor failures on the worker's part to share Mr. D'Agostino's exact feelings or to provide him with the positive responses he sought led him to become morose and withdrawn.

THE D'AGOSTINO CASE REVISITED Mr. D'Agostino, a gay Sicilian-American client, who presented with work problems, a negative self-concept, and depression, lacked mirroring and encouragement from his parents and teachers, idealizable and positive role models whom he could look up to, and those with whom he shared a sense of likeness. It was difficult for him to feel good about his own talents and capacities and to pursue his ambitions. When he developed a selfobject transference in treatment, he brought articles about Italian culture to the sessions, and worker and client exchanged views of movies and plays. Later, they discussed all of the minute details of the client's employment search. In addition to exploring the origins of his negative self-concept in his early life experiences, the worker tried to be validating and mirroring of Mr. D'Agostino's talents and capacities and encouraging of his creativity and literary interests. Although he began to be more positive about himself and his future, he became depressed and hopeless when he did not feel that the worker was completely in tune with him.

Mr. D'Agostino: I've had a lousy week. I really crashed. I haven't been motivated to do anything and I've been irritable and angry at everyone. I just don't see any light at the end of the tunnel.

Worker: Did something happen to upset you?

Mr. D'Agostino: Nothing, really. It's just who I am.

Worker: I wonder if you feel let down by me in some way?

Mr. D'Agostino: Sometimes I don't know what the point is in my coming to see you.

Worker: It does sound like I've disappointed you.

Mr. D'Agostino: What are you supposed to do? You can't make me become a great writer. You probably think I am fooling myself by thinking I have any talent.

Worker: What makes you think so?

Mr. D'Agostino: You really weren't very enthusiastic about the article that I want to write.

Worker: What gave you that feeling?

Mr. D'Agostino: It wasn't what you said. It was your tone of voice. You didn't seem very excited. I thought you were just going along with me because you thought that was what you were supposed to do.

Worker: If you feel that way, I can understand your questioning why you are coming here. But why be down on yourself?

Mr. D'Agostino: I value your opinion. I want you to believe that I have talent.

Worker: I do believe that, but I guess I didn't communicate that very well last week.

Mr. D'Agostino: No, you didn't.

Worker: It didn't have to do to with my not liking your idea. I was a little distracted. I'm sorry. It's important to you that I show you what I am feeling and that I am really here for you. Otherwise you lose faith in yourself. That's an understandable need and reaction, given the little interest and encouragement you have received from others in your life.

Mr. D'Agostino: I don't really want to stop coming.

Discussion

Although the worker thought she had been encouraging of the client, she recognized that she had momentarily been distracted in the previous session by an oncoming cold and may have been less present than usual. Mr. D'Agostino's response was to feel bad about himself and about the worker. Instead of pointing out his need for perfect attunement and his hypersensitivity, the worker was non-defensive about her lackluster comment and empathized with the client's feelings. She also linked his need for a strong show of support to the lack of responsiveness of others in his life.

A LACK OF EMPATHY

In the following case, the client, who looked to the worker for validation and mirroring, became enraged at the worker when she questioned the client's intentions and tried to help the client exert some restraint on her angry impulses on her job.

THE DESMOND CASE Ms. Desmond, a 28-year-old African-American laboratory technician, sought help for her depression following the breakup of a relationship in which she became pregnant and underwent an abortion. The client's self-concept was of a highly responsible, competent, loyal, and hardworking person, and she had difficulty acknowledging her often impulsive and provocative behavior. The client had a history of ill-fated relationships with men, whom she idealized until they mistreated her. She also moved from job to job because she did not feel sufficiently appreciated. Among her problems, which the client did not recognize as such, were her attitude of entitlement, need for special treatment, and bursts of temper when challenged in any way. After Ms. Desmond recovered from her acute depression, she and the worker focused on helping her in her relationships and work life. The client felt supported by the worker as long as the worker empathically related to her concerns and provided validation and mirroring.

On one occasion, Ms. Desmond arrived at a session after having recently started a new job. She complained bitterly about the orientation she had received from her supervisor.

Ms. Desmond: I can't believe that she felt it was necessary to go over all the rules and procedures. Doesn't she realize that I've worked in a lab before and know my way around? It was so stupid and insulting. I'm the best technician in the place. I just know it's not going to work. I'm tempted to march right into her office tomorrow and have a talk with her.

Worker: What would you say?

Ms. Desmond: I want to let her know that I did not appreciate her lecture because it made me feel like a child.

Worker: What do you feel that would accomplish?

Ms. Desmond: I want her to know that I'm not like all the others. I work hard and do a great job and I don't have to be monitored. I've been taken advantage of too many times. Don't you understand?

Worker: I can see that you feel strongly about what happened but I am having trouble understanding your feeling that your supervisor should have known all about you and did not need to orient you and I'm concerned about your actually confronting her.

Ms. Desmond: I am not going to actually do it. I just said that I was tempted to do it. You don't appreciate who I am either. I'm not stupid enough to tell her off, although I want to.

Worker: Let's go back. I understand that it is hard for you to have to start over, and understandably you want your new employer to appreciate your experience, skills, and good qualities, but wasn't she just doing her job rather than deliberately trying to put you down?

Ms. Desmond: I know that. I don't know why you are so dense. I just feel like leaving. You are not helping me.

Worker: I must be doing something wrong because you are getting angrier and angrier at me and are not feeling that I'm on your side.

Ms. Desmond: It's not that I feel you are not on my side. You aren't on my side. All you are interested in is getting me to see that I'm overreacting.

Worker: You are right that I was concerned about your reaction and to your acting-out your anger and losing your job. Perhaps my concern kept me from responding to how frustrated you were at having to start over again.

Ms. Desmond: I don't know if I can trust you.

Worker: I guess you feel that if I make a mistake, I can't be counted on.

Ms. Desmond: I haven't ever been able to count on anyone for very long.

Worker: That's the truth. Do you feel you can't give me another chance?

Ms. Desmond: You have been pretty good so far.

Discussion _____

In this example, the worker became anxious as a result of what she perceived as the client's extreme reaction and apparent threat that she was going to confront her supervisor. Thinking that the client was going to act on her impulses and sabotage her new job, the worker's comments were aimed at helping her to become more realistic and to exercise restraint rather than on expressing empathy for the feelings that were underlying her strong reaction. When the client reacted angrily, accused the worker of not helping her, and was on the verge of leaving the session, the worker regrouped and tried to repair the disruption in the client-worker relationship instead of pressing her point or confronting the client with her tendency to turn on those who failed to show her the appreciation and treatment that she felt she deserved.

AN UNATTUNED RESPONSE

The following case example shows how a disruption occurred when the worker made an insensitive comment that was based partly on her cultural countertransference to an African-American client.

THE THOMAS CASE Ms. Thomas, a 55-year-old moderately light-skinned and attractive African-American woman who worked as a schoolteacher in a private high school in New Jersey, sought help because of work stress. She was contemplating leaving her position in a school in which she had been employed for many years, but she was fearful of doing so. She had become upset when there was an influx of African-American students, most of whom did not seem to be motivated to learn and get ahead. She and her coworkers found the students to be difficult and did not enjoy having them in class. The other teachers in the school, who were mostly white, looked to her for help because she was African American. Ms. Thomas found herself angry at everyone—at her coworkers for associating her with the students on the one hand and for being critical of them on the other, at the African-American students for not caring about their education, and at herself for feeling so angry and out of control.

Ms. Thomas lived alone and had never married. She was raised by her adoptive parents, who were financially comfortable and lived in a white neighborhood in which there were few other African-American families. Her adoptive father was a respected doctor and her adoptive mother, to whom she was very close, was a teacher. She felt accepted by her white classmates but was a shy girl who often kept to herself. All through her life, Ms. Thomas gravitated to those who were white and felt uncomfortable with members of her own race, from whom she felt different in terms of her upbringing, education, and interests. She had mixed feelings about being African American. She was proud of her parents and extended family, most of whom had elevated themselves from poverty and had become professionals, but she held negative attitudes toward members of her race who were poor, uneducated, and sometimes antisocial and who did not "raise themselves up."

Unaccustomed to discussing her feelings with anyone, Ms. Thomas gradually opened up to the worker, who was white, and used her as a sounding board and as someone she looked up to to help guide her. Ms. Thomas spoke about her current school situation, background, particularly with respect to her feelings about herself and who she was, and her lifelong loneliness, which intensified after her mother's death five years earlier. Attracted to women, Ms. Thomas could not quite use the term "lesbian" to describe herself but did report having had some brief relationships. She spoke of her interest in meeting someone who would be a good companion. The worker asked Ms. Thomas if she had opportunities to meet other women who were lesbians. Ms. Thomas replied that she had attended a women's discussion group and liked some of the members but they did not seem interested in her. She had felt that she stood out in the all-white group in a way that was unfamiliar to her and wondered if her being African American was keeping other women from pursuing her. When the worker asked if she knew how to meet African-American women, the client said no and then became silent.

Worker: Something seems to be bothering you.

Ms. Thomas: It's nothing.

Worker: You can tell me.

Ms. Thomas: I think our time is up. Can I leave?

Worker: I seem to have really upset you. We can take a little more time.

Ms. Thomas: It was what you asked me. I don't know why it's bothering me so much, but it is. I feel terrible. All you did was to ask me if I knew how to meet other African-American women. Why did you ask me that?

Worker: You were talking about wondering if the other white women in the discussion group might not be interested in you because you are African American, so it seemed a natural question.

Ms. Thomas: So you think that the women in the group are avoiding me because I'm black and that I would be better off associating with other African Americans? Thanks a lot. It's been nice knowing you.

Worker: Please don't leave now. I can see that my question really hurt you. I guess it felt like I was taking their side against you and suggesting that you belong with your own. I guess I did what your coworkers do when they ask you for help with the African-American students and you feel demeaned and angry.

Ms. Thomas: Yes! I don't know how you could ask me such a stupid and insensitive question after all we have talked about. You don't understand me as well as I thought. What's worse is that when you look at me, all you see is that I'm black.

Worker: Part of what I see is an African-American woman, but that makes you feel that I'm making a negative judgment about you.

Ms. Thomas: Aren't you?

Worker: No, I'm not, but I think you are right that my question was insensitive. I should have just asked you what it was like for you to feel that your race was an obstacle in the group.

Ms. Thomas: Why didn't you? That would have been better.

Worker: At the time, I was feeling upset for you if what you were wondering was true, and I guess I wanted you not to be hurt. Maybe my question did reflect some feeling that you wouldn't expose yourself to as much potential rejection if you sought out other African Americans because many white people still are racist or have hangups about getting close to blacks. Even that feeling tells me that it's hard for me to overcome being a product of my own background, but I was not trying to put you down or to suggest that you are not good enough to attract a white woman.

Ms. Thomas: You are honest. That's good.

Discussion

When the client first reacted to her question by becoming silent, the worker did not immediately realize her insensitivity. When she did recognize that her question was both unattuned to the client—particularly in the light of what she did know about the client's self-concept—to her credit, the self-scrutinizing and non-defensive worker took responsibility for her comment. She acknowledged the possibility that it was based not only on her wish to be helpful to the client but also on an automatic assumption that an African American would be less prone to rejection were she to seek out a member of her own race for a romantic relationship. The worker's empathy, genuineness, and openness helped to repair the disruption in the client-worker relationship that occurred.

AN UNRESOLVED POWER STRUGGLE

The final example describes a case that has been discussed elsewhere (Goldstein, 1994: 424–427) in which the worker's inability to respond to the client's selfobject need resulted in an irreparable disruption of the treatment.

THE SAUNDERS CASE Ms. Saunders was a successful 43-year-old businesswoman who sought help for her depression. From adolescence, she had felt attracted to other women but was too ashamed and fearful to wholeheartedly identify as a lesbian. She had some short-lived romantic relationships in which she felt alive despite her sense of shame. After being encouraged by previous therapists to seek out relationships with men, she did so but did not feel emotionally connected to them.

The client described her parents as self-involved, cold, non-communicative about their feelings, secretive, and greatly concerned with appearances. She had two much older brothers and was quite isolated as a child. She longed for a sister whom she fantasized would be her friend. Her early life was devoid of close attachments with the exception of a youthful aunt who died when the client was 5. Ms. Saunders was told that she refused to eat for a time after the aunt's death. While a conscientious and good student, she remembers feeling different from her peers and seeking out the attention of older girls and teachers from whom she was able to get some affirmation. Her friendships were intense and she was sensitive to rejection.

In treatment, Ms. Saunders formed a twinship transference, which seemed to be reinforced by her perception of the worker as similar in age, general appearance, and sense of humor. A lesbian herself, the worker thought that the client's feelings of alienation and depression were rooted in never having had crucial aspects of her self experience validated, and that her sense of shame and difference were reinforced by her feelings of stigma around her sexuality. When the client began to verbalize wishes that the worker be a lesbian so that she could understand her better, the worker attempted to explore what this meant to the client. Although this led to their further exploring the client's long-standing feelings of being different and bad, it also heightened her feelings of aloneness, shame, and hopelessness. She repeatedly asked the worker to tell her whether the worker was a lesbian, stating that it would make her feel less alone to know that someone she respected and liked could be like her but that she could handle it if the worker turned out not to be gay.

The worker's supervisor at the psychotherapy institute clinic believed that Ms. Saunders's sexual orientation was still an open question and advised the worker not to answer the client's question. She felt that the worker's self-disclosure would inhibit the client's exploration of her sexual feelings and conflicts. The client could not accept the worker's refusal to answer her question and showed increasing frustration with the worker, accused her of not caring about her, and became more withdrawn and depressed. The worker felt quite dishonest and rejecting in the process and asked herself whether she had a need to share her sexual orientation with the client, as her supervisor had suggested. The treatment seemed stalemated. When the client missed her last appointment, the worker told her supervisor that she was very concerned that she was imposing an intolerable frustration on the client and wanted support for being experimental. The supervisor reluctantly agreed that the worker could self-disclose if she felt she had no other choice in order to keep the client in treatment but indicated that she felt that this would be a countertransference acting-out.

When the worker consulted with a former supervisor who was not connected to the institute, she asked for her opinion about what she should do. Then she laughed and said, "I guess my client and I are both looking for validation. But you know, I really don't need you to tell me that I'm right, but my client does need to have her question answered. She needs to stop hiding and to feel good about herself, yet I am being withholding and anonymous." Unfortunately, before their next session, the client canceled her appointment and left a message that she was terminating treatment. Despite the worker's calls, she angrily refused to come in one final time to discuss the matter.

Discussion

In this instance, the worker's failure to disclose whether or not she was a lesbian constituted a traumatic disruption of the selfobject transference. Ms. Saunders was expressing a need for someone who would validate her existence and aliveness. The human responsiveness reflected in the worker's self-disclosure rather than its exact content per se might well have been affirming to this client. She had experienced persistent lack of attunement on the part of her early caretakers with the exception of her aunt, who died when Ms. Saunders was a child. The trauma of her aunt's death contributed to her feelings of aloneness and vulnerability. Her shame over feeling different and about her longings for women contributed to her alienation from her own feelings and from others and to her lack of self-cohesion. Her years of therapy seemed to reinforce rather than repair her damaged self and fostered the suppression of her sexual orientation. The client's yearnings for a positive relationship were revived in the transference and provided her with another chance to make meaningful human contact and to complete her development. The worker's refusal to self-disclose dashed the client's hopes for a better solution, made her feel more hopeless, and led to an irreparable disruption in the treatment.

ADDRESSING PROJECTIVE IDENTIFICATION AND ENACTMENTS

A fundamentally different way of looking at what emerges in the client-worker relationship focuses on clients' use of projective identification and their tendency to recreate their internalized pathological object relations and relational patterns in treatment. Enactments are inevitable and can be beneficial if the worker is able to recognize what is occurring and help the client to understand the client-worker interaction and its significance. This approach requires that the worker consider the degree to which his or her countertransference reflects understandable responses to clients' objective personality traits, uncomfortable feelings that they are putting into the worker in order to get rid of them, or efforts to induce the worker to act in certain ways in relation to their behavior and to be like someone from their past.

Indicators that the client may be utilizing projective identification or enacting earlier relational configurations in the treatment appear in the worker's strong or repetitive reactions to the client, in the client's distorted views of the worker, and in the worker's sometimes unusual ways of responding to the client. For example, the worker may experience feelings of resentment, helplessness, inadequacy, or boredom; be perplexed by the client's accusations that the worker is angry and critical; act cautiously lest he or she say or do something to upset the client; refrain from implementing usual policies; or make special efforts to reach a client.

There are different ways of addressing the client's tendency toward the use of projective identification and enactment. The worker who is alert to the nature of his or her countertransference reactions, in the sense in which the term is being used here, may simply attempt to contain the turbulent nature of the client's inner life and distortions, withstand the client's attacks without counterattacking, and refrain from replicating pathological interactions. Often, the worker may try to help the client to examine, understand, and own his or her feelings, self- and object-representations, and relational patterns by drawing attention to and interpreting what is occurring in the client-worker interaction.

Although still a controversial subject, self-disclosure may be an important component of the worker's ability to use his or her countertransference to help clients understand their own inner life and what they are contributing to the client-worker interaction (Ehrenberg, 1995; Maroda, 1999; Renik, 1995). The worker may self-disclose what he or she thinks and feels about what is happening in the treatment or strong feelings that the worker has toward the client that may be stemming from the client's use of projective identification or attempts at enactment. In discussing her view of psychotherapy, Maroda (1999: 99) argues that the only way that the therapist has to complete the cycle of affective communication and to show the patient that he or she has gotten the message is to disclose the strong affects that the patient is inducing in the therapist. She also suggests that the therapist's truthfulness will help the patient to be more truthful and that when revealing strong countertransference feelings, one should distinguish between what the therapist feels and how the therapist behaves, since the goal is to provide new kinds of experiences for the patient. She further cautions therapists not to disclose strong feelings at times when they feel on the verge of being out of control and expresses caution about revealing erotic countertransference because of its being too stimulating and threatening generally.

A difficulty with the view that the client is causing the worker's countertransference is that the worker may be bringing his or her personal countertransference issues to the treatment. Likewise, enactments occur all the time on the part of both participants in therapeutic interactions, and it is difficult to know which member of the interaction started the enactment or when it began (Aron, 1996). Consequently, it is erroneous to view an enactment as stemming only from the worker's participation in what is being induced in him or her by the client. Maroda recognizes that a therapist's own personality and past can get together with the patient's need for pathological forms of enactment and that this is a serious therapeutic problem that also makes it difficult to know who is doing what to whom. The therapist may be at risk for participating in a repetition or enactment of both the patient's and therapist's earlier experiences without recognizing and understanding this (Maroda, 1999: 121–140).

Even if the client engages in projective identification, it is not always appropriate for the worker to share his or her induced feelings or to interpret the client's defense. There are times when containing such feelings temporarily may be necessary in order to help clients feel safe and to wait for them to come into contact with their feelings more gradually on their own. Alternatively, it may be useful for the worker to verbalize his or her uncertainty about how to understand what is happening between the client and worker and to invite the client to participate in the process of figuring this out. Because the client and worker are always influencing one another during the treatment, it may be beneficial for the worker to check with the client about what is occurring in the treatment on a regular basis rather than at times of special difficulty.

CASE EXAMPLES

The following case examples show how the workers addressed interactions between client and worker that could be considered to represent the clients' attempts to create enactments in the treatment.

THE WORKER'S MOUNTING FRUSTRATION
In the Morrison case, the worker began to wonder on whether her mounting frustration with the client's behavior both outside of sessions and in the treatment relationship reflected an enactment of a significant relational pattern.

THE MORRISON CASE Mr. Morrison was a 48-year-old man who was let go from a position that he had held for fifteen years, after several years of ruminating about quitting and finding another line of work. In view of his years with the company, which was downsizing, he was given six months' salary and health benefits. Initially relieved that the decision about leaving his job had been made for him and that he was now free to pursue another line of work, the client denied being angry at the firm.

Mr. Morrison had sought help earlier because of his dissatisfaction with his life. An underachiever, he had a job that he hated, was socially isolated, and fluctuated between feeling that he had some great but as yet hidden talent and that he was too damaged to be able to take on more responsibility and to succeed in or enjoy life. Born in the South, he was estranged from his parents and two younger siblings. He described his mother as physically abusive at times and as having very high expectations of him to which he felt he never could live up. He viewed his father as passive and unavailable. He did not feel close to his brother and sister, who shared his family's "middle class" values. He left home when he went to college.

Mr. Morrison anticipated rejection by others and was extremely anxious in interpersonal relationships. He had difficulty making and keeping friends and never felt that others liked him. He was quite judgmental of others and displayed a lack of sensitivity, flexibility, and willingness to compromise in relationships. He attended concerts and plays, mostly by himself, and he volunteered in church-related activities, in which he often experienced dissatisfaction. He searched for a niche in which he could be happy. His tedious and frustrating job was nevertheless a focal point of his existence. After incidents in which his managers and coworkers would distance from or become critical of him as a result of his having acted in grandiose and inappropriate ways in the office, he would consider quitting, but not having anywhere to go, he would remain. For example, he would take prolonged lunch hours, come in late repeatedly without calling or giving a good excuse, refuse to help out because he was too busy, and become irritated if others made even small mistakes. When confronted with his behavior, Mr. Morrison would become depressed and feel worthless and humiliated.

After losing his job, Mr. Morrison put off seeking employment, withdrew from the few social relationships and volunteer work in which he engaged, and spent most of his time operating his computer. He seemed to relish his "paid vacation" and attended sessions regularly and sought the worker's support for his taking some time off from work and his plans to change careers. As his money began to run out, however, he complained of depression and anxiety, and his symptoms became severe enough that he consulted with a psychiatrist and was put on antidepressants. When pressed to talk about what he was feeling, he acknowledged a sense of loss but said that he mainly dreaded the idea of having to start over. He was convinced that any job he might find would be boring and unbearable, and he hated the fact that he had to work at all.

Although the worker was empathic with his plight, Mr. Morrison seemed closed down and did not want to discuss his situation, even when he seemed less acutely depressed. He missed sessions and arranged to have telephone appointments at the last minute rather than making the trip to the city. When he did appear, he was non-communicative or filled the sessions with what felt like endless accounts of the minutiae of his various computer projects. If the worker suggested that Mr. Morrison was trying to avoid discussing his situation, he would complain about having to look for a job and about the tasks of everyday life that interfered with his pleasure. He was often testy with the worker if she did anything other than show an interest in how he was occupying his time and became annoyed with her no matter what she did or said. He dismissed her attempts to help him discuss his anger and sense of betrayal about having been fired and his anxiety about having to begin again, saying, "It doesn't help to talk about it"; he was impatient with the worker's efforts to empathize with his feelings of being overwhelmed and wanting to escape; he found numerous reasons why he did not want to see people and could not look for a job when the worker encouraged him to reach out to others and identify what he might like to do in the future; he was noncommittal when she tried to elicit his anger at the worker for not having saved him from being fired, for not being able to provide him with an enjoyable job or an income, or for having any expectations of him; and he shrugged off the worker's attempts to engage the client in reflecting on what was going on between them and to tell her how she could be of best help to him.

Mr. Morrison seemed to be engaged in a "sit-down strike," which she attributed to his anger, a narcissistic withdrawal, which she thought related to his having been fired, and escapism, which she believed was connected to his feeling overwhelmed. The worker became increasingly frustrated by the client's reactions to her interventions. Feeling inadequate and devalued, she found herself wanting to ask the client why he was still coming to see her at all. On one occasion, she found herself wishing he would leave treatment and even considered "firing" him. This reaction, as well as her feeling that she was more concerned about his plight than he was, led her to reflect on what was being enacted between them.

The worker thought that it was possible that several dynamics were operating in the client-worker relationship. It seemed likely that Mr. Morrison, instead of being in touch with his overwhelming feelings of rage, humiliation, inadequacy, and rejection about having been fired and his fear that he would not find another job had managed to induce a disturbing set of feelings in the worker, so that it was she who was experiencing them while the client was escaping into his computer. The worker also wondered if the client was trying to provoke her criticism and rejection of him, which would confirm his feelings of worthlessness and shame and would constitute a repetition of earlier experiences in his life, particularly with his family, personal relationships, and coworkers and employers.

The worker's speculations about the presence of these dynamics enabled her to be more relaxed in her interventions and more engaged rather than frustrated with the client. At what seemed an opportune moment, she raised with him what might be occurring between them in a nonjudgmental way. She did not self-disclose the nature of her own feelings but used them to frame her interpretations. For example, the worker said, "I'm wondering if in some ways you are expecting me to criticize and reject you the way you have been rejected so many times before in your life and may even be acting in ways that risk provoking those responses." Likewise, she commented, "Have you noticed that I've been more involved in trying to help you focus on your work issues than you have been? Could it be that your distress and feelings of desperation are so overwhelming to you that you have found a way of getting rid of them by transferring them to me? Although the client initially seemed to push aside the worker's interpretations, when she persisted in trying to help him consider what might be occurring and what the nature of his true feelings were and how they were linked to his past life experiences, the client began to speak of the fear he had that the worker was going to turn on him and blame him for losing his job and for not performing as he should, particularly because he felt guilty for having contributed to his having been let go by acting-out at work. He was able to connect his fear to his lifelong feeling that he was a failure, which began when his mother would do his homework over and over until it was perfect and would hit him if he grew restless. Mr. Morrison began to feel more of the pain, anger, and despair that he had been warding off and to allow the worker to help him to grapple with how to pick up the pieces of his life. Much later they were able to examine his self-sabotaging behavior in other situations in the light of his pattern of trying to provoke rejection before it happened to him.

Discussion

In this example, the worker did not initially focus on what was being enacted in the treatment. When her countertransference reactions seemed to be intense and unusual, she recognized that she had to better understand what was occurring in the client-worker relationship. In some ways, she was feeling like the client on the one hand and acting like his mother, whom he feared and from whom he needed protection, on the other. Based on what she was feeling in response to the client and on her knowledge of the client's background and major dynamics, she speculated about what was being enacted in their relationship. Her becoming more focused on understanding and exploring the enactment with the client allowed her to overcome her frustration with him and resulted in their being able to jointly explore the nature of the enactment and its origins and to overcome the impasse in the treatment and in the client's current life situation.

One could ask whether the worker was contributing to the enactment not only through experiencing the client's warded-off feelings and beginning to play the role that he expected her to assume but also through what she, herself, was bringing to the situation. What started this enactment? Was the worker actually feeling critical and blaming in her internal attitude toward Mr. Morrison for being fired and was it hard for her to sit back and let him escape into his computer if he wanted to without feeling that she had to mobilize him? Could she have communicated a judgmental attitude and strong work ethic that triggered the client's response? If this were true, then would it have been more appropriate for the worker to have viewed what was occurring in the treatment as a disruption in the client-worker relationship that she unwittingly helped to create and to have attempted to repair it through exploring and acknowledging her empathic failure? In this case, the worker felt she had not started the enactment but had become caught up in it, but it is difficult to know whether she was correct.

THE WORKER FEELS RESENTFUL

In the final example, the worker began to recognize that her increasing feelings of resentment toward the client were part of a pattern that the client exhibited in many of his relationships.

THE STANLEY CASE Mr. Stanley, a tall, stern-looking but mild-mannered 50-year-old small-business owner, sought help because of his difficulties maintaining satisfactory relationships with women. Divorced for five years, he wanted to remarry. He had dated a lot but felt he often was attracted to the "wrong" type of woman. He had engaged in relationships with women who were considerably younger than he, only to realize that they expected him to take care of them emotionally and financially. He said that he wanted a more self-sufficient partner who did not expect him to be the sole breadwinner and caretaker in the relationship. Mr. Stanley described his ex-wife as strong, controlling, and critical. He was vague about the reasons that she had initiated their divorce but considered himself fortunate to be out of the marriage. He had recently satisfied his financial obligations under the settlement, which he resented bitterly even though he knew that "I got off cheap because my ex-wife had an inheritance from her parents and wanted to marry a man she was seeing." He had one daughter who was 20 and attending a state university with the help of loans. Mr. Stanley was currently seeing a woman, Jane, who was his age and who was different from other women he had dated. He thought she might be the right partner for him. Also divorced, she had custody of an adolescent daughter. Like his ex-wife, she seemed to be strong and independent. She earned a solid income, and they shared many interests.

When Mr. Stanley began treatment, he appealed to the worker to understand his financial concerns. He explained that he was having a cash flow problem and asked the worker if he could pay her fifty percent of her fee at the end of each month and the rest when he received his insurance reimbursement, which paid for the balance. The worker asked the client if it wouldn't be better to have the insurance company send the worker the money directly, but he said that he wanted to stay on top of the situation as he had when he filed medical claims. The worker agreed to this seemingly reasonable request, but it turned out that she had to wait a considerable time for the insurance portion of the fee. It took one month after the client filed for him to receive the money and then it took him another few weeks to pay her. Additionally, two checks that Mr. Stanley gave her for the non-insurance portion of the fee were returned due to insufficient funds even though he seemed to have enough money support a fairly good lifestyle. When this occurred, Mr. Stanley explained in a matter-of-fact manner that he had failed to make a deposit and wrote out replacement checks. Although the worker had some reservations about the arrangement she had agreed to, she did not feel comfortable renegotiating it because of the client's sensitivity about being taken advantage of financially. She pushed aside some feelings of resentment that he was taking advantage of her.

In sessions, Mr. Stanley spoke about himself, his current and past relationships with women, and his background. After his divorce, he was attracted to women who touched him emotionally because of their neediness and fragility and who looked up to him for his seeming strength and competence. Soon he would become resentful that they were not there for him and that they expected him to be their financial and emotional caretaker. He would become disdainful of them and felt justified in breaking off the relationships. He did not see himself as contributing to the problems in the relationships.

Prior to meeting Jane, his new romantic interest, he had a disastrous relationship. His description of this affair disturbed the worker for what it seemed to reveal about Mr. Stanley. He had become involved with a woman who was twenty years his junior and who had a 10-year-old son. She had been sexually abused repeatedly by her stepfather until she was 16 and ran away from home. Her ex-husband was physically abusive to both her and her son. Initially, Mr. Stanley felt protective toward her and befriended her son, who became very attached to him. After several months, the client accused her of being infantile and demanding and not mature enough to be in a relationship with him. When he attempted to end the affair, she took an overdose of sleeping pills and had to be hospitalized briefly. She couldn't accept the breakup and he eventually changed his telephone number so that she could not reach him.

It became clear to the worker that the client saw himself in two main ways, as a benevolent protector of women and as a victim of women's greed and emotional demands. Feeling justified in "dumping" the women he dated when they became too demanding, he did not see himself as exploitative, controlling, needy, and callous. Although he had come for help in sustaining a good relationship, he blamed his problems on poor choices and lacked awareness of and rigidly defended against coming into contact with the true nature of his difficulties.

In one session, after several months of treatment, Mr. Stanley appeared upset and angrily described an argument he had had with Jane. He explained that he had borrowed a thousand dollars from her two weeks earlier to help him until the end of the month. She had given him the money willingly, so that he was shocked when she asked for the money back. He was upset that she was so impatient and didn't trust him to return the money to her when he could. They had a terrible verbal fight. "I've never seen her like that. She was an entirely different person." When the worker asked the client if Jane had asked for the money "out of the blue," he replied that they had been discussing his just having purchased some expensive new stereo equipment that he had wanted for a long time. "All of a sudden, she erupted and started asking me to return her money and accused me of being selfish and childish and of expecting her to put her needs aside so that I could have what I want. I thought she would be happy for me."

This incident occurred shortly after a check that the client had given the worker was returned. In listening to Mr. Stanley's account of his interaction with Jane, she understood why he reacted as he did but was aware that she felt more sympathetic to Jane than to her client. It also occurred to her that she was participating in a financial interaction with the client that resembled what had occurred in his relationship with Jane except that the worker had not yet acted on her growing resentment and confronted the client. She did not know what to do. She thought that if she commented on the similarity between the two situations in which the client expected the more emotionally strong and financially independent women in his life to sacrifice for and take care of him, the client would become angry, defensive, and accusatory. Alternatively, if she did not say anything, she would be allowing the enactment between the two of them to continue unexamined and would lose an opportunity for helping the client to own some of his contradictory and split-off behavior. She decided to share her dilemma and her under-standing of what was occurring, her realization of which helped her overcome her own feelings of resentment.

Worker: I am having some difficulty knowing how to respond to what you are telling me.

Mr. Stanley: What's the problem?

Worker: I know that you want me to agree that your anger at Jane was justifiable and to join you in seeing her as greedy and demanding like the other women in your life, but I feel it is important for you to consider what Jane might have been reacting to in you. But I'm concerned that my asking you to take a look at what you might have triggered in her will make you feel that I am on her side.

Mr. Stanley: How do you think I was contributing to her reaction?

Worker: I can imagine that Jane may have felt that you were taking advantage of her and not considering her needs when you chose to spend money on stereo equipment rather than pay her back immediately.

Mr. Stanley: She doesn't need the money.

Worker: Perhaps she doesn't, but you did agree to pay her back in a timely fashion. I wonder if you see any similarity between what happened with you and Jane and what happens between us with respect to our fee arrangement?

Mr. Stanley: I never thought about it, but you seem to think there is a connection.

Worker: It may be hard for you to hear this, but I have had some similar feelings as Jane did related to our financial arrangement.

Mr. Stanley: Why?

Worker: I agreed because I wanted to help you out and thought your request was reasonable even though it meant inconveniencing myself to a degree. Perhaps I should have not gone along, but I was okay with it until I began to feel that you were not keeping your end of the bargain when you were not prompt in your payment of the money and when your checks were returned. It made me feel that you were not considering me.

Mr. Stanley: I did not force you to go along with me. I did not make Jane lend me the money.

Worker: That's true, but perhaps you are not aware of your expectation that if a strong woman cares about you she will help you out and put her own needs aside and of your anger if she makes any demands on you.

Mr. Stanley: My ex-wife always accused me of that but my other relationships have been different. The women expected me to take care of them.

Worker: You do seem to have two different patterns. In one you are attracted to fragile women who look to you as their caretaker but you turn on them when they seem too needy or expect too much of you, and in another you are drawn to independent and strong women whom you want to take care of you and you cast them aside if they don't live up to your expectations.

Mr. Stanley: I don't know what the point of all this is.

Worker: I think it is hard for you to acknowledge and accept the different parts of yourself that are in conflict and this affects your relationships with women. Perhaps it's time for you to consider what creates problems for you in those relationships in a different way than you have previously.

Mr. Stanley: The problem is that I've never found a woman I could trust would be there for me.

Worker: We have to understand more about that. Your feelings go back a long time. I know you think that women just can't be trusted, but when we have had bad experiences with others in our lives, we sometimes recreate them over and over.

Mr. Stanley: I am tired of coming up empty.

Worker: I guess it's hard to trust me too.

Mr. Stanley: I think you are trying to help me. Maybe there is something I am doing wrong.

Discussion

The client's report of his argument with Jane enabled the worker to recognize what was being enacted in the client-worker relationship. She decided to use this understanding to help the client begin to focus on how he was contributing to his relationship problems. In order to do this, the worker chose to self-disclose both the dilemma she was experiencing in knowing what to say to the client and the feelings their financial arrangement were stirring up in her. The fact that the client did not completely view the worker as the enemy when she commented on the enactment was a good sign that he could begin to look at his role in creating unsatisfying relationships.

It is possible that the worker's lack of empathy for the client was based on her identification with Jane and that they both were too eager to please and were self-sacrificing women who gave too much and then resented it, allowing themselves to be victimized instead of just trying to be helpful and having a reasonable expectation of reciprocity. Even if this were true, however, it would still be appropriate to look at what occurred in the treatment as an enactment in which both participants played a role.

UNDERSTANDING SIMILARITIES AND DIFFERENCES BETWEEN CLIENT AND WORKER

Yet another way of thinking about what occurs in the client-worker relationship centers on the fact that workers and clients bring both similar and different organizing principles to treatment. Similarities can lead to understanding or to collusions because both worker and client may share the same but not necessarily helpful stance. Alternatively, differences can generate misunderstandings and misinterpretations (Stolorow & Atwood, 1992). In either case, the worker needs to explore the nature of the organizing principles of each participant in the treatment. This may require that the worker be self-disclosing at times, particularly in overcoming impasses and obstacles that arise.

In contrast to emphasizing the worker's role in empathizing with clients and bridging the differences that may exist between worker and client, there are those who underscore the importance of the worker's attempts at helping the client to recognize the worker's separateness (Hoffman, 1983; Aron, 1992). Drawing on the developmental view that children observe and study the parental personalities, need to make contact with the parents' inner world, and must come to recognize the parent as a separate other, Aron proposes that patients should be encouraged to think and share their ideas about who the therapist is. He suggests further, that in order not to be tantalizing, therapists should disclose at times in order to refute or confirm the patient's views and perceptions. He links this behavior in treatment to how parents feel and handle the child's attempts to get to know who they are and to penetrate their inner worlds. Aron recognizes, however, that this approach can be intrusive and divert the patient from his or her own concerns in favor of a focus on the therapist.

RECOGNIZING OTHER FORMS OF OBJECT RELATING

Not all forms of relating in the treatment situation stem from the client's selfobject needs on the one hand or from the recreation of pathological relational patterns on the other (Shane, Shane & Gales, 1997). The client may also express needs for new types of interaction that must be recognized and responded to by the worker. For example, some clients may never have experienced a satisfying form of relational intimacy, and their ability to participate in and sustain closeness with the worker may represent an important step forward that will also carry over into their relationships with others outside of the treatment.

SUMMARY

This chapter has discussed and illustrated two important but very different ways of understanding and addressing issues that arise in the worker-client relationship during the course of treatment. Repairing disruptions in the selfobject transference relies on the worker's empathic understanding of how he or she has often wittingly contributed to disturbances in the client-worker relationship through unattuned comments, mistakes, and failures to live up to the client's expectations. This process leads to a restoration of the selfobject transference, to an exploration of the origins of clients' archaic selfobject needs, and to an eventual strengthening of the client's self-structure. It requires that workers be self-scrutinizing with respect to how their personal countertransference reactions may be interfering with their ability to be optimally attuned to the client. In contrast, addressing enactments requires that the worker recognize those aspects of his or her objective countertransference that are being induced by the client and to use these to help clients to understand how their pathological internalized object relations or relational patterns are being re-created in the treatment.

This process leads to the exploration of the origins and manifestations of clients' images of themselves and others and problems in relating and to their owning more of their own feelings and behavior.

9

TREATMENT OF CLIENTS UNDERGOING STRESSFUL LIFE EVENTS

Stressful life events are disruptive not only because of the realistic challenges they present but because of the personal meaning that they have for the individuals undergoing them. Even seemingly minor occurrences can result in temporary periods of disequilibrium and distress when they trigger long-standing narcissistic vulnerability, undermine self-esteem, the self-concept, and compensatory self-structures, and stimulate deep-seated feelings of guilt and badness. This chapter will discuss and illustrate how object relations and self psychological thinking shed light on the meaning that some common types of occurrences, such as the death of significant others, illness and disability, and midlife issues, have for the individuals undergoing them and how they shape the treatment process.

DEATH OF SIGNIFICANT OTHERS

The death of a loved one is one of the most painful experiences in human life, whether or not an individual is prepared for such an event, and despite the age of the deceased (Nolen-Hoeksema & Larson, 1999). The tasks of accepting the reality of the death of a significant person, experiencing the feelings connected to the loss, becoming accustomed to living in a world without the loved one, and learning to go on with one's life are always difficult, but underlying narcissistic vulnerability and object relations pathology may complicate the grief process.

From a self psychological perspective, death may rob people of those who have served important selfobject functions and produce a loss of self-esteem and self-cohesion, prolonged depressive reactions, or states of depletion. The bereaved individual, who has been dependent on the selfobject functions that the deceased has provided, may experience a loss of self. "These losses are felt as critical injuries to the self, evoking intense pain. The pain leads to fears of fragmentation and to overpowering anxiety. The absent function results in a state of depletion in which the self experiences helplessness and hopelessness. In addition, the self experiences a sense of deficiency and defectiveness of the capacity to cope with reality" (Palombo, 1985: 38). In turning to others, who often do not share their pain, grieving individuals who feel depleted may feel ashamed of their being needy, impatient with themselves, and angry at those who are able to enjoy life.

From an object relations perspective, the loss of significant others can stimulate a persecutory superego that punishes the bereaved person for not living up to its perfectionist demands. The person may experience a loss of self-esteem, feel guilty, and inflict self-punishment. Sometimes guilt is related to the fantasied harm arising from aggressive impulses the bereaved individual felt toward the loved one, anger at the deceased for dying, and guilt about having survived.

ILLNESS AND DISABILITY

Illness or disability are physically and psychologically assaultive experiences that, like the death of significant others, involve losses, produce narcissistic injuries, and stimulate feelings of self-blame and guilt. Individuals who face illness or disability may experience the loss of health, bodily intactness, strength, youth, vitality, time, feelings of invulnerability, physical attractiveness, mental and sexual functioning, senses, and other characteristics, activities, and roles that have been mainstays of their self-concept and self-esteem. Even minor conditions may feel traumatic. Sometimes, people feel that they are being punished for past misdeeds, angry feelings, acts of independence, or for not having lived up to the unrealistic demands of their grandiose self. These onslaughts may be greater when there is a stigma attached to the condition, as is the case with HIV or cancer. The personal meaning of illness and disability plays a major role in how afflicted individuals respond to and cope with their physical challenges.

MIDLIFE ISSUES

It has been said that the most fundamental developmental tasks of adult life involve the maintenance of self-esteem and identity in the face of the biological, psychological, and social stresses and losses that occur as we grow older (Lazarus, 1991: 135). Midlife spans many years and contains events that create changes in and losses of selfobjects and meaningful roles, create or lessen opportunities for attaining desired goals, diminish feelings of attractiveness and physical well-being, and challenge values, ambitions, ideals, and life structures.

In the middle years, the self-concept often must undergo a shift. For narcissistic individuals, the bubble of perfection, self-sufficiency, and control of others and life may seem to erode or suddenly burst (Modell, 1975: 275–282). Children and partners display unacceptable characteristics or behavior or show emotional problems that make them appear flawed. Aging parents fail to change their attitudes, make new demands, and die without ever having been good selfobjects or allowing reparation or rapprochement to occur. The need for new and greater achievements brings overwork and exhaustion to some individuals, who feel empty, depressed, and anxious, yearn for what they are missing in themselves or in their relationships, and engage in frantic activity, extramarital relationships, substance abuse, or the like in a frantic effort to maintain their equilibrium. It may be necessary to shed certain illusions about the self and life. Feelings of regret or pressure to make changes may arise as a person becomes acutely aware of the limitations of time, the awareness of paths that have not been traveled, and the lives that have not been led (Goldstein, 1995c).

The middle years may also reflect a time of life when people have attained long-sought goals and relationships, experience a greater sense of emotional well-being, security, and empowerment than was true earlier, and face new and greater possibilities for personal fulfillment and creative expression. These positive achievements can have negative consequences psychologically when a person has a profound sense of not deserving them, of being fraudulent, or of not being able to bring about the approval, recognition, or love that the person has sought from parents and others or to live up to their internalized expectations.

Thus, whether one sees the door opening or closing in midlife (Brooks-

Gunn & Kirsh, 1984: 11), the middle years are fraught for most people, but for those who have narcissistic vulnerability or underlying object relations pathology, midlife events can stimulate severe reactions.

TREATMENT EMPHASES

There are ten special emphases in applying self psychological and object relations concepts to the treatment of clients who experience the death of a loved one, illness or disability, and other problems that arise in midlife.

ASSESSING THE PERSONAL MEANING OF LIFE EVENTS

It is particularly important for the worker to explore the nature of the client's self-concept and what has helped him or her to maintain it, the client's main selfobject needs and the compensatory structures that the client has established, and the impact of the death of a significant other, illness or disability, or other midlife event on a client's self-structures. Likewise, the worker must be aware of the ways in which these types of occurrences stimulate guilt, a sense of inner badness, and feelings of fraudulence.

EMPATHIZING WITH LOSSES AND BLOWS TO THE SELF

It is necessary to empathize fully with the sense of loss, rage, despair, bitterness, envy, and other catastrophic reactions of clients to both major and minor life events. There may be tendencies to underestimate their impact, point out what seem to be extreme reactions or unrealistic expectations and attitudes, offer false reassurance, hope, or incorrect advice, or become overwhelmed by the client's despair. Yet correct empathy itself will enable clients to feel less alone and, perhaps paradoxically, in many instances to feel some sense of hope. Furthermore, it is only within the context of this type of empathy that clients can explore themselves more deeply.

EMPATHIZING WITH NARCISSISTIC RAGE AND SHAME

Narcissistic rage and shame over their failure to meet the demands of the grandiose self may be acute in many instances and must be a focal point of the treatment. Believing that they should be able to control life, prevent death and illness, and be strong and self-sufficient, individuals with severe narcissistic vulnerability do not allow for human limitations or life's vicissitudes. Problems that others might regard as part of the human condition are experienced as humiliating or signs of failure. Narcissistic rage may be turned against the self, resulting in depressive and suicidal reactions. There may be a reality basis for the self-blame that these clients show, because they may have contributed to their own problems.

UNDERSTANDING GUILT, A SENSE OF INNER BADNESS, AND FEELINGS OF FRAUDULENCE

Life events often trigger guilt and a need for self-punishment that does not seem to be warranted by the objective situation confronting the individual, such as a death or illness over which the person has no control. Because of their human limitations and failings, sometimes people do play a small or inadvertent role in bringing about certain difficult situations, but they relentlessly attack and cannot forgive themselves for their actions or inactions, such as in not being able to prevent a suicide or an automobile accident in which they were a passenger. Likewise, when life deals certain blows, this may confirm underlying feelings of warranting bad treatment. Moreover, positive events—such as getting an important promotion, earning an advanced educational degree, or purchasing a new house—can stimulate feelings of worthlessness or of not being deserving. It is important for the worker to be able to empathize with and explore the origins of such feelings in his or her past rather than talk the person out of them before attempting to enable the client to relinquish the hold that they have.

MOURNING THE LOSS OF SELFOBJECTS AND COMPENSATORY STRUCTURES

Clients need help in understanding how the losses of meaningful selfobjects, characteristics, or activities that have supported their sense of self and self-esteem are affecting them. This can enable them to gain some perspective on their profound feeling states. An important part of the long process of helping clients to deal with the impact of these losses is the worker's ability to provide needed selfobject functions that stabilize the person and help him or her to feel less alone and to regain a sense of self-worth. The worker's ability to be a good selfobject will also provide leverage in enabling the client to discover and develop new relationships and activities and to take pride in other characteristics that can bolster his or her self-esteem.

TEMPERING THE DEMANDS OF THE GRANDIOSE SELF

Narcissistic individuals have carried with them unrealistically grandiose, omnipotent, or perfectionist expectations of themselves and what they should accomplish in life that would be difficult for anyone to achieve. The demands of the grandiose self need to be tempered. In order to achieve this, it is first necessary to help clients recognize that their reactions are not only related to the present situation but to long-standing ways of viewing themselves, and that they are understandable. The worker then must explore the conditions of the client's early life that led the client to adopt such high expectations and a need for control over life. Finally, the worker gently begins to question the client's major assumptions about himself or herself and attempts to help clients to become more accepting and forgiving of their human limitations and faults.

MOURNING THE LOSS OF ILLUSIONS, AMBITIONS, AND DREAMS

As the worker attempts to explore and understand the magnitude of a client's current sense of loss and despair and its relationship to his or her self-concept and to the childhood conditions that shaped the client's personality, it will be necessary to help clients to give up some of their illusions and mourn their losses (Pollock, 1987). The mourning process for those individuals who have more narcissistic vulnerability is complex and intense. Trapped by their own unrealistic and waning dreams, it may be necessary for them to get in touch with feelings that they have warded off, to grieve the childhood that never was, the roads not taken, the lives not led, aspects of the self that have changed, relationships that never were or that have been lost, and the future that never will be. Letting go of the grandiose fantasies and illusions that have been a mainstay of the self and facing the loss of opportunities and time are painful. Furthermore, each positive step that is taken may be accompanied by giving up what is famil- iar and safe. The working-through process may take a long time, and the worker must be able to balance the need to remain attuned to the client's feelings of despair and fear while believing in the client's ability to reach a better place.

MODIFYING FEELINGS OF GUILT AND THE NEED FOR SELF-PUNISHMENT

When guilt and a need for self-punishment are stimulated by events, the worker will need to help clients realize that their feelings, although under- standable, are not warranted by the situation and are being fueled by issues that the client has grappled with all of his or her life. It likely will be neces- sary to revisit the childhood experiences that gave rise to the client's chron- ic and underlying feelings of guilt. Sometimes, the current crisis permits the reworking of these earlier issues, but their resolution is not essential. What is critical is the client's ability to separate out what is happening in the here and now from the there and then.

MODIFYING FEELINGS OF INNER BADNESS AND FRAUDULENCE

As with feelings of guilt, the worker will need to enable clients to see that current events are triggering feelings of inner badness or fraudulence, to explore the origins of such feelings in the client's early life, to enable the client to make contact with his or her true self, and to help the client to feel a sense of worth.

STRENGTHENING THE SELF AND ENCOURAGING NEW RELATIONSHIPS AND ACTIVITIES

Helping clients to develop alternative ways of viewing themselves, to recognize and build on their own strengths and areas of achievement, to discover new outlets and selfobjects, and to restore and develop compensatory structures are important aspects of the treatment. Many clients are extremely negative about themselves and their past experiences. They eradicate their own history of achievement, since their lack of affirmation and recognition in the present causes them to forget previous successes. Their self-esteem can be enhanced by empathically helping them to retrieve memories, to review and reshape the way they view themselves and their own past life experiences, and to identify and support their strengths and the ways and areas in which they can regain and retain control of their lives (Butler, 1963; Greenes, 1987; Grunes, 1982). It is easier to accomplish these tasks with those individuals who have had areas of better functioning and success in their lives and when some avenues for self-expression, recognition, and achievement are possible.

Workers may need to selectively meet clients' selfobject needs for applause or other forms of self-affirmation rather than to interpret their efforts to get their needs met as "manipulations" or as unhealthy attempts to obtain approval from the outside world (Goldstein, 1990, 197–198). Furthermore, in order to empower those who lack role models for new behaviors, it may be important to hold out a vision of alternatives for them to actively encourage clients to take actions that are new and frightening if these are consistent with our assessment of their capacities.

COUNTERTRANSFERENCE ISSUES

Workers are not immune from the assaults to the self and narcissistic injuries that clients experience, or from their own object relations pathology. There are several common kinds of reactions, however, that workers may be vulnerable to in their helping efforts with those who are grieving, coping with illness and disability, and dealing with midlife issues. Palombo (1985: 46–48) offers a cautionary note in describing the difficulty that clinicians have when they work with clients who are in pain. Workers may feel overwhelmed and try to help clients overome their strong feelings too quickly. It is necessary to empathize with a client's despair while conveying hope. Other sources of strong reactions in the worker arise from having to face the reality of death and illness, to address a client's suicidal intent, and to experience the power of a client's narcissistic rage. Moreover, the setting in which treatment occurs also can be a source of stress for the worker. Just as it is difficult for a parent to establish a good-enough holding environment for a child when he or she is surrounded by a non-nurturing and stressful environment, it is difficult for workers to be emotionally present and to show empathy for clients when they are under siege in the workplace. A parallel process takes place in which workers pass along to their clients what they experience from their surrounding work environment, which itself is affected by the wider society. As the health care system is overburdened and there are serious threats to service delivery and to the very survival of social work and the biopsychosocial approach, the task of remaining available to clients is more difficult and workers must recognize how the impact of the surrounding environment affects their ability to be there for clients.

CASE EXAMPLES

The following case examples illustrate many of the points raised in the preceding discussion. They show clients who are struggling with different kinds of losses and how workers began to understand and address their concerns.

PROLONGED GRIEF INVOLVING THE LOSS OF SELF

In the case of Ms. Silver, the client's grief process was complicated by her having an underdeveloped and vulnerable self and her dependence on her partner of many years to provide selfobject functions.

MS. SILVER, a 45-year-old Jewish bookkeeper, sought help from the counseling center almost two years after the loss of Emily, her woman partner of fifteen years, who died of cancer after a long illness. Ms. Silver looked depressed and said that she felt almost as bad as she did right after Emily died except that she was not as acutely upset. In some ways, she felt worse because she had become more socially isolated and was impatient with those who were unable to share her pain. "I feel angry at people whose lives are going on and for their not realizing what I'm going through. Even worse, maybe they do know and don't want to be around me. I think of Emily all the time, and that makes me feel better until I realize that she's not here. I haven't even given away her clothes or possessions. It gives me some comfort to have her things around me. Most of the time I feel dead and that I'm going through the motions of life." When the worker asked what had prompted Ms. Silver to come for help at this time, she replied, "I'm really worried about myself. I can't go on like this. I'm not getting any better. I walk around in a fog. I almost got hit by a car last week. I can work because my job is pretty easy and my boss is afraid to get rid of me, but otherwise I don't know what I'm doing. I've been taking antidepressants and I don't think they really do very much except help me to sleep. I don't know if you can do anything."

During the rest of the session, the client talked about her relationship with Emily and the illness that overcame her. She was open about their having had some very difficult interactions but felt that they had been able to talk through and better understand their problems in the period before Emily's death. "People keep telling me that I am angry at Emily for leaving me, but I don't feel that way. She didn't want to die. I feel I was lucky to have known her. She made me laugh and feel alive. It's true that I had a lot of resentment toward her at times, but I wasn't easy either." When Ms. Silver talked about Emily, she became more animated and seemed less depressed.

The worker, who herself had experienced the loss of a partner some years earlier followed by a painful grief process and then a new and rewarding beginning, felt touched by the client's plight. She conveyed her empathy and concern for the client's sense of loss and despair but also held out hope that the client would recover. Interestingly, when the client returned the following week, she said she had actually felt better after she left the worker because "You encouraged me to talk about Emily, so I felt like she was present, and you didn't seem put off by my pain."

In discussing her life before she met Emily, Ms. Silver described herself as a fearful and shy person who always felt somewhat different from her peers. She was one of two daughters born to parents who lived in a poor neighborhood in the Bronx. Her father worked long hours, withdrew into his newspaper at home, and was non-communicative. Her mother, a depressed person, was a caring but needy woman who was controlling and possessive. As a child and adolescent, Ms. Silver was compliant, but at the age of 19 she left home in rebellion. Her mother was quite upset about her moving out, and Ms. Silver felt quite guilty about having done so. She had never been encouraged to attend college and began working as a bookkeeper. When she realized she was a lesbian in her early twenties, she went through a period of experimentation. She was never popular with others, and although she had some brief relationships with other women, she did not feel successful in "the gay scene." Her mother died when Ms. Silver was 28 and her sister, with whom she never got along, moved to California when she married ten years ago. Her father remarried and still lived in the Bronx.

When Ms. Silver met Emily, she was "blown away" by the strength of her personality. Emily became the sister she never had and was everything she would have wanted to be—smart, fun, outgoing, and popular. "She had a way with people. Even my parents liked her." The negative side of their relationship was that "I got lost. I let Emily's life be my life. She always encouraged me to do things on my own, but I didn't want to. Sometimes I became overwhelmed by how much I needed her. Then I would get sullen and withdraw, which made her 'crazy' and she would try to make me talk. The more she tried, the more I would withdraw until she would give up in frustration."

In the initial phase of treatment, the worker encouraged Ms. Silver to talk about her feelings about Emily and her illness and death in great detail. In addition to listening, the worker commented on how alive the client seemed to feel when she spoke about Emily. She explored and pointed out the ways in which Ms. Silver had depended on Emily to fulfill her selfobject needs. Once the selfobject transference of a twinship nature was established, Ms. Silver began to feel less alone and more present. She looked forward to coming to sessions as if they were her lifeline, even though she often used them to share her pain. The worker and client also were able to investigate what life was like for Ms. Silver before she met Emily, and the client began to recognize how little self-definition and self-confidence she had had even then and how much work she needed to do on herself.

As the client began to feel somewhat better, she set about beginning to sort out and give away some of Emily's possessions and to reach out to old friends. This ushered in new waves of mourning, not only for Emily but for Ms. Silver's past life experiences, which were associated with the possessions. In renewing relationships with others, she became aware of her tendencies to lose herself, and her fear of being "taken over" by others showed itself in the client-worker relationship. She became withdrawn and more depressed at times, and it became apparent that she was worried about her attachment to the worker. She was able to explore the origins of her fears in her relationships with her mother and the ways in which her parents had been unable to provide mirroring for her autonomous development, stifled her self expression, and contributed to her feeling responsible for their well-being. The worker also helped her to examine the nature of her guilty attachment to her mother, which heightened when she left home and became more open in her lesbianism. She felt she had deserted her mother and was never able to share any details of outside activities or relationships with her. At a later phase of the treatment, the worker took an active interest in Ms. Silver's work life and encouraged her to pursue interests that she had set aside much earlier in her life. Feeling stronger in her self, Ms. Silver expressed an interest in dating. The worker supported her efforts, and she and the client would discuss how she might meet women and the vicissitudes of her dating experiences. When the client would seem to fall back into a withdrawn and depressed state at times, the worker would empathically interpret her fear and guilt.

Discussion

When Emily died, Ms. Silver lost a major part of what made her feel whole and she had lacked a developed sense of self before she met Emily. The worker speculated that a major reason for her continuing depression and for her efforts to keep Emily alive was not so much related to her anger at Emily but to how bereft she was in losing her primary selfobject and being left with her underdeveloped and highly vulnerable sense of self. The worker's empathic immersion in the client's grief and in her recounting of her experiences with Emily enabled a selfobject bond to form and the mourning of the numerous losses that the client had undergone. The worker was able to help the client to explore the impact of her early background on the development of her sense of self and in producing a guilty attachment to her mother. She took an active role in encouraging Ms. Silver to pursue her interests and to reach out to others and in interpreting the client's regressive pulls.

A BLOW TO THE SELF-CONCEPT

In the following case, the death of the client's younger sister as a result of a fatal accident constituted the loss of someone who had shared the client's history. It also proved to be a blow to the client's self-concept because of her belief that it was her job to take care of her sister and prevent anything bad from occurring.

THE RUFOLO CASE Ms. Rufolo, a 39-year-old Irish-American housewife, sought counseling from a local family service agency a year after her younger 36-year-old married sister, Marie, was killed when a speeding and out of control car hit her when she was crossing a busy intersection. She was survived by her husband and an 11-year-old son, for whom Ms. Rufolo was the godparent. The client's priest had convinced her to seek help after she told him about her feelings of self-blame and guilt about her sister's death.

   When she saw the worker, Ms. Rufolo described the past year as having been "nightmarish." She said that it took her six months to accept that her sister was gone and "I'm not sure that I accept it even now. I can't believe that she's not going to just come back one day and say that this has all been a big mistake. We had our fights, but we were there for one another. She held my memories. We always used to talk about what it was like for us growing up. There's no one else with whom I can do that. I feel like a part of my self is missing. I feel depressed all the time. I even started taking antidepressants, but I don't know if they are doing anything except that I'm not crying all the time. I keep going over and over in my mind the minute by minute details of the hours before the accident. I think about what might have been different if I had called her before she left the house so that she would have left a few minutes later or if I had gone shopping with her like we usually did." When the worker commented on the fact that Ms. Rufolo seemed to blame herself for not being able to prevent the accident, she said, "I should have been able to. I've looked after her all my life."

In telling the worker about her family, Ms. Rufolo reported that because she was the oldest of three siblings, she was responsible for their well-being and in fact, from childhood, was often expected to look after them. Her younger brother developed a serious drug problem and Ms. Rufolo was instrumental in trying to convince her parents to get help for him, which they eventually did with her help. After many unsuccessful attempts, he did become abstinent but was having a difficult time keeping employment. Although they had meager funds themselves and viewed the brother as "lazy and difficult," the client and her husband, an Italian-American construction worker, contributed financially to his support.

Ms. Rufolo described her relationship with her sister, Marie, as close but competitive. Marie thought that their parents respected Ms. Rufolo because she was the smartest of the children, and Ms. Rufolo thought that her brother had been indulged and her sister had been doted on because she was especially attractive and had a pleasant and outgoing disposition. Ms. Rufolo, who had a weight problem from early childhood, was more serious and shy and envied Marie's looks and popularity. Her envy intensified when her sister married and had a son that the client's parents made the center of attention. Ms. Rufolo and her husband had decided not to have children, which distressed both sets of parents. The client said that she always thought her sister had everything and commented, "There have been many times in my life that I thought something bad was going to happen to me, not to her." In addition to feeling responsible for her siblings, Ms. Rufolo felt it was her job to take care of her parents from the time she was a child. They expected her to know what to do and to meet all of their needs from an early age, and she remembered feeling that they were not able to handle things on their own and did need her help. During her adolescence, she rebelled for a time and they repeatedly accused her of being selfish and self-centered.

In early sessions, several important themes emerged that served as a basis for exploration in months of later meetings. The first theme was the client's feelings of being abandoned by her sister because the client had no one with whom she could share her history. This was especially difficult for the client because she felt that her sister was the one person who had witnessed how difficult her parents were and helped her to feel that she was not a bad person for not always being there for them. A second theme was Ms. Rufolo's rage at herself for having failed to live up to her self-concept as being the responsible one, a view that had been reinforced from the time she was a child. She was unaware of what unrealistic expectations were placed on her, which she internalized, leading to feelings that she could control life and death. She berated herself as if she really could have prevented her sister's fatal accident. Yet a third theme was the client's feelings of anger, frustration, and rejection that her brother-in-law was not consulting with her about the raising of Ms. Rufolo's godson. A fourth and final theme that emerged somewhat later was Ms. Rufolo's guilt that her envious feelings toward her sister and her fleeting feelings of being glad that the sister was out of the way had somehow caused the sister's death.

In the treatment, the worker first addressed the client's painful feelings of aloneness because no one was there to validate her experiences in the family. By exploring the client's history in detail, the worker became the person who now could bear witness to what Ms. Rufolo had gone through earlier in her life. As part of this discussion, it was possible for the worker to identify the ways in which the client's parents had expected too much of Ms. Rufolo, had not sufficiently let her be a child, and had led her to feel that she really could and should control her environment. Because of the strength of the client's selfobject transference, the worker was able to temper the client's feelings of grandiosity and omnipotence that were contributing to her acute feelings of rage against her self and sense of failure. This tempering process also was relevant to Ms. Rufolo's feelings of responsibility for her godson. One of the reasons she was angry at her brother-in-law was that she viewed him as standing in the way of her fulfilling her promise to her sister and her obligations to the boy, despite the fact that she felt this responsibility to be a burden. The worker helped her to lessen her burden, to step back and relinquish control in order to allow her brother-in-law to raise his own son as he saw fit, and to find ways to be involved with the godson without threatening his father. Finally, it was necessary to help Ms. Rufolo accept her feelings of envy and competitiveness without feeling that they had caused her sister's death.

Discussion

In the above example, Ms. Rufolo's prolonged depressive reaction after her sister's death was influenced by the loss of a much-needed selfobject and the blow and narcissistic rage of not being able to live up to the demands of her grandiose self-concept. Through her empathic interventions and the strength of the selfobject transference, the worker was able to help the client to overcome her feelings of loss and aloneness, to understand and lessen her feelings of anger, self-blame, and guilt, and to help her maintain her relationship with her godson without fighting with her brother-in-law about playing a role in decisions about the boy's upbringing.

ILLNESS AS A PUNISHMENT AND LOSS OF COMPENSATORY STRUCTURES

In the next case, a serious illness and surgery made the client feel she was being punished and undermined the client's compensatory structures, triggering her underlying narcissistic vulnerability.

THE WILSON CASE Ms. Wilson, an African-American divorced hair stylist, was 48 when a malignant tumor of the breast necessitated a mastectomy. Despite a favorable pathology report, she became angry at everyone around her, cried easily, was inconsolable, did not want visitors, was uncooperative with the nurses, and refused to discuss the need for further preventive treatment, reconstructive surgery, and her attendance at a support group. When she was discharged, Ms. Wilson did begin to explore her options for treatment and rehabilitation but continued to be very depressed and angry. Her doctor referred her to a clinic social worker for counseling.

In her first meeting, the client railed against life. She felt she had been born unlucky. She didn't know why God was punishing her but felt powerless to change her fate. She gave numerous examples of having had "bad" things happen to her, including having been born into a poor family, being physically abused as a child, raped as an adolescent, undergoing numerous miscarriages, and marrying a philandering man who left her without a penny. "Now this! I've always prided myself on my looks. What man is going to want me now?" The client felt that she had no future.

Ms. Wilson's history showed that she was the oldest of four children. She lived with her mother, and her common-law father left the family when she was eight. Ms. Wilson described her mother in glowing terms despite the mother's alcoholism and maltreatment of her. Her mother was supported through welfare and had very little money and was overwhelmed by having to take care of all the children. Ms. Wilson was expected to help out and she was frequently punched and beaten by her mother when she was drinking if Ms. Wilson didn't perform her chores to her mother's satisfaction or made too much noise. Although many of her needs were neglected, her mother took some pride in Ms. Wilson's being an unusually attractive child whose appearance was a focus of positive attention. Her mother did buy her pretty clothes when she could. Popular among her peers, Ms. Wilson felt that people only responded to her because she looked good and that she basically had little to offer. She continued to place importance on appearing fashionable and perfectly groomed in later life. Ms. Wilson married when she was 18 to get away from home but her husband left her. They did not have any children. She studied to be a hair stylist and was able to support herself. Her relationships with men usually did not work out. She tended to respond to men who showed an interest in her without thinking about whether she liked them or whether they were worthy of her.

The client was filled with anger at her plight. The worker encouraged her ventilation and tried to understand the basis of Ms. Wilson's feelings that her cancer diagnosis and mastectomy were two more assaults in a series of punishments for someone who had a very hard life. She also explored the client's long-standing feelings of inner badness that stemmed from her childhood experiences. The worker was able to help the client overcome her idealization of her mother and accept her problems and limitations and to see that the "shortcomings" and "wrongdoings" for which she blamed herself were part of being a child and constituted human failings rather than being signs that she was a bad person who deserved to be punished.

The worker also showed her understanding of how important Ms. Wilson's appearance had been all of her life in getting her some positive attention, even from her mother as well as from others, and how devastated she felt at the prospect that her good feelings about her body had been taken away from her. She helped the client to mourn her illusion of being "perfect" with respect to her appearance, to accept that she could still look good despite her mastectomy, and to begin to identify and prize other aspects of her personality.

Discussion

Ms. Wilson's reactions to her cancer and mastectomy were particularly intense because of the significant blows to her compensatory structures. Thus, her diagnosis and surgery stimulated her rage, caused her to feel a sense of despair, and made her feel she was being punished for past misdeeds. Treatment provided her with a place in which she could vent her painful feelings, feel less alone, understand the reasons for her reactions, modify her sense of inner badness, and strengthen her self-esteem.

THE BUBBLE OF PERFECTION BURSTS

The following case example, which describes a client discussed elsewhere (Goldstein, 1995c), shows a woman's reaction to midlife events that burst the illusion of perfection that she had maintained to ward off her underlying narcissistic vulnerability.

MS. WEISS, a Jewish 49-year-old guidance counselor, sought help reluctant-ly because she was at her "wits' end" with respect to knowing what to do about her son, Mark, age 22. She had not ever asked for help from anyone before and was contemptuous of the therapists with whom she had come into contact over the years. She described herself as the strong one whom people sought out for help. "I'm the one people have envied because they thought I had it all, and I did. I had looks; I got straight A's in college; I married a doctor; I had a big house; and I had beautiful and healthy children. Mark, my son, was amazing. When he was a baby, I never realized what a star he would be. He was so talented in sports. Strangers would ask if I was Mark's mother and would say that he was their children's hero and tell me how proud I must be. He won several athletic scholarships to go to college." The look on Ms. Weiss's face then changed as she described what became of Mark. "He's not dead in a physical sense but he might as well be. The person he was is gone. I don't have a son anymore. I have a vegetable who can't get himself out of bed in the morning without my help, let alone work for a living. He decided to drop out of college, just like that. He came home and announced that he didn't know who he was. I told him that he was a star athlete and came from a wonderful home with par-ents who would do anything for him. He replied that there were others who were better than he was and if he couldn't be the best then he didn't want to have anything to do with sports. I've tried everything. I talk to him, give him pep talks, yell at him, threaten him. I get out of control, but nothing works. I can't stand myself. I can't stand him." Ms. Weiss went on to say that Mark was seeing a therapist who was not helping him. She described her husband as a "weakling" and her daughter as "selfish and self-centered." "I've done everything I was supposed to do. The best part of my life is over. I'm 49 going on 80."

An only child who was born when her mother was 40, Ms. Weiss related that her mother, an entertainer, was quite flamboyant and took center stage at home. Appearances and material possessions seemed very important to her. Although she praised her daughter for being smart, independent, and well-behaved, she rarely spent time with her, seemed unattuned to her feelings, and unaware of her real abilities. She described her father as a financially unsuccessful, unassuming and depressed businessman and stated that her mother was very critical of his economic mishaps, passivity, and weakness. Ms. Weiss felt somewhat ashamed of her father but admired her mother, nevertheless feeling unattractive, fearful, and inadequate in her presence. Ms. Weiss became self-sufficient and tried to be the perfect child, hoping that her mother would pay attention to her and fearing that she would be ashamed of her if she did not do well. She described developing an air of extreme self-reliance and aloofness from others but remembers being very anxious and driven. She studied music and was told by her teachers that she had a beautiful voice, but her mother actively discouraged her from pursuing this as a career, telling her that she should marry a professional man who would be a good provider and have a teaching career to fall back on if something happened to him. When Ms. Weiss graduated magna cum laude from college, she married a medical school graduate who was admiring of and attracted to her independence, vitality, and strength. He provided her with a comfortable life economically and they socialized, but she experienced him as self-involved and absent as a husband and father.

Ms. Weiss felt frightened when her children were born and never felt comfortable with either of them. She described herself as lacking in good maternal instincts but attempted to make up for this by being supermom and by being involved in what her children felt, thought, and did. Karen was an easy child and quite independent. Mark was more of a challenge, crying endlessly at night and not responding to his mother's efforts to soothe him. He frustrated her by not fitting into her routines and she resented his demands. Early in his school career he was singled out for his athletic abilities and Ms. Weiss became his enthusiastic supporter and fan. Despite her busy schedule, she attended his sports activities and cheered him on. His victories were hers. When Mark went to college, he encountered more serious competition and was no longer the fair-haired child. Prior to his dropping out of college, Ms. Weiss's husband became depressed and sought professional help following the suicide of his brother. She felt shocked by and ashamed of his "collapse." She concealed the facts of his and

Mark's situation from friends and family, becoming isolated, resentful, and depressed.

Ms. Weiss presented an outward appearance of high functioning and of having an ideal life that generated the admiration and envy of others at times. She had an illusion of total self-sufficiency, believing that she could control the events around her. Her success in evoking recognition and admiration from others met her constant needs for mirroring, and her seeming ability to maintain control over life reinforced her grandiose self-structure. Her need for her children to be selfobjects put them at risk, however, for developing self pathology themselves, since she was not attuned to their individual needs and they conformed to her expectations and perceptions of them. Suddenly, the bubble of perfection, self-sufficiency, and control of others burst.

Ms. Weiss's treatment was difficult. She seemed to require not only the worker's agreement with her point of view but constant affirmation. Yet, her rage was prominent. When she described her son, Mark, the star athlete, as dead because he was no longer pursuing his athletic career, the worker shuddered internally. She knew that it was important to help her express her anger at his failure and to explore what this meant to her, but it was difficult for the worker to listen to her vent her anger at her son and at her husband for taking antidepressants after his brother committed suicide and to experience the degree to which her self-esteem and self-concept rested on his success. Likewise, her initial abrasive and distrustful attitude was hard to take, but her suffering was very real and compelling and the worker was able to find an empathic connection to her pain.

The client filled the sessions initially with the details of her most recent frustrating interactions with Mark and her husband. The worker sometimes had to consciously control her impatience with her self-involvement, anger, her lack of awareness of her impact on others, and her demands for guidelines on how to help Mark. Gradually she was able to shift a little after the worker told her that she could not promise her that she would be able to help her cure Mark, but that she did think she could help her get beyond her understandable pain if they could understand why his problems were so devastating to her. As she related more of her history, Ms. Weiss became more in touch with her own early life experiences and feelings of aloneness, how her needs for mirroring had been thwarted, how she had managed to adapt, how she protected herself from painful feelings, and how her husband's and Mark's problems had been challenging her self-concept and self-esteem. She began to grieve for her own lost childhood, the superstar that she never felt she truly was, and for the loss of dreams for Mark. She recognized that she, not only her husband, had made mistakes with Mark, and while this was an upsetting realization, she began to accept her own failings. She became less driven by her need to appear in control and perfect, tried to modify her destructive interaction with him, became more empathic to her husband, and redirected her energies to her work life and to renovating her house.

Discussion

Life went out of control for Ms. Weiss as her husband and children displayed unacceptable behavior and emotional problems that made them appear flawed. The extreme nature of her reaction was related to her grandiose self-structure, archaic mirroring needs, and underlying and persistent feelings of inadequacy. Just as Ms. Weiss experienced her husband's depression as a narcissistic injury reflecting her failure to have a perfect husband, she experienced Mark's identity crisis as a devastating personal blow that showed everyone her own profound sense of deficiency. Treatment aimed at helping her to modify her needs for control and perfection, to mourn her lost childhood and unfulfilled ambitions, to accept the limitations of life, to support her efforts to find outlets for her interests, and to go on with her life.

DEPRESSION FOLLOWING THE ACHIEVEMENT OF A GOAL

In the final example, the client experienced a painful depression following his achievement of a long-sought-after goal because it stimulated his deep-seated feelings of being unworthy.

THE CRUZ CASE Mr. Cruz, a 45-year-old Latino man who worked as an administrative assistant at a local university, was hospitalized briefly following a suicide gesture in which he ingested fifty aspirins and then called emergency medical services, which arrived immediately. He was placed on antidepressant medication, convinced his doctor that he was not a suicidal risk, and was discharged after a week with a referral to outpatient treatment. When Mr. Cruz saw the worker, he said he was still very depressed and hopeless but knew that killing himself was not a solution. "I didn't really want to die, I just wanted to get away from the constant thoughts that were going on in my head. The medication seems to be helping but I still feel pretty awful. My life has been a failure."

Mr. Cruz began to feel depressed a few months earlier when he received his college degree following many years of part-time course work. He had realized his wish to be a college graduate. The client described that he was numb during the graduation. When he attended a dinner with friends to celebrate his achievement, he drank a lot and the next day slept till noon. When he awoke, he was plagued by disturbing thoughts that mocked his achievement, such as "You don't really think that you can amount to anything," "Whom do you think you are fooling?" and "You're nothing but a lazy bum." He became afraid to answer the telephone, thinking that he was going to be called and told that the school had made a mistake and that he still had to take another course. The thoughts got worse, and he impulsively swallowed a bottle of aspirin.

Mr. Cruz was born in Cuba and came to the United States early in his life with his older siblings and parents when they fled the Castro regime. Their emigration led to a drastic change for the worse in their economic situation but the parents were quite enterprising and gradually were able to reestablish themselves financially. Before leaving Cuba, Mr. Cruz attended school but was an average student, which was the source of constant fighting in the family. His father, a strict disciplinarian, was angry at and critical of Mr. Cruz, punished him physically when he did not receive excellent grades or reports from his teachers, forced him to study long hours, restricted his activities, and compared him unfavorably to his four older brothers and sisters. His mother would try to soothe him when the father was not present but would not stand up to her husband.

When the family emigrated to the United States, Mr. Cruz's school performance deteriorated further. He missed his relatives and friends, did not learn English quickly, and felt adrift while his family members were preoccupied with their own survival. His only source of pleasure was playing baseball. He recalled a recurrent fantasy in which he became a professional baseball player and appeared in the World Series. He imagined that his father would be sitting in the stadium and that Mr. Cruz would hit a grand slam home run that would win the game while everyone cheered him and that his father would be proud of him. In sharing this fantasy, Mr. Cruz began to cry. "He will never be proud of me." Mr. Cruz's father had died ten years earlier. At the time, Mr. Cruz was trying to complete his high school equivalency, having dropped out of school when he was 17 in order to go to work. Mr. Cruz's siblings had all graduated from college and his oldest brother helped him to get a job at a local university. Mr. Cruz was well liked and found a place for himself. He was promoted several times and much to his surprise was admitted to college when he applied.

The worker thought that Mr. Cruz's completion of his college degree meant the same to him as did his fantasy of hitting a grand slam home run. He hoped that graduating from college would earn him his father's respect and acknowledgment. Unfortunately, the father was dead, and to make matters worse his critical attitudes toward and harsh treatment of his son were alive in Mr. Cruz, who felt deeply undeserving. The father was not present in reality to mirror Mr. Cruz's achievement but he was present internally to mock him. The client wished that a proud father would be at his graduation from college but was thrown back on his disappointing and frustrating internal relationship with his critical father.

The worker helped Mr. Cruz to see that his depression and obsessive thoughts stemmed from his feelings of unworthiness and his relationship with his father and post-emigration experiences. To enable him to overcome these feelings, it was necessary to help him to explore his early life and the messages that he received and how these shaped his deep-seated negative attitudes toward himself. Dealing with his relationship to his father was a major focus of the treatment. It was necessary for Mr. Cruz to connect with his own suffering as a child, to overcome his view that if he had been different, his father would have been more supportive and validating, to recognize his father's limitations, to get in touch with his anger at his father, and to mourn never having had a close relationship with him and of being able to elicit his pride. The worker showed pride in Mr. Cruz's achievements and provided selfobject responsiveness that affirmed his strengths and supported his efforts to improve himself.

Discussion

Instead of being proud of and happy with his achievement when Mr. Cruz attained the long-sought-for goal of graduating from college later in his life, he experienced a severe depressive reaction. The internal voice of his critical father tortured him and stimulated his feelings of worthlessness. The treatment helped him to understand what was causing his reaction and to help him rework his internalized relationship with his father and to modify his self-concept.

SUMMARY

Using self psychological and object relations perspectives, this chapter has considered the impact of certain stressful life events, such as the death of a significant person, illness and disability, and the range of those occurring in midlife. Then it discussed and illustrated numerous treatment foci, including assessing the personal meaning of life events, empathizing with losses and blows to the self, narcissistic rage, and shame, understanding and modifying guilt, a sense of inner badness, a need for self-punishment, and feelings of fraudulence, helping clients to mourn the loss of selfobjects, compensatory structures, illusions, ambitions, and dreams, tempering the demands of the grandiose self, and strengthening the self and encouraging new relationships and activities.

10

THE TREATMENT OF CLIENTS WITH SPECIAL PROBLEMS

Object relations theory and self psychology offer new perspectives on the causes and treatment of many types of problems presented by clients in today's practice arena. Among some of the more difficult of these are substance abuse, child maltreatment, and the effects of childhood sexual abuse on adult survivors.

SUBSTANCE ABUSE

Clients from all social classes and walks of life use alcohol and drugs to varying degrees, and substance abuse takes an enormous toll on personal, family, and occupational functioning. It is clearly associated with child maltreatment and domestic violence. Many clients who seek help are not open about the extent of their substance abuse and attempt to conceal or deny it. Consequently, practitioners should be alert to the possibility that clients may be using alcohol and drugs, particularly when there are signs that an individual is unpredictable or volatile and is having problems in his daily life and social roles that are not readily explainable. Straussner (1993: 15–18) outlines a series of questions that can be used to assess the nature and severity of the substance abuse and advises that the practitioner also assess the effects of the abuse on the client's life.

THE CAUSES AND TREATMENT OF SUBSTANCE ABUSE

Psychodynamically oriented practitioners have tended to regard substance abuse as an attempt at self-medication or as an expression and way of dealing with underlying personality difficulties. They believe that the substance use will diminish if the client's long-standing personality problems are addressed in treatment. In contrast, specialists in the chemical dependency field have regarded substance abuse as a disease for which many individuals have a biological predisposition, and they focus directly on treatment of the addiction. Because the potential for becoming a substance abuser is always present in certain persons, they can never consider themselves to be "cured." In the recovery model that flows from this view, self-help groups, such as Alcoholics Anonymous or Narcotics Anonymous, and more structured treatment programs require that the afflicted person accepts the presence and chronicity of his or her disease and engages in lifelong, total abstinence. More recently, harm-reduction programs have come into vogue. They emphasize helping individuals gain control over their substance abuse through controlled use of alcohol or drugs.

Increasingly, there is recognition that the causes of chemical dependence are varied and complex and that substance abusers are not uniform in their treatment needs. A multifaceted rather than singular approach to understanding and treating substance abuse seems desirable. One way of integrating diverse views has been through the use of the concept of "dual diagnosis," which refers to the fact that an individual may present with both the syndrome of substance abuse and a personality or mental disorder. Proponents of the dual-diagnosis perspective argue that those who present with multiple disorders have special treatment needs that require a blending of techniques that address both the substance abuse and the concurrent personality or mental disturbances (Evans & Sullivan, 1990; Mulinski, 1989).

THEORETICAL AND CLINICAL PERSPECTIVES

In the context of an integrated approach to work with substance abusers, object relations theory and self psychology offer important insights into the psychological components of addictive behavior. Self psychologists are likely to view those who become addicted to substances as lacking in internal self structures that make them vulnerable to using substances to make up for their deficits. Thus, they use alcohol and drugs for tension regulation, self-soothing, and self-esteem regulation (Levin, 1991: 203). Ulman and Paul (1990: 129) hold the view that the use of substances is associated with "archaic fantasies and moods of narcissistic bliss" and that alcohol and drugs are selfobject experiences. They describe three types of addicts: the manic addict, who self-anesthetizes the pain of disintegration or hypomanic anxiety; the depressive addict, who uses substances to elevate, stimulate, and inflate his or her self experience; and the manic-depressive addict, who uses drugs and alcohol both to calm and stimulate the self (Ulman & Paul, 1990: 131–132).

In keeping with a self psychological view of the causes of substance abuse, treatment generally should aim at helping substance abusers to develop a selfobject transference, to understand the ways in which alcohol and drugs fulfill selfobject needs, to help them find other ways of meeting those needs, and to strengthen their self structures. Levin (1991: 214–238) outlines numerous foci in working with alcoholics, in particular, but many if not all of his suggestions also apply to the treatment of those who abuse drugs. He recommends that the worker needs to appreciate the narcissistic injury to substance abusers of not being able to use alcohol or drugs; their sense of failure, humiliation, low self-esteem, and self-hatred that stems from their addiction, which has often caused occupational and economic setbacks, ill health, and relationship problems and losses; their emptiness; their absence of a firm identity; their incapacity to be alone; the nature of their selfobject transference to drugs and alcohol; the role of substances in confirming their sense of grandiosity and omnipotent control; the presence of low self-esteem; and the prevalence of feelings of shame.

From an object relations perspective, substance abuse may serve to express or soothe deep-seated feelings of inner guilt, badness, emptiness, and lack of worth, problems in intimacy, and separation-individuation issues; to form connections with and replicate earlier interactions with and internalizations of significant others; and to quiet anxiety, feelings of aloneness, boredom, or angry impulses with which the person has no other ways of dealing. Defenses such as denial or splitting prevent the substance abuser from acknowledging the severity and negative consequences of their addictive behavior.

Substance abusers are not easy to engage in treatment. Although the provision of a therapeutic holding environment that may include environmental structuring in order to help substance abusers to refrain from substance use is necessary, it may first be necessary for the worker to point out and modify their use of denial and resistance to stopping their use of alcohol and drugs. Sometimes this can be done early in treatment, but at other times it may have to wait until the worker has more therapeutic leverage with the client because of the strength of the client-worker relationship. In order for many clients to sustain their sobriety, it generally will be necessary for them to become aware of and to modify the underlying dynamics and relational patterns that give rise to their substance abuse and to strengthen the clients' internal capacities for managing their strong impulses and affective states.

CHILD MALTREATMENT

Child maltreatment is a social problem of great magnitude. Working with parents who maltreat their children through neglect or outright physical abuse presents practitioners with enormous challenges. Workers may be responsible for life-and-death decisions and face ethical, medical, and legal dilemmas. Most parents do not seek help voluntarily but only because they are fearful of the negative consequences of not doing so. They often are mandated or ordered by legal authorities to be involved in treatment, or are required to undergo counseling in order to receive other services. Even when they do seek help on their own, they are difficult to engage in treatment. They may be distrustful of the helping process and of those whom they perceive as representing authority. Because many of these clients may be overwhelmed by a lack of adequate environmental resources and multiple stressors or problems, they may have little hope, energy, or motivation to work on improving their situation. Moreover, even when they become engaged in treatment, it is not easy to break the cycle of abuse or to transform neglectful parents into more adequate caretakers (Gonzalez-Ramos & Goldstein, 1989: 21; Mishne, 1989: 51).

THE EFFECTS OF CHILD MALTREATMENT

Child maltreatment can be life-threatening and has devastating effects, including psychosomatic complaints, chronic low-grade depression, suicidal impulses, anger and aggression, shame and guilt, self-hatred, and numerous other psychiatric disorders (Wagner, 1991: 244). Moreover, there appears to be a generational transmission of child abuse and neglect in that a high proportion of those who have been maltreated by their parents repeat the pattern with their own children (Steele, 1980: 52).

There is not a single cause of child maltreatment, and parents who abuse and neglect their children do not have one type of clinical diagnosis or personality type. There appears to be a complex interaction of biological, psychological, environmental, and societal factors that lead to child maltreatment and that necessitate a multifaceted and integrated treatment approach (Goldstein & Gonzalez-Ramos, 1989: 21–37). Many, but by no means all, parents who abuse and neglect their children have a history of having been abused themselves. They often show an early disturbance of attachment to their parents that influences the bonding process with their children, reflect a lack of self-esteem and have unresolved developmental needs that make them vulnerable to stress in their parenting role, and abuse alcohol and drugs. They share numerous traits and psychosocial characteristics, including heightened anxiety, impulsiveness, aggression, dependence, lack of maturity, apathy-futility, difficulties in problem-solving, discomfort in their parenting role, lack of knowledge about parenting, and social isolation. Sometimes, the child's own behavior and characteristics, the particular nature of the parent-child relationship, the absence of social supports, and stressful life events play a role in child maltreatment (Gonzalez-Ramos & Goldstein, 1989: 11).

THEORETICAL AND CLINICAL PERSPECTIVES

In the context of an integrated approach to understanding and working with clients who maltreat their children, object relations theory and self psychology offer important insights into the psychological and interpersonal causes of child maltreatment and suggest numerous treatment foci. It has long been recognized that parents reexperience their own childhoods as they perform their parenting roles (Benedek, 1959). Parenthood can be a time that stimulates past experiences of both good and bad parenting. Although it may allow for a reworking of the parents' earlier issues in more positive ways, it also can lead to a repetition of poor parenting.

From a self psychological perspective, parents who are vulnerable to acts of child maltreatment suffer from severe narcissistic personality disturbances, are lacking in self-esteem and the capacity for parental empathy, and are prone to archaic selfobject longings for mirroring, idealization, perfection, and omnipotent control. They are not prepared psychologically to be parents or to be nurturing to others and become easily overwhelmed. They may be depleted themselves, or their archaic selfobject needs are stimulated by having to perform the parenting role. They look to the child to provide selfobject functions. When the child fails to fulfill the parent's pressing selfobject needs, the parent experiences a primitive rage reaction and strikes out (Eldridge & Finnican, 1985: 53–56; Wagner, 1991: 246–250).

The development of a selfobject transference to the worker is viewed as especially important in the individual treatment of maltreating parents following self psychological principles, which may be one component of a more comprehensive treatment approach. The worker should provide some of the selfobject functions that the parent looks to the child to fulfill, thereby easing the pressure on the child. Additionally, the worker should use the selfobject transference to help parents to develop firmer self-structures, to increase their capacity for empathy with their children, to find better ways of relating to them, to reach out to others who can be good selfobjects, and to find social supports.

Although there is an overlap between the self psychological and object relations perspectives with respect to their view that maltreating parents are unable to parent because of their own early deprivation and deficits, the object relations perspective also emphasizes maltreating parents' impulsiveness, primitive defenses of splitting and projective identification, unmodulated aggression, incapacity to relate to the child as a separate person who has needs of his or her own, tendency to exploit children to meet their own needs, and predilection to repeat past pathological interactions. Such parents become like the parent who maltreated them through the defense mechanism of identification with the aggressor, which involves taking on the characteristics of a powerful person in order to avoid the anxiety and painful feelings of helplessness and fear experienced in the early relationship with that individual.

A second important dynamic involves the parent's use of the splitting and projective identification. When taking care of children who stimulate their unmet needs and earlier painful childhood interactions to which they have little conscious emotional connection, they may identify with a child's helplessness and demandingness, which is seen as "bad." To get away from these urgent and disturbing feelings, they take on the role of the "bad" parent, which temporarily makes them feel powerful and "good" (Fraiberg, Adelson & Shapiro, 1975). Sometimes maltreating parents see one child in particular as representing their "bad" self and relate to that child in a fixed and abusive pattern. The child becomes a "scapegoat" for the parent.

In addition to providing a holding environment in treatment and through environmental structuring that will help parents who are vulnerable to maltreating their children to contain their impulses, an important element of the treatment approach stemming from this view is to help parents make an emotional connection to their own past histories of trauma and to see the connection between how they were treated as children and how they are treating their own children. It also may be necessary for the worker to be quite active in pointing out the splitting and projective identification or scapegoating mechanisms occurring in the family and to help parents gain control over their impulses. The strength of the positive relationship between the worker and the client also is an important means by which parents can be helped to expand their capacity for parenting.

Whether one employs a self psychological or object relations approach, the engagement of maltreating parents in treatment will not be easy. It will be necessary to give such clients opportunities to express their negative feelings about having to see the worker and to discuss their previous experiences with social workers and social service agencies as well as other representatives of authority. It also will require the worker's acceptance of clients' resentment, anger, or indifference. In order to accomplish these tasks, it is helpful for workers to put themselves in the clients' shoes and to see the world through their eyes, to help them identify some positive value that derives from their involvement in the interventive process, even if the only benefit is to avoid negative consequences. Additionally, the worker needs to demonstrate in a tangible way his or her interest in and capacity to help the client in even some small area of his or her life and to locate clients' strengths, to help clients appreciate them, and to use them in working on and ameliorating their problems. Speaking in ways that clients can understand, becoming familiar with the customs and mores of their cultural background, reaching out to them repeatedly, entering their life space, and participating with them by accompanying them to court hearings or medical appointments are ways in which workers can demonstrate their commitment to helping the client (Goldstein & Noonan, 1999: 235–239).

ADULT SURVIVORS OF CHILDHOOD SEXUAL ABUSE

There has been growing interest in the treatment of adult survivors of sexual abuse who are thought by many to have a distinct type of disturbance and special treatment needs. Although there is reason to believe that there is a sizeable percentage of male as well as female survivors, the following discussion will focus on women who have been sexually abused, as increasing numbers of women are coming for help in dealing with the aftermath of their traumatic experiences.

Many women who are aware of having been sexually abused may seek help for other problems and do not readily disclose their abuse history. Still others seek help for a variety of problems but have little if any conscious memory of having been abused. Although women in the first category identify themselves as survivors, those in the second group often conceal their abuse out of shame and guilt or reveal it later in the treatment or when asked directly about it. The presence of sexual abuse in the third group may go unrecognized unless the practitioner is alert to the clues that it has occurred.

THE EFFECTS OF CHILDHOOD SEXUAL ABUSE

Childhood sexual abuse leads to characteristic defenses, personality traits, and symptoms in later life. Some of the more common symptoms that adult survivors display are severe apprehension and anxiety attacks; sleep disturbances, nightmares, flashbacks or intrusive thoughts; fears, phobias, and chronic depression; suicidal thinking and behavior; low self-esteem and negative views of themselves; physical problems and complaints such as headaches, stomach ailments, skin disorders, backaches, and other pain; hypervigilance, distrust of others, and interpersonal disturbances; compulsive, impulsive, and addictive behavior; problems in social functioning; difficulties in sexual functioning; and a tendency toward revictimization (Courtois, 1988: 104–115).

Because of the presence of severe trauma in their histories, the resultant changes in their personality, and the repetitive nature of their characteristics in adulthood, Herman (1992: 115–29) argues that the term "complex post-traumatic stress disorder" be used in diagnosing their particular problems. She feels that the survivor's symptoms mimic a personality disorder but have very different origins. In fact, Herman decries the diagnostic mislabeling and mistreatment of those who have been sexually abused that she believes occurs in the mental health field. She notes that a large percentage of women who are given diagnoses of borderline personality disorder, multiple personality disorder, and somatization disorder have a history of sexual abuse.

THEORETICAL AND CLINICAL PERSPECTIVES

Whether one sees adult survivors of childhood sexual abuse as suffering from a type of post-traumatic stress disorder or from other clinical syndromes, object relations theory and self psychology contribute important insights into the effects of childhood sexual abuse on the adult personality and identify important treatment foci. Self psychologists tend to view survivors of childhood sexual abuse as having been denied the selfobject responsiveness essential to their forming a cohesive and positive sense of self and also as having been deprived of basic safety, ownership of their own physical being, and the feeling of being loved in their own right. Because they have been exposed to overstimulation and trauma, they may have trouble regulating their level of excitation and developing adequate self-soothing mechanisms.

From an object relations perspective, the adult survivor may have internalized relational patterns based on being victimized by those closest to them and negative self- and object-representations that they play out in later relationships. In order to deal with their early trauma, they may have relied on certain common defenses, the most important of which is dissociation, in which they totally repress the memories of disturbing events and/or the painful and overwhelming affects associated with them. While the use of dissociation may result in a survivor not even remembering that she has been abused, it also may lead to recall of the event without the affects. As Blake-White and Kline (1985: 397) note, women who have been sexually abused do not feel the stronger emotions of terror, despair, abandonment, betrayal, pain, and total aloneness that they experienced as children.

As part of the dissociation process, survivors often distrust their own memories. Sometimes this is accompanied by idealization of the abuser and a tendency to protect the memory of the "good" aspects of the perpetrator through the use of splitting. The survivor finds it emotionally preferable to blame themselves for being "bad" even though this causes them low self-esteem, guilt, and shame. These feelings may be particularly intense when the abuser played a kind and nurturing role in the child's life.

Although helping adult survivors to recover their lost memories and painful affects so that they can recover from their earlier trauma is usually advocated in both self psychological and object relations approaches, this work must be based on an individualized assessment of clients' personality functioning and their ability to tolerate the exploration of their overwhelming earlier experiences. An assessment of the current support systems that clients have in their lives also is important, as the recovery work can become quite intense and anxiety producing, sometimes necessitating emergency interventions. Work with adult survivors is easier when the clients have recall of the painful events and have sufficient self-esteem, strengths, and social supports to endure the exploration of the original traumatic experiences.

Because of their lack of a sense of safety and their deficits in internal self-structures, which make it hard for them to tolerate the working through of their traumatic experiences, the treatment process is difficult. The therapist must pay particular attention to creating a secure holding environment for these clients, validate their survival skills, avoid the use of confrontative techniques, help them to avoid situations in which they are revictimized, and sensitively time interventions that engage them in the trauma recovery work.

It is difficult for many survivors of abuse to trust others, including those from whom they seek help, and to develop and sustain a selfobject transference. Having been exploited by the most significant people in their lives, they expect people to have hidden agendas and to violate their boundaries. Empathy may have been used as a manipulative tool in earlier relationships. Some survivors may unwittingly act in ways that lead to their revictimization. This tendency also may show itself in the therapeutic relationship, and the worker must be alert to its manifestations and refrain from being drawn in to a destructive re-creation of the original abuse situation.

Acceptance, consistency, empathy, genuineness, safety, and validation are important ingredients of a therapeutic holding environment in the beginning stages of working with survivors, and it is likely that the client will test the worker's intentions and steadfastness. Likewise, as the client begins to feel closer to the worker, she may begin to feel more frightened and try to distance or flee. The worker will need to understand the client's fear and help her to stay connected to the treatment.

When clients are reluctant to disclose or discuss their abuse or when they literally lack the memory of the abuse experiences, the worker must proceed with caution. Although it is important for the practitioner to be alert to the possibility that sexual abuse has occurred and to become comfortable in exploring the client's early experiences, the timing of this must be well thought out. All too often, inexperienced and zealous workers push for details of the abuse situation or attempt to recover traumatic memories before the client feels safe or has experienced some lessening of her defenses and feelings of fear, badness, shame, and guilt.

When sufficient safety has been established and the client has a greater feeling of self-esteem and diminished feelings of fear, shame, and guilt, the memory work can be started and the process of recovery begun. This may take a long time, and the client may undergo periods of resistance or show intense and overwhelming affects. The worker will need to be available and sustaining in order to help the client to contain her feeling states. Sometimes crises will occur during this process as the client reexperiences her pain. Anger usually accompanies the retrieval of the abuse experience and the client undergoes a mourning process for her lost childhood. This work can be very difficult for the practitioner as well as the client. Ultimately the treatment helps the client to connect the effects of her past experiences on her current life and to learn to reshape relationships and to reconnect to others in new ways.

COUNTERTRANSFERENCE ISSUES

There is general consensus that practitioners who work with certain populations are especially vulnerable to countertransference reactions that can obstruct their work. For example, because of the substance abuser's urgent needs and manipulative, aggressive, and sometimes antisocial behavior, acting-out, use of denial, self-involvement, and tendency toward slips and relapses, workers must be vigilant with respect to their reactions and refrain from judgmental attitudes, an overreliance on confrontative techniques, becoming angry at provocative behavior, or being naively trusting of the client's promises. Likewise, it is not easy to work with those who maltreat their children without feeling horrified at times by their neglectful and abusive acts and outright cruelty. The worker needs to be particularly careful not to blame clients, to withdraw from them, to try to meet all their needs, to become provoked by their distrust and noncompliance, and to identify with the children against the parents. It may be difficult for many workers to understand what is behind the clients' presenting attitudes and behaviors and not to personalize them. Even when workers recognize what is operating for these clients, they still may react with distress, feelings of rejection, and anger when their intentions are rebuffed, not appreciated, or attacked Goldstein & Noonan, 1999: 233–235). At the same time, there is a risk with such clients that workers will have difficulty being firm, setting appropriate limits, exercising authority, reporting suspected incidents of child abuse or neglect, and helping parents to relinquish parental rights in certain instances (Mishne, 1989: 48–51). Finally, in the treatment of adult survivors of childhood sexual abuse, there is a risk that the workers will experience the client's trauma vicariously and that this will affect their outlook on life and cause a type of burnout or that they will become caught up in the client's tendency to replicate earlier pathological interactions.

The overwhelming and disturbing nature of clients' difficulties, the absence or minimal amount of resources available to help them, and the limited amount of time allotted to address their problems also may lead workers to experience feelings of helplessness, impotence, revulsion, depletion, exploitation, and frustration. Because of their own values and backgrounds, which may be at great variance from or similar to those of the client, workers may be highly judgmental and critical in their attitudes toward such clients and may not wish to work with or try to impose their own values on them. Moreover, workers and agencies are not immune from the effects of racism and other types of discrimination. Practitioners' awareness of their own negative and stereotypical views, their skill in creating a safe, respectful, and accepting environment, their ability to help empower clients and advocate for them are crucial elements of effective intervention, and their participation in efforts to identify and modify prejudicial and nonresponsive agency policies and practices all are important ingredients to effective intervention (Goldstein & Noonan, 1999: 233–235).

CASE EXAMPLES

The following case examples are illustrative of how self psychological and object relations concepts and treatment principles are useful in the treatment of clients who are substance abusers, perpetrators of child maltreatment, and survivors of childhood sexual abuse.

SUBSTANCE ABUSE AND A GRANDIOSE SELF-STRUCTURE

In the example of Mr. Moore, which is based on a case that has been previously discussed elsewhere (Goldstein, 1995c), the client, who had an underlying narcissistic personality, had a relapse in which he began to abuse alcohol again when his grandiose self-structure was challenged by life events.

THE MOORE CASE Mr. Moore, a 54-year-old personnel recruiter, with a history of abstinence from alcohol for many years, began drinking excessively after being fired from work due to economic cutbacks and poor performance. This job was the last in a long series of ill-fated positions that had held out the promise of financial rewards that never materialized. Mr. Moore hid his drinking from his wife and pretended to look for work. Each day, he spent hours fantasizing about either going back into the theater or into his own business. His wife's income and their meager savings enabled them to survive. Mr. Moore was consumed with anger at himself for having ruined all of his opportunities for financial success and personal happiness as well as his sobriety. In response to his wife's threats to leave, he finally sought help from an outpatient psychiatry clinic, where he was given antidepressants and urged to return to Alcoholics Anonymous. He dropped out of treatment and then sought help again several months later after he caused a minor automobile accident while drinking and lost his license.

In sharing his background, Mr. Moore described his parents as self-involved, valuing performance, material success, and the opinions of others. He experienced them as emotionally unavailable, while his role in the family appeared to be one in which he provided admiration for his parents, both of whom were successful in business. He felt that they expected him to project the appearance of perfection to the outside world through his achievements. As long as he could remember, they told him he was destined for greatness, should not associate with others who were not as good as he was, and that he was lucky to come from such an intelligent family. At the same time, they were perfectionist in their expectations and hypercritical of him and were unavailable for companionship and nurturing. Mr. Moore spent time alone, enacting plays in front of the living room mirror and fantasizing about being famous, wealthy, and admired.

Although his parents wanted him to follow in their footsteps occupationally, they reluctantly allowed him to study music and theater. Rather than going to business school after college, Mr. Moore performed in small theater groups for a time and received some positive notices but began to feel that acting was beneath him. He found a position directing a small theater company, but his escalating drinking sabotaged his work. Dating attractive women who made him "look good" and upon whom he lavished whatever money he had, he found himself eventually bored by and resentful of them. After becoming sober with the help of Alcoholics Anonymous, he did not return to the theater, believing that others would remember that he was a "drunk." Instead, he opted to make money in various aspects of the business world while continuing to think of himself as an entertainer. Usually hating his jobs and employers, he felt he was too good for what he was doing and disappointed his management with his low productivity, inability to take even minor criticism, and surly attitude. He gave up several opportunities to return to acting and it was becoming more difficult for Mr. Moore to obtain work as he aged. He had squandered what little savings he had on the stock market in the hopes of making a killing. He often collected unemployment insurance and lived on a meager income with the help of his wife. When they met, she was charmed by his seeming self-confidence and dreams for the future. He found her attractive and enjoyed her admiration but always took her for granted and demeaned her intelligence. Over the years, she became disillusioned with him, and their relationship was characterized by silent resentment and little closeness. Mr. Moore sought one-night affairs with other women with whom he played the role of a wealthy businessman. It was harder for him to attract women now and to afford their company. He and his wife had one son, who was in college on scholarship. He was handsome, personable, and talented, but Mr. Moore was hypercritical of him.

Mr. Moore's drinking maintained his self-concept and regulated his self-esteem through grandiose fantasies that were at odds with his actual achievements and enabled him to drown his underlying low opinion of himself, his sense of failure, and his deep feelings of shame. His life was strewn with failed opportunities that reflected feelings of unworthiness, a lack of a sense of competence, and an inability to engage in the step-by-step process by which his goals and ambitions could be realized, reflecting severe problems in early idealization of his parents and their failure to provide attuned mirroring. Told that he was expected to be great but having never received attuned mirroring, and unable to idealize his parents, Mr. Moore's grandiose self became fixated as well. As he aged, the possibility of gaining acclaim, status, wealth, the ideal relationship, children, or the like became illusive and beyond reach. He began to feel that life had passed him by and he envied others who seemed successful. He negated any past achievements and became overwhelmed by feelings of failure, worthlessness, a sense of betrayal, bitterness, rage, and self-hatred that led to self-destructive behavior.

In the beginning of treatment, Mr. Moore described feeling deeply humiliated. Although he knew he should return to Alcoholics Anonymous, he could not bring himself to do so because he did not want to acknowledge his relapse to those who admired his apparently successful recovery from alcoholism. He was adamant about wanting to try drinking less, which he was able to do for a time.

The worker helped Mr. Moore to identify the role drinking was playing in helping him to maintain his view of himself and his fantasies about the future and to help him ward off his sense of failure and hopelessness about the future. He was able to acknowledge that he had lived in a dream world all his life, sustaining himself with fantasies of ultimately reclaiming his theatrical career and that now he felt that time had run out. As he became more in touch with his sense of despair, sessions were draining as the client expressed his bitterness about his relationships with his wife and son, his envy of anyone around him who was young, successful, or who loved their work, and acknowledged his own lack of capacity to love anyone. The worker and client were able to weather this period in the treatment with more frequent contact. This helped to solidify his feeling that the worker might be able to help him and he began to relinquish some of his need for control.

In exploring his past, the worker questioned some of the negative ways in which his parents had appeared to treat him and related to what this must have been like for him and how this led to his own early feelings of depression, failure, and inadequacy. Mr. Moore was able to understand how his active fantasy developed alongside his inability to pursue his goals and ambitions. Even in his desperation, he found it more acceptable to collect unemployment and depend on friends than to try to find a job.

During one period in which Mr. Moore was feeling particularly depressed about his life, his drinking escalated. The worker told him that she felt his efforts to control his drinking were not working and that she could not help him unless he returned to Alcoholics Anonymous, and offered to accompany him. Her stance both scared and touched him. Surprisingly, after some initial anger, he did what she asked, and quickly became abstinent. He remembered this later as a turning point.

When abstinent, Mr. Moore went through a very difficult period in which he began to mourn his relationships with his parents, his lost opportunities, wasted talent, and future opportunities. The sessions were extremely emotional and fraught. Any empathic lapses on the worker's part were followed by sullenness and withdrawal or accusations that the worker did not care about him. The worker acknowledged Mr. Moore's role in sabotaging his success during his life but also validated aspects of his struggles that he devalued. Mr. Moore began to be more hopeful and actually found work, albeit in a low-paying position. His twelve-step meetings enabled him to revitalize his friendship network, and his relationship with his son improved. While he tortured himself less, he still regarded his life as drudgery and did not really experience much pleasure. In response to his complaints that he could not write although he wanted to, the worker began encouraging him more actively by discussing ideas with him and suggested that he bring his writing into their sessions. As he began to do this, Mr. Moore seemed lighter in his mood and began to become more hopeful about the future. "Maybe I can't have what I always wanted, but I can find something that will make me feel productive." He and his wife had a rapprochement during this time, although they continued to live separately. Feeling better about himself and that he had something to offer as a father, Mr. Moore began to reach out to his son.

Discussion

Mr. Moore did not have any solid sense of self nor was he able to work toward achieving his goals and ambitions. He maintained a grandiose self-concept despite continual disappointments and failures through fantasies that one day he would "make it." The bubble that sustained this patient burst when his long-held belief that the future would be better dimmed. He returned to drinking to bolster his grandiosity and to ward off his despair. When he entered treatment, he still was not ready to give up drinking. His abstinence required that he develop a strong selfobject bond to the worker and overcome his sense of shame. Eventually he was able to return to Alcoholics Anonymous when the worker insisted that he do so. He was able to use the treatment to come to better terms with his failings and lost opportunities and to renew his investment in life.

CHILD MALTREATMENT AND THE FRUSTRATION OF SELFOBJECT NEEDS

In the following example, the client began to see her daughter as "bad" and strike out at her when she failed to meet the mother's selfobject needs.

THE NAPOLI CASE Ms. Napoli, a 19-year-old separated Italian-American mother of fraternal twins, Lisa and Anthony, ages 2 ½, was referred for help by a nurse in the hospital clinic that she attended for pediatric care. The nurse saw Ms. Napoli, who looked distraught, pulling Lisa's hair and yelling at her in the waiting room when the child was running around the waiting area and became concerned about the mother's parenting. She had no grounds for reporting Ms. Napoli to the child welfare authorities as a potentially abusive mother. She decided to urge her to speak to the social worker to get some pointers about how to deal with an active child and set up an appointment.

When Ms. Napoli met with the worker, she said she did not know why the nurse had referred her and had only kept the appointment because she had said she would. When the worker commented that she seemed angry and frightened, Ms. Napoli said, "How would you feel having someone tell you that you needed help taking care of your kid? I don't know what got into her or what she will do next if I didn't show up." The worker said that she would probably feel angry and frightened too but added that in her brief talk with the nurse, she had indicated that Ms. Napoli seemed overwhelmed and might benefit from talking things over with someone. The client shot back, "I don't know what you think you can do to help me. How do you know I need any help?" The worker responded that she didn't know whether she could be of help either because she did not know Ms. Napoli but that mothers with young children often feel a lot of demands on them and there were things that she could do to be helpful. "Maybe if you told me a little about yourself and your family, we could decide whether or not I can be of some assistance to you. I'd like to try."

Surprisingly, Ms. Napoli sat back in her chair and sighed. She apologized for her outburst and said that she has not been herself since her husband left her a year ago for another woman and then her mother passed away. "We never got along that well but she helped me out with the kids. It's funny, she was never there when I was young but she loved my kids." The worker learned that Ms. Napoli had been working as a waitress until she became pregnant and then had to stop. Her husband did not make enough money to support them, drank a lot, and was physically abusive to her. She was glad that he left, but she had to go on welfare. "I didn't know what else to do." Ms. Napoli was defensive about her parenting but acknowledged that she was not patient with the kids, especially Lisa. "I always wanted a daughter but I did not want to have children when I was so young. So I had twins. Anthony is okay. He was a good baby. He's very loving and affectionate and he listens to me and doesn't like it if he's not with me. Lisa's different. When I was pregnant, all I thought about was having a little girl and how close we would be, but right from the beginning, she was colicky and wouldn't stop crying. I couldn't stand that. I couldn't seem to calm her. My mother was better at it. Now she doesn't let me get close to her and she defies me. She has to learn that I'm her mother." The worker asked Ms. Napoli what she did to try to get Lisa to obey her. "I would never hurt her." The worker said that she could see that Ms. Napoli cared about her children but that if she was having trouble controlling her angry feelings, it was important for them to be able to talk about that so that they could prevent further problems. The client asked if the worker was going to report her to the child welfare authorities. The worker replied, "I hope that I don't have to. I will only do that if I think you have hurt or neglected the children or are at risk for doing so but I will tell you if I need to do that." The client started crying and said that she did not want to lose them. "I worry about myself sometimes. I get so angry. I mostly yell and sometimes I hit Lisa or pull her hair but I always stop myself from really hurting her. Something just comes over me when she doesn't listen to me or pushes me away. My father used to beat me as a child and I don't want to be like him. I don't know why I'm telling you all this. I don't know you. Why should I trust you?" The worker replied, "It's true that you don't know whether or not you can trust me, but it also sounds like you want to be a good mother and don't know how to reach Lisa. This is something I can help you with if you agree to come in to talk to me."

In later meetings, the worker learned more about Ms. Napoli's background. She was the youngest of four children and her mother went back to work when she was 2 or 3 years old because her father became disabled as a result of a work accident and his drinking worsened. Her mother was away all day and preoccupied with household chores and her husband's unreasonable demands in the evening. The mother delegated her care to her older adolescent sister, who wanted to have a life of her own. As a child, Ms. Napoli was expected to be perfect by her father, who would threaten and beat her if she cried or made too much noise. Her mother seemed not to be aware of what was going on at home in her absence or didn't care. The father died when Ms. Napoli entered adolescence. The mother seemed relieved and she was more attentive to Ms. Napoli. She was attending high school and dropped out in order to get a job. She had a relationship with an older man who seemed "crazy about her." They married when she became pregnant but he was an alcoholic and was verbally and at times physically abusive to her. He became sexually involved with another woman, moved out of the house, did not pay child support, and rarely visited. Soon after their separation, Ms. Napoli's mother, who had lived nearby and was her only source of support, died of a heart attack. Subsequently, Ms. Napoli felt more alone and frustrated.

Ms. Napoli had been abused a child and also had been deprived of the parental protection, nurturing, and attunement that was necessary for her to develop firm self-structures. She had low self-esteem, was unable to complete her education, and became involved in an abusive relationship with an alcoholic man with whom she had two children and who abandoned her. Unprepared for her parenting role and looking to her children to meet her own selfobject needs, Ms. Napoli struggled, with the help of her mother, to manage the children. After her husband left her and her mother died, Ms. Napoli, who was socially isolated, was thrown back on her own insufficient parenting resources. She became impatient with and frustrated by Lisa and wanted to hurt her but not wanting to repeat her own past history of being beaten, was able to exercise some restraint on acting-out her angry and violent impulses.

The worker tried to develop a relationship with Ms. Napoli in which some of her selfobject needs could be met in ways that had not been done previously, that would diminish her need for Lisa and Anthony to fulfill her needs, that would decrease her narcissistic rage when her needs were not met, and that would strengthen her ability to control her angry impulses and to parent Lisa and Anthony more effectively. The worker related empathically to Ms. Napoli's life experiences, especially to how her needs were not met and how this was affecting her current relationships with her children. She helped her to mourn for her mother and for the childhood she never had. She also enabled her to become more understanding of Lisa's and Anthony's needs as differentiated from her own and suggested new ways of trying to interact with them, and validated her efforts in this regard. The worker encouraged Ms. Napoli to join a mothers' group and to attend church activities in order to help her overcome her social isolation and gain support from others. The client gained considerable relief from the treatment process and became able to relate to her children in more nurturing ways. The worker also began to focus on helping Ms. Napoli identify how she might better herself and get on with her own life.

Discussion

In the case of Ms. Napoli, when her daughter, Lisa, whom she looked to as a selfobject, stimulated Ms. Napoli's feelings of childhood experiences of deprivation, abuse, and badness and frustrated her selfobject needs, Ms. Napoli experienced a narcissistic rage and lashed out at her to a degree and saw her as her "bad" child. With the help of an empathic and sustaining relationship with the worker, treatment enabled Ms. Napoli to get some of her selfobject needs met, to exercise control over her impulses and narcissistic rage, to become more able to nurture her children, to reach out to others, and to begin to move on with her own life.

INTRUSIVE THOUGHTS AND MEMORIES OF CHILDHOOD SEXUAL ABUSE

In the following example, the effects of the client's earlier sexual abuse began causing her more distress when the demands of her close relationships and work life stimulated her traumatic memories.

THE ESPINOSA CASE Ms. Espinosa, age 24, came for treatment at her boyfriend's urging because of her difficulties in allowing physical intimacy. She loved him and did not want to lose him. Her new job working as a legal secretary was another source of stress for her. She found herself to be quite agitated by the overtly critical comments, rude behavior, and unrealistic demands of many of the attorneys. Becoming anxious and not knowing how to assert herself appropriately, Ms. Espinosa withdrew and become less effective in her work, and she feared being let go.

Because of her feelings of shame and her fear of being judged, it was difficult for Ms. Espinosa to talk about what she was currently experiencing. The worker learned that the client was having intrusive thoughts and fragmented memories of her earlier sexual abuse when she and her boyfriend were physically intimate and this restricted her sexual performance and pleasure. Although her boyfriend said that he loved her and wanted to marry her, she became suspicious of his motives toward her when he approached her sexually. She wanted to avoid sex in order to keep herself from being overtaken by her unpleasant thoughts. She also was contemplating leaving her job despite the fact that it was the best one she ever had. She felt frightened every morning before leaving for work and continued to be anxious on the job lest an attorney speak to her in a harsh voice or show disappointment in her work. She suffered from headaches quite frequently and often had trouble sleeping through the night.

Ms. Espinosa was the oldest of two sisters born into a poor family who had immigrated to this country from Puerto Rico. Her father was a construction worker who was killed in an accident when Ms. Espinosa was a child. Her mother remarried several years later, and initially Ms. Espinosa liked the attention of her stepfather. She began to recall that starting when she was 12 to 15 years of age, he would repeatedly come into her room and lie on top of her and force her to engage in sexual behaviors. He repeatedly forced her to perform oral sex on him, stimulated her genitals manually to the point of orgasm, and threatened to have her sent away if she told anyone. She thought that her now-deceased grandmother found him in her room on at least one occasion, but her mother has denied any knowledge of the abuse. When Ms. Espinosa finally told her grandmother about the abuse, she was angry with her and told her she was imagining everything, but her stepfather's more flagrant behavior stopped. She felt he continued to stare at her, however, in peculiar ways. Her sister also did not believe her when she told her about these events recently, and her sister's attitude, along with the mother's denial, had been major sources of stress. She still felt frightened when she went to sleep at night and would stay awake listening for footsteps. She felt estranged from her family, and when she graduated from high school she got a job and went out on her own. She first worked as a waitress and then learned word processing. She had a series of poorly paying jobs but lacked the confidence to look for a better one until recently, when she took a position in a law firm.

Although Ms. Espinosa dated, she managed to avoid having sexual relations, which was a reason the relationships ended. When Ms. Espinosa met her current boyfriend, a law student, she felt he was different from the others and confided her past experiences and her fears of sex to him. He was gentle and patient with her, and she gradually became able to have some limited sexual contact and hoped he would be satisfied. He told her that he had a cousin who had been sexually abused and who had received help and was now happily married and had three children. He encouraged her to seek help and she finally did so reluctantly.

Although Ms. Espinosa did share the fact that she had been sexually abused by her stepfather and had some fragmented memories of the events, she felt too humiliated and frightened to go into these in any detail in the beginning of treatment. At the same time, the client felt pressured by her boyfriend and at work and verbalized feeling overwhelmed. "I have to do something fast, but I don't know what I can do." The worker tried to establish an accepting and safe therapeutic environment and also problem-solved with the client about how she could reduce the immediate stressors in her relationship and on the job in the short run in order to give herself some time and space to deal with her issues. The worker's attitude seemed to relieve the client and she was able to use the worker's suggestions to help her talk to her boyfriend about what she needed from him and to arrive at an understanding of what she could do to enable them to have at least some physical intimacy. Likewise, she was able to ask her supervisor at work to help her to negotiate her work assignments and relationships with the attorneys better.

Gradually, the client responded to the worker's empathic and gentle approach and her identifying and exploring Ms. Espinosa's understandable fear of trusting the worker by becoming more open in talking about herself. She was unsure about what anyone would find attractive and lovable about her. She was fearful of rejection, had difficulty knowing what she needed, wanted, or felt, and often complied with the wishes of others because it was easier to do so rather than assert herself. She liked her work but had to push herself because she worried about being able to meet employers' demands. She wished that sex were not that important in relationships because it was hard for her to imagine that she might feel more comfortable in a physical relationship. She knew that it was important for her to talk about her past sexual abuse but she didn't really want to. The worker tried to identify and support the client's strengths. An idealizing selfobject transference formed slowly and the worker and client were able to begin to delve more into Ms. Espinosa's earlier abuse.

The sessions in which the client spoke about her relationship with her stepfather and his actual abuse of her were painful to the client and to the worker. Starting with her intrusive thoughts and fragmented memories, the worker was able to help the client to fill in the details of what had occurred and how it had affected her. Worse than the sexual abuse was the client's feelings of having been betrayed by someone she looked to for nurturing, her loss of control and feelings of powerlessness, her fear, her sense of shame and guilt that her neediness had somehow caused the abuse to occur, and her sense of aloneness and feelings of being soiled and damaged. Likewise, Ms. Espinosa experienced great distress in discussing her relationship with her mother, whom she felt she had let down. She did not realize that it was her mother who had let *her* down, in failing to protect her and then in not believing her and that her stepfather had actually exploited and damaged her. As the client became more aware that she had not been allowed to be a child and that she was not to blame for her own abuse, she began to experience some anger at her family.

The worker helped the client to connect her earlier childhood experiences to the feelings that she was having in her relationship with her boyfriend and at work and focused on how to help her to exercise more control in those situations, to separate the current people with whom she was interacting from her family members, and to develop ways of soothing herself when she became anxious. Ms. Espinosa became increasingly able to engage in physical intimacy without feeling so frightened, although she still had trouble letting herself go completely. What was more important was that she felt more trusting of her boyfriend and more assertive with him. The two became emotionally closer and became engaged. The client kept her job and was fortunate in being assigned to an attorney who was "less obnoxious" than most. She was able to see that his moods did not always have to do with her and that "his bark was worse than his bite." She felt more hopeful about the future and for the first time since she was a child felt the lifting of a chronic low-level depression.

Discussion

In the Espinosa case, the client's childhood sexual abuse had interfered with the development of a solid sense of self, and the effects of her trauma affected many areas of her functioning. When she finally came for help, she was not able to deal with the memory work of the abuse until she felt accepted, safe, understood, and supported by the worker and formed a self-object transference. The worker was then able to help the client become more emotionally connected to what had befallen her, how it had influenced her personality and functioning, and how it was affecting her current relationship and work life.

SUMMARY

This chapter has described and illustrated some major implications of self psychology and object relations theory for understanding and working with clients who abuse alcohol and drugs, maltreat their children, and are survivors of childhood sexual abuse. It has emphasized the importance of the development of a selfobject transference, the provision of a highly individualized therapeutic holding environment, the meeting of selected selfobject needs, the development of insight and the establishment of an emotional connection to childhood experiences that contributed to clients' current problems, the strengthening of clients' personality structures, and the encouragement of new ways of relating to others and the world.

11

COUPLE AND FAMILY TREATMENT

There are many instances in which couples and families come for help because of difficulties in their interaction that they cannot resolve. Sometimes in work with children and adolescents in particular, the family itself requires treatment. Couples who come for treatment often show a history of chronic disharmony that has escalated, distance that has become painful, or disturbing symptoms in a child or adolescent in an otherwise seemingly "perfect" family. Difficulties in expressing feelings, problem-solving, and sustaining closeness, disappointments and misunderstandings, blaming, power struggles, competition, verbal aggression, and even physical violence may dominate couple and family relationships. Conflicts around autonomy and dependence, as well as fears of rejection, separation and abandonment, are commonplace. The partners cannot live together in peace and harmony but are unable to live apart. Offspring become triangulated into the couple interaction, are expected to meet the needs of both partners, are scapegoated, or are neglected and rejected.

Many couples and families who come for treatment find it hard to listen to and hear one another. This stems not only from their heightened degree of conflict but also from the fact that each member of the couple has a fixed view of and is unable to empathize with the other. They interpret one another's behavior in terms of their own reactions and cannot understand or accept that a partner may have different motivations and feelings than they have themselves. Sometimes each partner accuses the other of feeling and acting in ways that they feel and act themselves or they become upset with and try to control a child or adolescent's undesirable traits that resemble characteristics that the parents possess but cannot own up to. Even if partners or family members show an accurate perception of the unique ways a partner thinks and feels, they do not respect these differences and label them as "wrong" or "stupid."

Object relations and self psychological concepts and treatment principles can be applied to the treatment of couples and families. This chapter will present and illustrate these two somewhat different approaches.

OBJECT RELATIONS PERSPECTIVES

Object relations theory views couples as sharing problematic patterns of internalized object relations (Scharff & Scharff, 1987; Siegel, 1992; Slipp, 1988; Stewart, Peters, Marsh & Peters, 1975). Displaying intense transference reactions to one another, members of the couple often experience themselves as victimized children in relation to powerful parents. Each partner denies and splits off undesirable traits in himself or herself, projecting these onto the partner. He or she then reacts negatively or punitively to the object of the projections. As each partner projects selected split-off traits onto the partner, the other collusively accepts what has been projected and acts in accordance with the projection. Each may complain of feeling "set up" to respond in a particular way by the mate, only to be criticized or rejected for his or her reactions. Sometimes, it appears as if one member of the couple carries all the "badness" and the other all the "goodness," even if they sometimes exchange roles.

Because of the use of primitive defenses, each partner lacks an accurate perception of the provocative ways he or she behaves. In some situations, couples take on the appearance of possessing only "good" or idealized qualities so that their partnership seems "perfect" while they split off and project "bad" qualities outside the relationship, including onto offspring. As long as the splitting and projective identification continue, neither member of the dyad is forced to confront his or her own "unfavorable" traits.

SELF PSYCHOLOGICAL PERSPECTIVES

Alternatively, applications of self psychological theory to the treatment of couples and families view both partners as having selfobject needs—that is, needs for others to fulfill functions that they themselves cannot provide, that are archaic, urgent, and extreme (Schwartzman, 1984; Solomon, 1985, 1989). They tend to live out their earlier unfulfilled parental relationships quite dramatically when they mate, since fantasies of wholeness, total acceptance, and approval are activated (Solomon, 1985: 144). Selfobject failures and traumas at the hands of parents and significant others in childhood are reawakened. When selfobject needs are not met as a consequence of one or both partners failing to function as a mirroring or idealizing selfobject for the other, rage, depressive reactions, injured self-esteem, and fragmentation of the self may result.

The repetitive lack of recognition and failure to gratify one another's selfobject needs lead to mutually frustrating interactions. Each partner utilizes sometimes primitive defenses to protect him/herself from narcissistic injury and to preserve self-esteem and self-cohesion. Conflict, power struggles, and feelings of victimization result as one partner, for example, withdraws in order to preserve his or her autonomy and the other provokes a fight in order to maintain contact.

TREATMENT PRINCIPLES

Despite important differences, object relations and self psychological couple treatment share certain common features. Both models require a therapeutic atmosphere that is safe and facilitating and aims at helping the partners to perceive and relate to one another in terms of their "here and now" qualities rather than as representatives of their troubled development.

The worker who draws on object relations concepts and principles tries (1) to create a clear, firm, and consistent structure with boundaries against destructive acting-out, to show acceptance and neutrality, tolerate intense and unpleasant affects, and limit aggression so as not to permit excessive blaming, scapegoating, or loss of control; (2) to help the partners to identify their difficulty in supporting and providing "holding," the distortions in the way they perceive and relate, and the repetitive and rigid behavioral sequences that thwart sustained intimacy, collaboration, and appropriate dependence and autonomy; (3) to actively foster the partners' ability to provide more optimal "holding" for one another through suggestion and example; (4) to help partners accept traits and feelings in themselves that they have denied, disavowed, and projected onto one another, thereby lessening their distortions of one another; and (5) to identify the transference component of certain reactions by connecting them to past family-of-origin experiences, thereby helping the partners to separate the present from the past in order to free them to interact in terms of their "real" rather than their transference characteristics. Because the partners are entrenched in their feelings, attitudes, and behavioral patterns, even the worker's most tactful interventions may be experienced as confrontative and arouse considerable resistance.

While sharing some similarities to the object relations model, the self psychological treatment of couples and families has some major differences in emphasis and ways of intervening. Self psychological treatment relies more on the use of the worker's empathy and attunement to each partner's or family member's subjective experience and on interpreting and repairing selfobject failures, in contrast to the pointing out and interpretation of primitive defenses and collusive behavior that are employed in object relations therapy. The self psychologically informed worker attempts (1) to be attuned to each person's subjective experience through empathic immersion, acknowledge their individual and sometimes conflicting selfobject needs, and in some instances function as a selfobject; (2) to sensitize each partner to the other's needs and ways of thinking and feeling, thereby expanding the capacity for empathy; (3) to empathically comment on and relate to the needs underlying the repetitive dysfunctional interactions and the defensive patterns that take place; (4) to interpret the connection between past and present in order to help the partners understand and appreciate the origin of their own needs and fears, lessen the hold that developmental failures have on their relationship, and find better ways of gratifying their needs; (5) to help the partners learn to repair and restore their own positive connection when disruptions in their relationship occur; and (6) to non-defensively examine and acknowledge the worker's own empathic failure in order to repair and restore the selfobject transference between the couple and the worker.

When empathy is not sufficient to contain destructive behavior, the worker may need to be more active in setting limits and providing structure. This should be done, however, with an attitude of empathy and in collaboration with the couple rather than in a rigid and authoritarian manner. Some couples of this type display such unrelenting and destructive interactions, particularly in the beginning phase of treatment, that the worker may need to set limits or see each partner separately. Structuring the sessions in these ways may calm the system and allow the worker to engage each member of the couple more easily.

COUNTERTRANSFERENCE ISSUES

Object relations theory and self psychology embody different views of countertransference and its management. A major emphasis in object relations couple therapy is on the worker's role as a container for denied and disavowed feelings in the partners that are projected onto one another and onto the worker in order to relieve them of internal conflict. During the treatment, the worker becomes the object of the couple's projective defenses, which, because of their intense nature, stimulate strong feelings, or what has been termed "induced countertransference," in the worker. It is thought that such reactions can be used to inform the worker about the nature of internalized self- and object-representations that become manifested in interactions with partners and other family members (Siegel, 1992: 103–108). The worker uses his or her own countertransference in understanding the couple. He or she may sit with these feelings or use them to interpret the couple's defenses and dynamics.

The provision of optimal "holding" and "containment" necessitate that the worker understands and uses his or her countertransference positively; however, there is a tendency for those who work with certain highly charged and primitive couple or family interactions to experience feeling out of control and to become highly reactive. Anger, feelings of being shut out, rejected, devalued, and abandoned, retaliatory impulses, taking sides, and avoidant behavior are common. Frequently, workers may feel totally overwhelmed by the couple or are swept up into the unfolding drama, thereby losing their ability to intervene effectively.

The thrust in self-psychological treatment with respect to countertransference involves the worker's ability to remain empathically attuned to each partner. Rather than viewing the client as responsible for "inducing" reactions in the worker, self psychology sees both worker and client as shaping all aspects of the therapeutic situation. The worker must strive to understand how his or her own personality, belief systems, and needs influence therapeutic understanding and responses. For example, a worker, by virtue of his or her family-of-origin issues, relationship preferences and experiences, communication style, gender, age, ethnicity, values, personality, and archaic selfobject needs, will probably be better able to empathize with one partner than the other. The worker may have difficulties tolerating and accepting, let alone empathizing with, the attitudes and behavior of one or both of the partners. Even if the self psychologically informed worker is able to empathize equally with each partner, one or both may become upset if the worker seems too understanding or supportive of the other or when the worker is empathic with a partner who has conflicting needs or polarized perceptions. Striking a balance between helping each partner feel validated without appearing to be taking sides is a major therapeutic task. This is especially difficult with couples who are extremely needy of affirmation, competitive for nurture, and volatile.

In contrast to the object relations approach, self psychologists argue that a major countertransference pitfall is the worker's interpretation of apparently aggressive or provocative behavior as a manifestation of resistance or primitive defenses. Instead, the worker using self psychological concepts and treatment principles must relate empathically to the archaic selfobject needs and defenses against them that members of a couple show. Thus he or she must understand that individuals' needs for constant affirmation, feelings of rejection and disillusionment, outbursts of rage, sullenness and withdrawal, noninvolvement, glibness and superficiality, devaluation, missed appointments, nonpayment of fees, self-destructiveness, and acting-out are understandable reactions to actual failures in attunement, inabilities to meet selfobject needs, or anticipation and fear that such needs will not be met. This knowledge enables the worker to refrain from reacting to clients in countertherapeutic ways as he or she helps the partners identify their own selfobject needs, how these are frustrated, and how dysfunctional patterns result.

CASE EXAMPLES

The following case examples show the application of self psychological and object relations concepts and treatment principles to work with couples and families.

FRUSTRATED SELFOBJECT NEEDS AND NARCISSISTIC RAGE

In the example below, the couple, described elsewhere (Goldstein, 1997b), displayed a quite intense and volatile interaction that was related to the frustration of each of the partner's different selfobject needs and to the narcissistic rage reactions that ensued.

THE CASE OF PHIL AND JUDY Phil and Judy, a Jewish couple, ages 42 and 34 respectively, were married three years when they sought help at Phil's urging. Judy was six months pregnant when the new worker met with the couple. Phil began by launching an angry litany of accusations against Judy, who remained silent. When she did try to defend herself, Phil talked over her, saying, "You just don't get it" and seemed to be in a rage. After listening to Phil vent and watching Judy become more and more withdrawn, the worker asked Phil to take a deep breath so that Judy could react to what he was saying. Phil would not be stopped. When the worker suggested that in order to help both of them, it was important for her to understand Judy's point of view too, Phil allowed Judy to speak briefly and then interrupted her. Phil sought the worker's approval for his point of view. He asked, "What do you think of a person who acts the way Judy does?" He did not wait for an answer. In response to the worker's comment that he seemed to feel like he was "at the end of his rope" but that his continuous attack on Judy was not constructive, Phil said that he knew his attitude "stunk" but he did not care anymore. He wanted Judy to know how it felt to be yelled at and criticized all the time. Borrowing a line from the film *Network,* he said, "I'm not going to take it anymore. It's not my fault that I'm acting this way. It's her. She does not know how to be a partner and does not understand that our situation is urgent." By this he meant that he had told his wife repeatedly of his increasing business problems and the likelihood of declaring bankruptcy. He felt she did not hear him, since she kept spending as usual and asking him for money. Phil also complained that when Judy begrudgingly agreed to work in his office some months earlier, he had to fire her because she was so arrogant and insulting to the other employees. "I'm working as hard as I can to keep everything together, and I never once get a word of encouragement or appreciation from her or her parents." The worker commented that it was clear that Phil felt totally unsupported in the relationship but that Judy, too, seemed to be suffering. She went on to say that it was important for them to begin to hear one another. To her amazement, Phil and Judy thanked the worker for listening to them and agreed to return the following week.

In the second session, Phil continued with his diatribe against Judy but finally attempted to give her some opportunity to talk when the worker commented that she knew that he was obviously under enormous financial pressure, was feeling alone, and needed to get a lot "off his chest," but that if he truly wanted the situation to improve, he had to let Judy speak even if he totally disagreed with what she said. A different Judy then appeared, who began to systematically rebut each of Phil's accusations and to counterattack him in a condescending fashion for being irresponsible, sneaky, reckless with money, totally undisciplined, and secretive and too trusting of and generous with his business associates, who were taking advantage of him, while he gave her no priority at all. She recounted examples of Phil's impulsive spending, his lack of planning for the future, his extravagance with others financially, and his tightness with her. "You can buy a new sound system. Why do I have to keep asking you for the rent money?" Phil replied angrily, "Judy, there is *no* money." To which Judy responded, "I've heard that for two years. What's different? How do you expect me to believe you, when every time I look at your American Express bill, I see more charges for dinners, compact discs, clothes, and car rentals because of another accident? I need clothes and furniture for the baby. You say I'm not dealing with reality. What about you?" Phil retorted that he was trying to save his business, and Judy looked as though she wanted to kill him.

"You only think about your business but never about me and the baby. Do you ever ask me how *I'm* feeling? Do you ever try to get involved in the fact that you're going to be a father? You'll never be a success. You have great ideas, but you don't know how to follow through. You deal with your business the way you do everything else. You should just get a job. We don't have to make a lot of money." Turning to me, Judy said, "He's a total slob. He leaves his clothes all over the house. He's always losing his keys. He doesn't care how fast he's going when he's driving. Now he doesn't even have his license or own a checkbook. On some days he comes home early and watches television until he falls asleep. If he's so concerned about his business, why doesn't he work harder? I try to be there, but he completely shuts me out." Phil could not contain himself and said, "All I get is lectures from you. That's not listening." Judy replied that Phil wasn't telling me about how he sabotaged his own business by making completely wrong decisions. "If I try to help him he gets furious at me. Then he tries to punish me by not talking to me, and I'm supposed to want to jump into bed with him." At points when Phil yelled over her, Judy would also turn to the worker for approval, saying in an exasperated tone as if she were speaking about a bad child, "This is what it's like to try to talk to him. Yes, I do yell too much and I am critical, but do you blame me? How am I supposed to work right now? I'm expecting a baby in three months. He thinks that I don't worry about money, that I enjoy not working, and that I'm not looking for a job deliberately." Just at the point that Phil settled down but made a comment that upset Judy, she ran out of the office. Phil remained for another five minutes and spoke about how he didn't want the marriage to end.

In the next session, the worker decided to verbalize her understanding of how Phil and Judy were mutually frustrating one another and to stress the importance of their exploring each of their needs and disappointments in a calm way. "I see how frustrated, alone, hopeless, and fearful both of you are feeling. You can't even hear one another. Each of you seem to feel quite disappointed in the other. We need to talk about what you need from one another and how your needs are not being met." The couple became calmer until their battle reescalated. With each upsurge in fighting, the worker repeated that she understood that whenever they experienced one another as frustrating their needs they became more hopeless, and that this stimulated their attacking one another.

The worker asked Phil and Judy how they wanted to structure the sessions to ease their tension enough so that they could begin to sort out their difficulties and move forward. Both said that they wanted to try to make the marriage work and asked if the worker could meet with them separately before they came together again. Although the worker sensed that each wanted to make the worker an ally against the other, she nevertheless thought that seeing them separately would help them to feel more connected and might also calm the system.

The following picture of the couple's background emerged. Phil was the youngest of three sons and a daughter and grew up in their shadow, always feeling less competent than his siblings. He nevertheless was successful at sports until he suffered a knee injury. His father, a successful entrepreneur whom Phil admired, never gave him positive attention. He declared bankruptcy when Phil was an adolescent and the family experienced severe financial reversals. While they eventually recovered with his mother's help, Phil had to struggle financially and he lost faith in his father. He was closer to his mother and sister, who were sources of companionship and encouragement.

Judy never got along with her mother, who was extremely critical and self-involved, but idealized her father, who was very successful in business. Although they fought a great deal, he taught her a lot about the "tricks of the trade." Judy's mother was highly emotional and volatile; her father was the steadier one in the relationship and catered to her mother. Judy was quite dependent on her father still and had an angry and charged relationship with her mother; both parents were quite intrusive in her present life.

It seemed likely that Phil and Judy had very specific and highly charged expectations of one another that stemmed from their own families of origin. The worker learned that initially Phil found Judy's sense of independence and her admiration of him appealing. He thought she would be a steady and supportive force in his life and would not expect him to take care of her. He also hoped that Judy's father might take him into his successful business or help him in other ways should the need arise. Judy was excited by Phil's ambition, creativity, and energy and responded to his attention and willingness to share his ideas and feelings with her. Their relationship began to sour for Phil after he dissolved his business partnership with his oldest brother. Judy's father reneged on his offer to take Phil into his business. Meanwhile, Judy had stopped working and had difficulty finding a suitable job. Working in Phil's business at his request was highly stressful for both of them as Judy saw a different side of Phil and his dealings with others that distressed and frightened her. She became more vocal in offering him advice and more critical of his lack of organization and his difficulties managing his employees and clients. Phil felt Judy was making his business situation worse. After he fired her, they hardly spoke. Judy became more demanding and argumentative, and Phil became secretive, withholding, and punishing. Nevertheless they impulsively agreed to try to have a child and Judy quickly became pregnant.

In individual sessions, the worker was able to show empathy for each partner's ways of viewing the other and to validate and support each of them. Phil was able to deal with his anger at and resentment of Judy, to discuss his business problems and options, and his concerns about staying in a frustrating marriage. Judy was able to share her disappointment in and devaluation of Phil, to deal with her concerns about becoming a mother, and to cope with her parents more effectively.

Although Phil was impulsive, volatile, contradictory, self-sabotaging, unreliable, and much better at being insightful than integrating any of his perceptions into his behavior, he was dependent and overtly needy. This propelled him into relating to others and to developing a selfobject transference to the worker. He had some observing ego, which appeared in his sense of humor about himself. Phil was overwhelmed by his business problems and felt very alone. He demanded a great deal of ventilation time and validation for his efforts and used the worker as a sounding board with whom he could discuss concrete strategies for managing his business affairs and his relationship problems.

Judy, who was the more logical, organized, and responsible partner, protected her needy self with a somewhat rigid pseudo self-sufficiency, a grandiose and self-righteous sense of the correctness of her point of view, a shallowness in her capacity for intimacy or even more than superficial relatedness, a suspiciousness about seemingly positive motives that others showed, a lack of empathy for her own or others' feelings, which she viewed as weak, and a lack of psychological-mindedness. It was hard for the worker to feel connected to her as a person and she often felt inadequate along with a pressure to somehow prove her worth. In was necessary to spend what felt like an endless amount of time staying with Judy's accounts of day-to-day activities and her disappointments in and anger at Phil and her mother. Any attempt the worker made to show empathy for Judy's plight felt to her as if the worker was pitying her, so that the worker shifted to conveying her understanding of Judy's need to be self-sufficient. The worker allowed Judy to move at her own pace in her own way rather than comment on her seeming lack of connection and her contemptuousness. Gradually and repeatedly, the worker commented on how important it was to Judy, given her background, to have developed the characteristics that she had and how these had helped her survive, but also how she had paid a price in terms of her not knowing and valuing her own feelings, her fear of being emotionally dependent on someone who could hurt her, her anxiety about being made to feel wrong and bad as she had experienced so often in her life, and her lack of acceptance of her own needs for approval and support, which often made her see this need in others as weakness. Judy slowly began to become more interested in her own experiences growing up as they related to the ways she perceived herself and others and related to Phil. A turning point in the worker-client relationship came after the birth of her son, Josh. Because Judy did not have child care, she brought him to sessions and sometimes nursed him, changed his diapers, and played with him there. Although the worker felt quite self-conscious about her reactions to and behavior with the baby, she realized that Judy was presenting her needy infant self to the worker through bringing Josh to the sessions, and that the worker's ability to accept and show interest in her and the baby was important to her.

In working with the couple together, the worker helped both partners to become more aware of and empathic with one another's needs and expectations and how these were being frustrated, how their reactions were creating further obstacles to their supporting one another, and how some of their individual and couple problems stemmed from their own families of origin. It was necessary to manage their efforts to get the worker to take sides and to deal with their disappointment and frustration when the worker failed to respond as they wished. Although Phil and Judy's relationship was stormy, the couple was able to make considerable progress over six months of treatment with respect to establishing a sense of teamwork, managing finances, planning for the future, dealing with their in-laws, and parenting their son. Phil was able to bring his business to a conclusion and to take a reasonably well paying job that gave him an income and time to recoup his sense of well-being and professional reputation. Judy threw herself into being a rather attentive, if not somewhat mechanical and compulsive, mother. Phil gradually allowed himself to bond with his son and was quite attentive, although not always sensitive in his handling of Josh, which angered Judy. Their relationship showed an underlying tension, as Judy was quick to criticize Phil and remained disillusioned with him, to which Phil often reacted with volatility or withdrawal, but they found ways of coming together.

Discussion

In this case, the couple's rageful accusations of one another can be understood as their responses to the frustration of their selfobject needs at times of stress for both of them. In this connection, it seemed possible that Phil's anger was related to his loss of self-esteem as a result of his business problems, to his not being sufficiently appreciated by Judy, and to his feeling abandoned by her. He felt fearful of a business collapse, burdened that he had to do everything by himself without validation, disappointed in Judy as a partner, and apprehensive about becoming a father. Likewise, it seemed possible that Judy's demeaning and critical attitude toward Phil and her seeming denial of their financial problems reflected her deidealization of and disappointment in Phil, her fear of what would happen when she gave birth, her awareness of her dependence on him, and to her feelings of abandonment. Individual sessions helped each partner to form a selfobject transference to the worker and to get some selfobject needs met, and couple sessions enabled them both to become aware of and empathic with one another's needs and how they were being frustrated.

MUTUAL BLAMING RELATED TO SPLITTING AND PROJECTIVE IDENTIFICATION

In the following example, the couple's angry and accusatory interaction was related to their extensive use of primitive defenses.

THE CASE OF RICH AND NANCY When Rich, age 34, and Nancy, age 36, sought couples counseling, they were on the verge of separating again. Married for four years, they wanted to have a child but were fearful of doing so because of their constant fighting and incompatibility. Nancy felt pressured by her "biological clock." She wanted to resolve their problems and get on with their marriage or dissolve it so that she would have time to meet someone else and have a child. Counseling represented a last-ditch effort to see if they could make a go of the marriage.

The first session was acrimonious from the start. Nancy described Rich as critical, controlling, selfish, withholding of affection, and irresponsible. Rich's complaint was that Nancy had no right to accuse him of being irresponsible when she acted like a baby, expected him to take care of everything in addition to working to support them, and then got mad when he was too tired to listen to her or make love. Moreover, Rich accused Nancy of withholding sex when she wanted money and only being concerned about whether she had enough shoes. Nancy's response was that she could not believe that Rich thought she acted like a baby, when he was the one who had never grown up. "You always want everything your way or you pout, and if you buy one more piece of stereo equipment, I'm going to throw it out." Rich replied, "Fuck you! You always have to be in control." In an exasperated voice, Nancy said, "I have to be in control. Do you ever tell me anything about our financial situation or give me anything unless I beg you?"

From this interaction and information about the couple that the worked gleaned, it appeared that Rich and Nancy took turns assuming the roles of "good" parent and "bad" child. This pattern seemed to repeat the types of relationships that they had experienced earlier in their lives in their families of origin, in which they had been the youngest of their siblings and had parents who were very demanding, critical, domineering, and non-supportive. Each partner accused the other of displaying the very same qualities that each possessed and provoked the other into acting-out those characteristics in extreme ways, thus confirming the accusation. Both partners acted irresponsibly and were critical, controlling, selfish, and withholding. When they were angry at one another, they felt hatred that verged on violence. When their relationship was calmer, they acted as if they had no problems and never tried to talk anything through. Thus, Rich and Nancy either wanted to kill one another and erased anything good about their relationship or they denied all their differences.

In sessions the couple needed help in moving beyond their fighting. The worker accepted and showed empathy for what each partner was feeling but also set limits on their angry accusations and structured their communication so that they could listen to and be more empathic with one another. She was able to help them identify the ways in which they alternately played the role of parent and child and how each tended to see the other as having bad qualities and to deny having the very same characteristics. Likewise, the worker was able to help the couple to own their "black and white" or "all or nothing" ways of seeing their relationship.

In exploring their backgrounds, the worker helped the couple to get in touch with the issues in their early family relationships that they were replaying in their current relationship. This approach proved to be an eye opener for both partners and ushered in a very fruitful period in which they were able to take some distance from their acrimonious interaction and examine the family-of-origin dynamics that were contributing to their dysfunctional ways of relating. Finally, the worker was able to help the partners to be more sensitive to and supportive of one another.

Discussion

In this example, Rich and Nancy's tendencies to engage in splitting and projective identification were creating a highly tumultuous and frustrating interaction that bore some resemblance to what they each had experienced in their families of origin. Treatment helped to structure their communication, to help them recognize and modify their tendency to use primitive defenses, to enable them to link their family-of-origin issues to their current interaction, and to develop more positive ways of relating to one another.

THE FAMILY SCAPEGOAT

In the following case, the parents portrayed themselves as perfect and blamed their daughter for upsetting the family.

THE BUSH CASE Mr. and Mrs. Bush and their daughter Darlene, age 19, were referred for family therapy as part of a discharge plan. Darlene had been hospitalized for several days for tests after the parents learned of her deliberate vomiting episodes as part of her bulimia. She became frightened when she saw blood and told her parents, who called the family doctor.

In their first session, both parents spoke about their inability to understand and their frustration with Darlene. They were clearly furious at her "for not wanting to help herself." They felt they had given her everything and didn't know why she was wasting her life. By this they meant that Darlene had dropped out of college after her first semester, was not working, and was much too dependent on them for companionship. They were tired of giving her money, which she spent on food. Almost in unison, the parents said, "We don't know what to do to help you. You have your life ahead of you. Why are you messing it up?" In response to their harangue, Darlene became increasingly withdrawn and self-disparaging, commenting on her having disappointed them because she was just not smart or independent enough. The more silent Darlene became, the more the parents attacked her. "Why don't you say something? Are you listening to us?" Over a number of meetings, the worked gathered the following picture of the family. Both parents grew up in Boston and came from poor Irish Catholic families. They were the oldest of many siblings, and a great deal was expected of them while little was given to them in terms of nurture or encouragement. Nevertheless, the parents prided themselves on having been independent, hardworking, ambitious, and as "pulling themselves up by the bootstraps." When they married after finishing college, which they attended with the help of scholarships and part-time work, they moved to New York and Mr. Bush began a successful career in business. The couple achieved what they thought was a financially secure and perfect life that was a far cry from their wretched childhoods. They said that they always got along well and had no real conflicts. Their first child, a son, was all that they wanted him to be. "We are very proud of him. From the time he was a baby, he never has given us a moment's concern. He's strong, independent, intelligent. He graduated college *cum laude* and is in law school." In contrast, the parents described Darlene as different from everyone else in the family. "She was a needy child and has always been dependent, sensitive, shy, and easily hurt. We always tried to encourage her to be independent and outgoing. She just doesn't try. She gives up. We have always had busy lives. We can't always be there for her." Darlene said that her parents' description of her was accurate. She never felt very confident about herself and was very lonely as a child and never was a good student. She felt lost when she graduated from a small suburban high school and went to a large university in Boston, where her bulimia began. She wished that she could make her parents proud of her but felt that the only thing she was good at was having problems.

Both the parents and Darlene seemed to agree that she was the problem in the family, but it seemed to the worker that Darlene was locked into her role as the inadequate and dependent member of the family because she carried these "bad" traits for the parents while her brother embodied all their "good" characteristics. The worker thought that the parents maintained their own sense of perfection and goodness by disavowing any qualities in themselves that did not conform to their idealized self-images and then projecting them onto Darlene. She accepted their projections and acted in accordance with them.

In sessions, the worker tried to diffuse the family scapegoating of

Darlene. Initially, she had to actively intervene repeatedly to interrupt and set limits on their verbal accusations in order to enable them to listen to one another. The worker tried to create an accepting and nonjudgmental therapeutic environment in which she related empathically to each family member's feelings—for example, the parents' disappointment and frustration with Darlene and Darlene's feelings of failure and tendency to give up. The worker began to point out some of the dysfunctional ways in which both the parents and Darlene spoke to and interacted with one another, particularly their collusive pattern of the parents blaming Darlene and her accepting the blame. The worker indicated that she thought that the parents were locked in a pattern of relating to Darlene that was being influenced by their past family-of-origin experiences.

Through the exploration of the parents' backgrounds, the worker helped them to get in touch with some of the pain of their own childhoods that they had tried so hard to get away from. It was possible to help the parents to reflect on how important it was for each of them to see themselves as strong and independent and to block out their more vulnerable qualities, and to consider how their view of Darlene as embodying all of their undesirable traits forced her into a rigid role from which she could not escape and which did not accurately reflect Darlene's true self. Likewise, the worker helped Darlene to see how she had taken on the role her parents had assigned to her in order to please them in some way but that her bulimia was an expression of her need to break out of that rigid and distorted role. The worker also tried to foster better communication and more positive ways of relating—for example, asking questions rather than lecturing, asserting needs and feelings rather than withdrawing into silence, and supporting and encouraging rather than admonishing. Over time, the parents were able to lessen their scapegoating of Darlene and she was able to assert more of her self.

Discussion

In this example, the parents projected their own disavowed traits onto Darlene and she accepted them, so that a rigid collusive pattern was established. Family treatment provided a safe environment in which the blaming, splitting, projective identification, and collusive interaction could be identified and modified and in which more positive forms of relating could be established.

SUMMARY

This chapter has considered the practice applications of self psychological and object relations concepts and treatment principles to couple and family therapy. It has identified some of the salient features that are common to and distinctive of each approach and has illustrated their use. Of particular importance in couple and family treatment are the worker's ability to create a therapeutic holding environment in which each family member can feel safe to express himself or herself, the enhancement of each person's capacity for empathy, the identification of how selfobject needs are frustrated and how primitive defenses and dysfunctional interactions are distorting perceptions, the improvement of each member's capacity to fulfill selfobject needs and to provide holding, the modification of primitive defenses and dysfunctional patterns of relating, and the enhancement of more positive interactions.

REFERENCES

Adler, G. (1985). *Borderline psychopathology and its treatment.* New York: Jason Aronson.

Adler, G. & Buie, D. H. (1979). Aloneness and borderline pathology: The possible relevance of child development issues. *International Journal of Psycho-Analysis,* 60, 83–96.

Ainsworth, M. D. S. (1973). The development of mother-infant attachment. In B. Caldwell & H. Ricciuti (Eds.) *Review of child development research* (Vol. 3, pp. 1–94). Chicago: University of Chicago Press.

American Psychiatric Association (1994). *Diagnostic criteria from DSM-IV™.* Washington, DC: American Psychiatric Association.

Applegate. J. S. & Bonovitz, J. M. (1995). *The facilitating partnership.* Hillsdale, NJ: Jason Aronson.

Aron, L. (1992). The patient's experience of the analyst's subjectivity. *Psychoanalytic Dialogues,* 1, 29–51.

——— (1996). *A meeting of minds: Mutuality in psychoanalysis.* Hillsdale, NJ: Analytic Press.

Asbury, H. (1990). The evolution of the self through optimal gratification. *Clinical Social Work Journal,* 18, 131–144.

Bacal, H. A. (1985). Optimal responsiveness and the therapeutic process. In A. Goldberg (Ed.), *Progress in self psychology,* (Vol. 1, pp. 202–227). Hillsdale, NJ: Analytic Press.

——— (1991). Notes on the relationship between object relations theory and self psychology. In A. Goldberg (Ed.), *The evolution of self psychology: Progress in self psychology,* (Vol.7, pp. 36–44). Hillsdale, NJ: Analytic Press.

Bacal, H. A. (Ed.). (1998). *Optimal responsiveness: How therapists heal their patients.* Northvale, NJ: Jason Aronson.

Bacal, H. A. & Newman, K. M. (1990). *Theories of object relations: Bridges to self psychology.* New York: Columbia University Press.

Baker, H. S. (1991). Short-term psychotherapy: A self psychological approach. In J. P. Barber & P. Crits-Christoph (Eds.), *Handbook of short-term dynamic psychotherapy* (pp. 287–318). New York: Basic Books.

Balint, M. (1968). *The basic fault: Therapeutic aspects of regression.* New York: Brunner/Mazel.

Basch, M. F. (1988). *Understanding psychotherapy.* New York: Basic Books.

Beebe, B. & Lachman, F. (1988a). Mother-infant mutual influence and precursors of psychic structure. In A. Goldberg (Ed.), *Frontiers in self psychology: Progress in self psychology,* (Vol. 3, pp. 2–26). Hillsdale, NJ: Analytic Press.

——— (1988b). The contribution of mother-infant mutual influence to the origins of self and object representations. *Psychoanalytic Psychology,* 5, 305–337.

——— (1994). Representation and internalization in infancy. Three principles of salience. *Psychoanalytic Psychology,* 11, 127–165.

Bellak, L., Hurvich, M. & Gediman, H. (Eds.), (1973). *Ego functions in schizophrenics, neurotics, and normals.* New York: John Wiley.

Benedek, T. (1959). Parenthood as a developmental phase: A contribution to the libido theory. *Journal of the American Psychoanalytic Association, 7*, 389–417.

Benjamin, J. (1988). *The bonds of love: Psychoanalysis, feminism, and the problem of domination.* New York: Pantheon.

Berzoff, J. (1996). Psychodynamic theory and the psychology of women. In J. Berzoff, L. M. Flanagan & P. Hertz (Eds.), *Inside out and outside in* (pp. 247–266). Northvale, NJ: Jason Aronson.

Berzoff, J., Flanagan, L. M. & Hertz, P. (Eds.). (1996). *Inside out and outside in.* Northvale, NJ: Jason Aronson.

Bion, W. (1962). *Learning from experience.* New York: Jason Aronson.

—— (1967). *Second thoughts.* New York: Basic Books.

Biringen, Z. (1994). Attachment theory and research: Application to clinical practice. *American Journal of Orthopsychiatry, 64*, 404–420.

Blake-White, J. & Kline, C. M. (1985). Treating the dissociative process in adult victims of childhood incest. *Social Casework: The Journal of Contemporary Social Work, 66*, 394–402.

Blanck, G. & R. (1974). *Ego psychology in theory and practice.* New York: Columbia University Press.

—— (1979). *Ego Psychology II: Psychoanalytic developmental psychology.* New York: Columbia University Press.

Bowlby, J. (1958). The nature of the child's tie to the mother. *International Journal of Psycho-Analysis, 39*, 350–373.

—— (1969). *Attachment and loss. Vol. I: Attachment.* New York: Basic Books.

—— (1973). *Attachment and loss. Vol. II: Separation: Anxiety and Anger.* New York: Basic Books.

Brandchaft, B. & Stolorow, R. D. (1984a). The borderline concept: Pathological character or iatrogenic myth? In J. Lichtenberg, M. Bornstein & D. Silver (Eds.), *Empathy II.* (pp. 333–358). Hillsdale, NJ: Analytic Press.

Brandchaft, B. & Stolorow, R. D. (1984b). A current perspective on difficult patients. In P. E. Stepansky & A. Goldberg (Eds.), *Kohut's legacy: Contributions to self psychology* (pp. 117–134). Hillsdale, NJ: Analytic Press.

Brandell, J. R. & Perlman, F. T. (1997). Psychoanalytic theory. In J. R. Brandell (Ed.), *Theory and practice in clinical social work* (pp. 38–82). New York: Free Press.

Brooks-Gunn, J. & Kirsh, B. (1984). Life events and the boundaries of midlife for women. In G. Baruch & J. Brooks-Gunn (Eds.) *Women in mid-life* (pp. 11–30). New York: Plenum Press.

Burch, B. (1988). Melanie Klein's work: An adaptation to practice. *Clinical Social Work Journal, 16*, 125–142.

—— (1997). *Lesbian/bisexual experience and other women: Psychoanalytic views on women.* New York: Columbia University Press.

Butler, R. (1963). The life review: An interpretation of reminiscence. *Psychiatry, 26*, 65–76.

Cashdan, S. (1988). *Object relations therapy.* New York: W. W. Norton.

Cheschier, M. W. (1985). Some implications of Winnicott's concept for clinical practice. *Clinical Social Work Journal, 13*, 218–233.

Chodorow, N. (1978). *The reproduction of mothering.* Berkeley: University of California Press.

Consolini, G. (1999). Kernberg versus Kohut: A study in contrasts. *Clinical Social Work Journal, 27*, 71–86.

Corwin, M. D. (1996). Early intervention strategies with borderline clients. *Families in Society: The Journal of Contemporary Human Services, 77*, 40–49.

Courtois, C. A. (1988). *Healing the incest wound*. New York: W. W. Norton.

DeLaCour, E. (1996). The interpersonal school and its influence on current relational theories. In J. Berzoff, L. M. Flanagan & P. Hertz (Eds.), *Inside out and outside in* (pp. 199–220). Northvale, NJ: Jason Aronson.

Drescher, J. (1998). *Psychoanalytic therapy and the gay man*. Hillsdale, NJ: Analytic Press.

Dublin, P. (1992). Severe borderlines and self psychology. *Clinical Social Work Journal, 20,* 285–294.

Dyer, R. (1983). *Her father's daughter: The work of Anna Freud*. New York: Jason Aronson.

Edward, J., Ruskin, J. & Turrini, P. (1981). *Separation-individuation: Theory and application*. New York: Gardner Press.

Edward, J. & Sanville, J. (Eds.). (1996). *Fostering healing and growth*. Northvale, NJ: Jason Aronson.

Ehrenberg, D. B. (1995). Self-disclosure: Therapeutic tool or indulgence? *Contemporary Psychoanalysis, 31*, 213–228.

Eldridge, A. & Finnican, M. (1985). Applications of self psychology to the problem of child abuse. *Clinical Social Work Journal, 13*, 50–61.

Elson, M. (1986). *Self psychology in clinical social work*. New York: W. W. Norton.

Erikson, E. (1950). *Childhood and society*. New York: W. W. Norton.

——— (1959). Identity and the life cycle. *Psychological Issues*, I, 50–100.

Evans, K. & Sullivan, J. M. (1990). *Dual diagnosis: Counseling the mentally ill substance abuser*. New York: Guilford Press.

Fairbairn, W. R. D. (1940). Schizoid factors in the personality. In W. R. D. Fairbairn, *Psychoanalytic studies of the personality* (pp. 2–27). London: Routledge & Kegan Paul, 1952.

——— (1943). The repression and return of bad objects (with special reference to the 'war neuroses'). In W. R. D. Fairbairn, *Psychoanalytic studies of the personality* (pp. 59–81). London: Routledge & Kegan Paul, 1952.

——— (1952). *Psychoanalytic studies of the personality*. London: Routledge & Kegan Paul, 1952.

——— (1954). *An object relations theory of the personality*. New York: Basic Books.

Fish, B. (1996). Clinical implications of attachment narratives. *Clinical Social Work Journal, 24*, 239–254.

Fosshage, J. L. (1992). The selfobject concept: A further discussion of three authors. In A. Goldberg (Ed.), *New therapeutic visions: Progress in self psychology* (Vol. 8, pp. 229–240). Hillsdale, NJ: Analytic Press.

——— (1998). Self psychology and its contributions to psychoanalysis. *Journal of Analytic Social Work, 5*, 1–18.

Fraiberg, S., Adelson, E. & Shapiro, V. (1975). Ghosts in the nursery. *American Academy of Child Psychiatry, 14*, 387–421.

Freud, S. *The standard edition of the complete psychological works of Sigmund Freud*. 24 vols. J. Strachey (Ed.). London: Hogarth Press, 1953–1956.

——— (1900). The interpretation of dreams. In *The standard edition*. Vols. 4 and 5. London: Hogarth Press, 1955.

——— (1905). Three essays on the theory of sexuality. In *The standard edition*. Vol. 7. London: Hogarth Press, 1953.

——— (1923). The ego and the id. In *The standard edition*. Vol. 19. London: Hogarth Press, 1961.

———— (1926). Inhibitions, symptoms, and anxiety. In *The standard edition*. Vol. 20. London: Hogarth Press, 1959.

———— (1933). Anxiety and the instinctual life. Lecture XXXII. New introductory lectures in psychoanalysis. In *The standard edition*. Vol. 23. London: Hogarth Press, 1964.

———— (1940). An outline of psychoanalysis. In *The standard edition*. Vol. 23. London: Hogarth Press, 1964.

Galatzer-Levy, R. M. (1991). Introduction: Self psychology searches for its self. In A. Goldberg (Ed.), *The evolution of self psychology: Progress in self psychology* (Vol. 7, pp. xi–xviii). Hillsdale, NJ: Analytic Press.

Gay, P. (1988). *Freud: A life for our time*. New York: W. W. Norton.

Gilligan, C. (1982). *In a different voice: Psychological theory and women's development*. Cambridge, MA: Harvard University Press.

Glassgold, J. M. & Iasenza, S. *Lesbians and psychoanalysis*. New York: Free Press, 1995.

Goldberg, A. (1988). *A fresh look at psychoanalysis*. Hillsdale, NJ: Analytic Press.

Goldstein, E. G. (1983). Issues in developing systematic research and theory. In A. Rosenblatt & D. Waldfogel (Eds.), *Handbook of Clinical Social Work* (pp. 5–25). San Francisco: Jossey-Bass.

———— (1984). *Ego psychology and social work practice*. New York: Free Press.

———— (1990). *Borderline disorders: Clinical models and techniques*. New York: Guilford Press.

———— (1994). Self-disclosure in treatment: What therapists do and don't talk about. *Clinical Social Work Journal, 22*, 417–433.

———— (1995a). *Ego psychology and social work practice* (2nd ed.). New York: Free Press.

———— (1995b). The psychosocial approach. In *Encyclopedia of Social Work* (19th ed., pp. 1948–1954). Washington, DC: National Association of Social Workers.

———— (1995c). When the bubble bursts: Narcissistic vulnerability in the middle years. *Clinical Social Work Journal, 23*, 401–416.

———— (1996). What is clinical social work? Looking back to move ahead. *Clinical Social Work Journal, 24*, 89–104.

———— (1997a). To tell or not to tell: Self-disclosure of events in the therapist's life to the patient. *Clinical Social Work Journal 25*, 41–58.

———— (1997b). Countertransference reactions to borderline couples. In M. F. Solomon & J. P. Siegel (Eds.), *Countertransference in couples therapy* (pp. 72–86). New York: W. W. Norton.

———— (1999). Short-term treatment of the borderline patient. *Psychoanalytic Social Work, 6*, 87–111.

Goldstein, E. G. & Gonzalez-Ramos, G. (1989). Toward an integrative clinical practice perspective. In S. M. Ehrenkranz, E. G. Goldstein, L. Goodman & J. Seinfeld (Eds.), *Clinical social work with maltreated children and their families: An introduction to practice* (pp. 21–37). New York: New York University Press.

Goldstein, E. G. & Noonan, M. E. (1999). *Short-term treatment and social work practice*. New York: Free Press.

Gonzalez-Ramos, G. & Goldstein, E. G. (1989). Child maltreatment: An overview. In S. M. Ehrenkranz, E. G. Goldstein, L. Goodman & J. Seinfeld (Eds.), *Clinical social work with maltreated children and their families: An introduction to practice* (pp. 3–20). New York: New York University Press.

Greenberg, J. R. & Mitchell, S. A. (1983). *Object relations in psychoanalytic theory*. Cambridge, MA: Harvard University Press.

Greenes, J. M. (1987). The aged in psychotherapy: Psychodynamic contributions to the treatment process. In J. Sadovy & M. Leszcz (Eds.), *Treating the elderly with psychotherapy.* (pp. 64–75). Madison, WI: International Universities Press.

Greenson, R. (1974). Transference: Freud or Klein. *International Journal of Psycho-Analysis,* 55, 37–48.

Grunes, J. M. (1982). Reminiscence, regression and empathy—A psychotherapeutic approach to the impaired elderly. In S. I. Greenspan & G. H. Pollock (Eds.), *The course of life* (Vol. 3, pp. 545–560). Washington: DC: National Institute of Mental Health.

Gunderson, J. G. & Chu, J. A. (1993). Treatment implications of past trauma in borderline personality disorder. *Harvard Review of Psychiatry,* 1, 75–81.

Guntrip, H. (1961). *Personality structure and human interaction.* New York: International Universities Press.

———— (1969). *Schizoid phenomena, object relations, and the self.* New York: International Universities Press.

———— (1973). *Psychoanalytic theory, therapy, and the self.* New York: Basic Books.

———— (1975). My experience of analysis with Fairbairn and Winnicott. *International Review of Psychoanalysis,* 2, 145–156.

Hamilton, G. (1958). A theory of personality: Freud's contribution to social work. In H. J. Parad (Ed.), *Ego psychology and dynamic casework* (pp. 11–37). New York: Family Service Association of America.

Hanna, E. A. (1993a). The implications of shifting perspectives in countertransference on the therapeutic action of clinical social work part I: The classical and early-totalist position. *Journal of Analytic Social Work,* 1, 25–52.

Hanna, E. A. (1993b). The implications of shifting perspectives in countertransference on the therapeutic action of clinical social work part II: The recent-totalist and intersubjective position. *Journal of Analytic Social Work,* 1, 53–80.

Hartmann, H. (1939). *Ego psychology and the problem of adaptation.* New York: International Universities Press.

Herman, J. (1992). *Trauma and recovery.* New York: Basic Books.

Herman, J., Perry, J. C. & van der Kolk, B. (1989). Childhood trauma in borderline personality disorder. *American Journal of Psychiatry,* 146, 490–495.

Hoffman, I. Z. (1983). The patient as interpreter of the analyst's experience. *Contemporary Psychoanalysis,* 19, 389–422.

Horney, K. (1945). *Our inner conflicts.* New York: W. W. Norton.

Hughes, J. M. (1989). *Reshaping the psychoanalytic domain.* Berkeley: University of California Press.

Isay, R. A. (1989). *Being homosexual: Gay men and their development.* New York: Farrar, Strauss, & Giroux.

Jackson, H. (1991). *Using self psychology in psychotherapy.* Northvale, NJ: Jason Aronson.

———— (1964). *The self and the object world.* New York: International Universities Press.

———— (1971). *Depression.* New York: International Universities Press.

Jones, E. (1953). *The life and work of Sigmund Freud* (Vol. 1), New York: Basic Books.

Jordan, J. (1990). Relational development through empathy: Therapeutic applications. *Works in Progress* (40, pp. 11-40). Wellesley, MA: The Stone Center for Developmental Services and Studies.

Kaplan, A. & Surrey, J. L. (1984). The relational self in women: Developmental theory and public policy. In L. Walker (Ed.), *Women and mental health policy*. Beverly Hills, CA: Sage Publications.

Kernberg, O. F. (1974). Further contributions to the treatment of narcissistic personalities. *International Journal of Psycho-Analysis, 55*, 215–240.

——— (1975). *Borderline conditions and pathological narcissism*. New York: Jason Aronson.

——— (1976). *Object relations theory and clinical psychoanalysis*. New York: Jason Aronson.

——— (1984). *Severe personality disorders*. New Haven: Yale University Press.

Kernberg, O. F., Selzer, M. A., Koenigsberg, H. W., Carr, A. C. & Appelbaum, A. H. (1989). *Psychodynamic psychotherapy of borderline patients*. New York: Basic Books.

Khan, M. M. R. (1975). Introduction. In D. W. Winnicott, *Through paediatrics to psycho-analysis* (xi–xxxxix). New York: Basic Books.

Klein, M. (1948). *Contributions to psychoanalysis, 1921–1945*. London: Hogarth Press.

——— (1957). *Envy and gratitude*. New York: Basic Books.

Kohut, H. (1957). Introspection, empathy and psychoanalysis. An examination of the relationship between mode of observation and theory. In P. H. Ornstein (Ed.), *The search for the self: Selected writings of Heinz Kohut: 1950–1978*, (Vol. 1, 205–232). New York: International Universities Press.

——— (1966). Forms and transformations of narcissism. *Journal of the American Psychological Association, 14*, 243–278.

——— (1971). *The analysis of the self*. New York: International Universities Press.

——— (1977). *The restoration of the self*. New York: International Universities Press.

——— (1984). *How does analysis cure?* A. Goldberg & P. Stepansky (Eds.), Chicago: University of Chicago Press.

Kohut, H. & Wolf, E. S. (1978). Disorders of the self and their treatment. *International Journal of Psycho-Analysis, 59*, 413–425.

Kroll, J. (1993). *PTSD/borderlines in therapy*. New York: W. W. Norton.

Lazarus, L. W. (1991). Elderly. In H. Jackson (Ed.), *Using self psychology in psychotherapy* (pp. 135–149). Northvale, NJ: Jason Aronson.

Levin, J. (1991). When the patient abuses alcohol. In H. Jackson (Ed.), *Using self psychology in psychotherapy* (pp. 203–222). Northvale, NJ: Jason Aronson.

Levine, S. S. (1996). *Useful servants*. Northvale, NJ: Jason Aronson.

Lichtenberg, J. (1989). *Psychoanalysis and motivation*. Hillsdale, NJ: Analytic Press.

Linehan, M. M. (1993). *Cognitive-behavioral treatment of borderline personality disorder*. New York: Guilford Press.

Magid, B. (1984). Some contributions of self psychology to the treatment of borderline and schizophrenic patients. *Dynamic Psychotherapy, 2*, 101–111.

Main, M. & Solomon, J. (1990). Procedures for identifying infants as disorganized-disoriented in the Ainsworth strange situation. In M. Greenberg, D. Cicchetti & M. Cummings (Eds.), *Attachment in the pre-school years* (pp. 121–160). Chicago: University of Chicago Press.

Mahler, M. S. (1951). On child psychosis and schizophrenia: Autistic and symbiotic infantile psychosis. In *Psychoanalytic Study of the Child* (Vol. 7, pp. 286–305). New York: International Universities Press.

———— (1968). *On human symbiosis and the vicissitudes of individuation.* New York: International Universities Press.

———— (1971). A study of the separation-individuation process and its possible application to borderline phenomena in the psychoanalytic situation. *Psychoanalytic Study of the Child* (Vol. 26, pp. 403–424). New York: International Universities Press.

———— (1972). On the first three phases of the separation-individuation process. *International Journal of Psycho-Analysis,* 53, 333–338.

Mahler, M. S., Pine, F. & Bergman, A. (1975). *The psychological birth of the human infant.* New York: Basic Books.

Maroda, K. J. (1999). *Seduction, surrender, and transformation.* Hillsdale, NJ: Analytic Press.

Masterson, J. F. (1972). *Treatment of the borderline adolescent.* New York: Wiley-Interscience.

———— (1976). *Treatment of the borderline adult.* New York: Brunner-Mazel.

Masterson, J. F. & Rinsley, D. (1975). The borderline syndrome: The role of the mother in the genesis and psychic structure of the borderline personality. *International Journal of Psycho-Analysis,* 56, 163–77.

Mattei, L. (1996). Coloring development: Race and culture in psychodynamic theories. In J. Berzoff, L. M. Flanagan & P. Hertz (Eds.), *Inside out and outside in* (pp. 221–246). Northvale, NJ: Jason Aronson.

McMillen, J. C. (1992). Attachment theory and clinical social work. *Clinical Social Work Journal,* 20, 205–218.

Miller, J. B. (1977). *Toward a new psychology of women.* Boston: Beacon Paperback.

Mishne, J. M. (1989). Individual treatment. In S. M. Ehrenkranz, E. G. Goldstein, L. Goodman & J. Seinfeld (Eds.), *Clinical social work with maltreated children and their families: An introduction to practice* (pp. 38–61). New York: New York University Press.

———— (1993). *The evolution and application of clinical theory.* New York: Free Press.

Mitchell, S. A. (1988). *Relational concepts in psychoanalysis: An integration.* Cambridge, MA: Harvard University Press.

———— (1993). *Hope and dread in psychoanalysis.* New York: Basic Books.

Mitchell, S. A. & Black, M. J. (1995). *Freud and beyond.* New York: Basic Books.

Modell, A. H. (1975). A narcissistic defense against affects and the illusion of self-sufficiency. *International Journal of Psycho-Analysis,* 56, 275–282.

Mulinski, P. (1989). Dual diagnosis in alcoholic clients: Clinical implications. *Social Casework: The Journal of Contemporary Social Work,* 70, 333–339.

Nolen-Koeksema, S. & Larson, S. (1999). *Coping with loss.* Mahwah, NJ: Lawrence Erlbaum Associates.

Ornstein, E. D. & Ganzer, C. (1997). Mitchell's relational conflict model: An analysis of its usefulness in clinical social work. *Clinical Social Work Journal,* 25, 391–406.

Ornstein, P. (1991). Why self psychology is not an object relations theory: Clinical and theoretical considerations. In A. Goldberg (Ed.), *The evolution of self psychology: Progress in self psychology* (Vol. 7, 17–30). Hillsdale, NJ: Analytic Press.

Palombo, J. (1985). Depletion states and selfobject disorders. *Clinical Social Work Journal,* 14, 32–49.

Perez Foster, R. (1999). An intersubjective approach to cross-cultural clinical work. *Smith College Studies in Social Work,* 69, 269–291.

Perez Foster, R., Moskowitz, M. & Art, J. (Eds.). (1996). *Reaching across boundaries of culture and class.* Northvale, NJ: Jason Aronson.

Phillips, D. G. (1993). Integration and alternatives: Some current issues in psychoanalytic theory. *Clinical Social Work Journal,* 21, 247–256.

Pine, F. (1988). The four psychologies of psychoanalysis and their place in clinical work. *Journal of the American Psychoanalytic Association,* 36, 571–596.

Pollock, G. H. (1987). The mourning-liberation process: Issues in the inner life of the older adult. In J. Sadovy & M. Leszcz (Eds.), *Treating the elderly with psychotherapy* (pp. 3–30). Madison, WI: International Universities Press.

Racker, H. (1957). The meaning and uses of countertransference. *Psychoanalytic Quarterly,* 26, 303–357.

Rapaport, D. (1960). The structure of psychoanalytic theory. *Psychological Issues,* 2, 39–85.

Reich, W. (1949). *Character analysis.* New York: Orgone Institute.

Renik, O. (1995). The ideal of the anonymous analyst and the problem of self-disclosure. *Psychoanalytic Quarterly,* LXIV, 466–495.

Rowe, C. & MacIsaac, D. (1989). *Empathic attunement—The "technique" of psychoanalytic self psychology.* Northvale, NJ: Jason Aronson.

Sable, P. (1995). Attachment theory and post-traumatic stess disorder. *Journal of Analytic Social Work,* 2, 89–109.

Scharff, D. E. & Scharff, J. S. (1987). *Object relations family therapy.* Northvale, NJ: Jason Aronson.

Schwaber, E. (1983). Psychoanalytic listening and psychic reality: *International Journal of Psycho-Analysis,* 10, 379–392.

Schwartzman, G. (1984). Narcissistic transferences: Implications for the treatment of couples. *Dynamic Psychotherapy,* 2, 5–14.

Segal, H. (1974). *Introduction to the work of Melanie Klein.* New York: Basic Books.

Seinfeld, J. (1990). *The bad object: Handling the negative therapeutic reaction in psychotherapy.* Northvale, NJ: Jason Aronson.

——— (1991). *The empty core: An object relations approach to psychotherapy of the schizoid personality.* Northvale, NJ: Jason Aronson.

——— (1993). *Interpreting and holding.* Northvale, NJ: Jason Aronson.

——— (1996). *Containing rage, terror, and despair.* Northvale, NJ: Jason Aronson.

Settlage, C. F. (1994). On the contribution of separation-individuation theory to psychoanalysis: Developmental process, pathogenesis, therapeutic process, and technique. In S. Kramer & S. Akhtar (Eds.), *Mahler and Kohut: Perspectives on development, psychopathology, and technique* (17–52). Northvale, NJ: Jason Aronson.

Shane, E. (1991). Self psychology expanding: A consideration of recent books of Michael Basch, Arnold Goldberg, and Robert Stolorow, Bernard Brandchaft, and George Atwood. In A. Goldberg (Ed.), *The evolution of self psychology: Progress in self psychology,* (Vol.7, pp. 157–166). Hillsdale, NJ: Analytic Press.

——— (1992). The latest word: A discussion of three major contributions to self psychology by Ernest Wolf, Howard Bacal and Kenneth Newman, and Joseph Lichtenberg. In A. Goldberg (Ed.), *New therapeutic visions: Progress in self psychology,* (Vol. 8, pp. 215–228). Hillsdale, NJ: Analytic Press.

Shane, M., Shane, E. & Gales, M. (1997). *Intimate attachments.* New York: Guilford Press.

Siegel, J. (1992). *Repairing intimacy.* Northvale, NJ: Jason Aronson.

Slipp, S. (Ed.). (1988). *The technique and practice of object relations family therapy.* Northvale, NJ: Jason Aronson.

Solomon, I. (1995). *A primer of Kleinian therapy.* Northvale, NJ: Jason Aronson.

Solomon, M. F. (1985). Treatment of narcissistic and borderline disorders in marital therapy: Suggestions toward an enhanced therapeutic approch. *Clinical Social Work Journal, 13,* 141–156.

Solomon, M. F. (1989). *Narcissism and intimacy.* New York: W. W. Norton.

Specht, H. & Courtney, M. (1994). *Unfaithful Angels.* New York: Free Press.

Spitz, R. (1945). Hospitalism: An inquiry into the genesis of psychiatric conditions in early childhood. *The Psychoanalytic Study of the Child, 1,* 53–74.

——— (1946a). Hospitalism: A follow-up report. *The Psychoanalytic Study of the Child, 2,* 113–117.

——— (1946b). Anaclitic depression: An inquiry into the genesis of psychiatric conditions in childhood. *The Psychoanalytic Study of the Child, 2,* 313–342.

——— (1946c). The smiling response: A contribution to the ontogenesis of social relations, with the assistance of K. M. Wolf. *Genetic Psychology Monographs, 34,* 57–125.

——— (1959). *A genetic field theory of ego formation: Its implications for pathology.* New York: International Universities Press.

——— (1965). *The first year of life: A psychoanalytic study of normal and deviant development of object relations.* New York: International Universities Press.

St. Clair, M. (1996). *Object relations and self psychology.* Pacific Grove, CA: Brooks/Cole.

Steele, B. (1980). Psychodynamic factors in child abuse. In C. H. Kempe & R. E. Helfer (Eds.), *The battered child* (3rd ed., pp. 49–85). Chicago: University of Chicago Press.

Stern, D. (1985). *The interpersonal world of the infant.* New York: Basic Books.

Stewart, R. H., Peters, T. C., Marsh, S. & Peters, M. J. (1975). An object relations approach with marital couples, families, and children. *Family Process, 14,* 161–172.

Stolorow, R. D. (1992). Subjectivity and self psychology: A personal odyssey. In A. Goldberg (Ed.), *New therapeutic visions: Progress in self psychology* (Vol. 8, pp. 241–250). Hillsdale, NJ: Analytic Press.

Stolorow, R. D. & Atwood, G. E. (1979). *Faces in a cloud: Subjectivity in personality theory.* Northvale, NJ: Jason Aronson.

——— (1992). *Contexts of being: The intersubjective foundations of psychological life.* Hillsdale, NJ: Analytic Press.

Stolorow, R. D., Atwood, G. E. & Brandchaft, B. (1994). *The intersubjective perspective.* Northvale, NJ: Jason Aronson.

Stolorow, R. D., Brandchaft, B. & Atwood, G. E. (1987). *Psychoanalytic treatment: An intersubjective approach.* Hillsdale, NJ: Analytic Press.

Stolorow, R. D. & Lachmann, F. M. (1980). *Psychoanalysis of developmental arrests.* New York: International Universities Press.

Straussner, S. L. A. (Ed.). (1993). *Clinical work with substance-abusing clients.* New York: Guilford Press.

Strean, H. S. (1979). *Psychoanalytic theory and social work practice.* New York: Free Press.

——— (1993). Clinical social work: An evaluative review. *Journal of Analytic Social Work, 1,* 5–23.

Strom, K. (1994). Social workers in private practice: An update. *Clinical Social Work Journal, 22,* 73–89.

Strozier, C. B. (1985). Glimpses of a life: Heinz Kohut (1913–1981). In A. Goldberg (Ed.), *Progress in self psychology,* (Vol. 1, pp. 3–12). Hillsdale, NJ: Analytic Press.

Sullivan, H. S. (1953). *Interpersonal theory of psychiatry.* New York: W. W. Norton.

——— (1956). *Clinical studies in psychiatry.* New York: W. W. Norton.

Teicholz, J. F. (1999). *Kohut, Loewald, and the postmoderns.* Hillsdale, NJ: Analytic Press.

Tolpin, P. (1980). The borderline patient: Its make-up and analyzability. In A. Goldberg (Ed.), *Advances in self psychology* (pp. 115–128). New York: International Universities Press.

Ulman, R. B. & Paul, H. (1990). The addictive personality and "addictive trigger mechanisms" (ATM'S): The self psychology of addiction and its treatment. In A. Goldberg (Ed.), *The realities of transference, Progress in self psychology* (Vol. 6, pp. 113–128). Hillsdale, NJ: Analytic Press.

Wagner, G. (1991). When a parent is abusive. In H. Jackson (Ed.), *Using self psychology in psychotherapy* (pp. 243–259). Northvale, NJ: Jason Aronson.

Weinberg, L. (1991). Infant development and the sense of self: Stern vs. Mahler. *Clinical Social Work Journal,* 19, 9–22.

Wells, M. & Glickhauf-Hughes, C. (1986). Techniques to develop object constancy with borderline clients. *Psychotherapy,* 23, 460–468.

White, R. F. (1959). Motivation reconsidered: The concept of competence. *Psychological Review,* 66, 297–333.

——— (1963). Ego and reality in psychoanalytic theory. *Psychological Issues,* II (3). New York: International Universities Press.

Winnicott, D. W. (1960). The capacity to be alone. In D. W. Winnicott, *The maturational processes and the facilitating environment* (pp. 29–36). Madison, CT: International Universities Press.

——— (1965). *The maturational processes and the facilitating environment.* Madison, CT: International Universities Press.

——— (1975). *From peaediatrics to psycho-analysis.* New York: Basic Books.

Wolf, E. S. (1988). *Treating the self.* New York: Guilford Press.

——— (1991). Toward a level playing field. In A. Goldberg (Ed.), *The evolution of self psychology: Progress in self psychology,* (Vol. 7, pp. 185–200). Hillsdale, NJ: Analytic Press.

Woodroofe, K. (1971). *From charity to social work in England and the United States.* Toronto: University of Toronto Press.

Wyss, D. (1966). *Depth psychology: A critical history.* New York: W. W. Norton.

INDEX

Abstinence, in the therapeutic relationship, 98–100
Adversary
  need for, 81
  transference and, 111
Affects, 55
Aging, 88
Alter ego, 81
  hungry, 87
  transference, 111
Ambitions, 221–22
American Psychoanalytic Association, 41
Anxious resistant attachment style, case example, 135–37
Archaic parental imago, 80, 82
Assessment, 126–34
  case examples, 135–53
  data sources, 131–34
  guidelines, 127–31
Attachments
  -affiliation motivation system, 91
  anxious resistant, 61
  disorganized-disoriented, 61
  secure, 61
Austin, Lucille, 4
Aversive motivational system, 92

Bacal, Howard, 10, 48, 49
  view of self psychology as a form of object relations theory, 92–93
Balint, Michael, 39
Basch, Michael Franz, 10, 42, 48
Beebe, Beatrice, 10, 48
Benjamin, Jessica, 51
Bion, Wilfred, 32, 39–40
Biopsychosocial factors, in treatment approaches, 7
Bipolar self, 82–83
Blame, case example, 280–81
Blanck, Gertrude, 64–65

treatment of object relations pathology, 103–4
Blanck, Rubin, 64–65
  treatment of object relations pathology, 103–4
Bowlby, John, 40
  patterns of attachment and their pathological outcomes, 60–61
British Psychoanalytic Society, 30
Britton, Claire, 35–36
Burlingham, Dorothy, 21

Case examples
  of anxious resistant attachment style, 135–37
  of "bad" internal objects, 140–42
  of blow to self-concept, 228–31
  of child maltreatment, 258–62
  of confronting splitting and projective identification, 165–72
  of countertransference, 224–40, 253–66
  of couple and family treatment, 273–84
  of depression following achievement of a goal, 237–40
  of false self organization, 144–47
  of family scapegoat, 282–84
  of frustrated selfobject needs, 147–49
  of grandiose self, 253–58
  of illness as punishment and loss of compensatory structures, 231–33
  of intrusive thoughts and memories of childhood sexual abuse, 262–66
  of lack of empathy, 191–94
  of lack of sufficient mirroring, 189–91
  of narcissistic vulnerability, 233–37
  of negative self- and object representations, 137–39
  of projective identification, 139–40, 202–13
  of prolonged grief involving the loss of self, 224–28

Case examples (*cont.*)
of repairing disruptions of selfobject
transference, 189–200
of re-traumatization, 162–65
of schizoid tendencies, 142–44
of selfobject functions, 178–79
of selfobject needs, 273–79
of splitting, 139–40
of substance abuse, 253–58
of unattuned response, 194–97
of unresolved power struggle, 197–
200
of worker's frustration, 202–7
of worker's personal countertransference,
173–75
of worker's resentment, 207–13
Charcot, Jean, 15
Child development, 18–19
grandiose-exhibitionistic self, 80
mothering and, 36–37
psychoanalysis and, 31
Children
adult survivors of sexual abuse
effects of, 248–49
theoretical and clinical perspectives,
249–52
capacity for concern, 76
capacity to be alone, 76
maltreatment
case example, 258–62
effects of, 244–45
theoretical and clinical perspectives,
245–48
"marasmus" in, 25–26
Clients, 132–34
understanding similarities and differences
between worker and, 213–14
Compensation, 84
Confrontation, 100–104
in self psychological treatment, 117–18
Contact-shunning, 87
Countertransference, 118–19
case examples, 174–75, 224–40, 253–66
in couple and family treatment, 271–72
in object relations treatment, 104–9
in treatment approaches, 6–7
worker's personal, 173–75

Couple and family treatment, 267–85
case examples, 273–84
countertransference issues, 271–72
object relations perspectives, 268
self psychological perspectives, 268–69
treatment principles, 269–71
Culture
case examples, 150–53, 178–79

Death, of significant others, 88, 216–17
Defenses
manic, 73
moral, 60
primitive or lower level, 57–58
Dependence, evolution to independence,
77–78
Depression
case example of depression following
achievement of a goal, 237–40
Jacobson's view of, 71–72
Disability, 88, 217
Disappointment, 88
Discrimination, case example, 150–53
Diversity, 50–52
Divorce, 88
Dreams, 221–22

Efficacy, 81
Ego, 56
alter (twin), 81
anti-libidinal, 74
central, 74
ideal, 58–59
libidinal, 74
regressed, 75
-relatedness between mother and infant, 76
in stages of internalized object relations, 68
Ego psychology, 18–22
comparison with Freudian theory, 23–25
Empathy
case example, 162–65
case example of lack of, 191–94
with client's fears of re-traumatization,
162–65
interpretation of selfobject needs and
failures, 182–83
Heinz Kohut's views, 41–42

Empathy (*cont.*)
  with losses and blows to the self, 219
  with narcissistic rage and shame, 219–20
  in self psychological treatment, 110
  in treatment approaches, 9
Endopsychic structure, 73–75
Environment
  impediments, 175–76
  therapeutic holding, 155–61
    containment and transitional
      phenomena, 157
    general considerations, 156–57
    role of experience-near empathy, 158–59
    use of limits and structure, 159–61
Erikson, Erik, 20–22
Ethnicity, 51–52
Exciting object, 74
Explanation, in therapeutic treatment, 179–84
Exploratory-assertive motivational systems, 91

Facilitating environment, 75–76
Fairbairn, W. R. D., 10, 32–35
  endopsychic structure and the bad object,
    73–75
  use of interpretations in object relations
    treatment, 100–101
False self organization, case example, 144–47
Family scapegoat, case example, 282–84
Fantasy, real object and, 54
Feelings, fraudulent, 220, 222
Ferenczi, Sandor, 30
Freud, Anna, 18–19, 21
Freud, Sigmund
  biography of, 15–16
  comparison with ego psychology, 23–25
  developmental theory, 17–18
  guilty man concept, 84–85
  theories into social work, 4, 15–18
  theories modified and transformed, 4–5
  writings, 16–17
Frustration, of the worker
  case example, 202–7

Gales, Mary, 93
Garrett, Annette, 4
Gedo, John, 42
Gender, 50–52

Geography, changes in, 88
Goals, 88
  in self psychological treatment, 110
Goldberg, Arnold, 10, 42, 48
Grandiose self, 81–82
  case examples, 253–58
  tempering the demands of, 221
Grief, case example of prolonged, involving
    the loss of self, 224–28
Guilt, 220, 222
Guntrip, Harry, 10, 37–39
  regressed ego and the schizoid problem, 75
  object relations treatment, 104

Hamilton, Gordon, 4
Hartmann, Heinz, 19–20
Helmholz School, 15
Hollis, Florence, 4
"Hospitalism," 25–26
Human development, self psychology and, 9
Hypnosis, evolution of, 15

Idealization, 58
  of others, 81
Idealized object, 74
Idealizing transference, 111
Identification, 56–57
Illness, 88, 217
  case example as punishment and loss of
    compensatory structures, 231–33
Illusions, 221–22
Images, internal, 7
Independence, evolution from dependence,
    77–78
Individuation, 28
Infant-caretaker interactions, 8
Infants
  escape from reality and, 34
  evolution from dependence to
    independence, 77–78
  Jacobson's writings and, 55
Insight, as treatment for object relations
    theory, 97–98
Internalization, 56–57
  case example, 140–42
  interpretation of, 183–84
  transmuting, 83

Interpretation, 100–104
  of the presence of "bad" internal objects,
    183–84
  of resistance to selfobject transference,
    181–82
  of selfobject needs and empathic failures,
    182–83
  of separation-individuation subphase
    issues, 180–81
  in therapeutic treatment, 179–84
Intersubjectivity, 94
  in the client-worker relationship,
    172–73
  Stolorow's theory of, 93–94
"Intersubjectivity," 49–50
Introjection, 56–57

Jacobson, Edith, 10, 22, 26–27
  view of early object loss and depression,
    71–72
Jordan, Judith, 51
Joseph, Betty, 40

Kaplan, Alexandra, 51
Kernberg, Otto, 10, 22, 28–30
  object relations approach in
    treatment of borderline personality
    organization, 101
  stages of internalized object relations and
    borderline and narcissistic pathology,
    67–71
Klein, Erich, 35
  paranoid/schizoid and depressive positions,
    72–73
Klein, Melanie, 10, 28, 30–32, 35
Kohut, Heinz, 10, 41–44, 79
  tragic man concept, 84–85
Kris, Ernst, 19

Lachmann, Frank, 10, 48
Latent negative transference reactions, 101
Libido, ego and, 74
Lichtenberg, Joseph, 10, 48
  five motivational systems, 91–92
Life events
  treatment emphases, 219
Lowenstein, Alfred, 19

Mahler, Margaret, 10, 22, 27–28
  separation-individuation process
    and subphase inadequacies,
    61–67
Manic defenses, 73
"Marasmus," 25–26
Marcus, David, 42
Mental health, attitude in self psychological
    treatment, 109
Merger experiences, 81
Midlife issues, 218–19
Miller, Jean Baker, 51
Mirror-hungry, 87
Mirroring, 81
  case example of lack of sufficient,
    189–91
Mirror transference, 111
Mitchell, Stephen, 10
Moral defense, 60
Mothering, 36–37. *See also* Women
  "good enough" mother and the true and
    false self, 75–77
Motivation, Lichtenberg's five systems of,
    91–92
Multiculturalism, 51–52

Narcissistic disorders, 86
  alter-ego hungry, 87
  behavior, 86
  borderline states, 86
  case example of narcissistic vulnerability,
    233–37
  contact-shunning, 87
  empathizing with, 219–20
  encouraging healthy narcissism, 116–17
  Heinz Kohut and, 42
  ideal-hungry, 87
  Kernberg's stages of internalized object
    relations and, 70–71
  merger-hungry, 87
  mirror-hungry, 87
  personality, 86
  rage as a disintegration product, 83–84
  vulnerability and, 85
National Association of Social Workers
    Register of Clinical Social Workers
    (1991), 3–4

Neutrality, in therapeutic relationship, 98–100
New York Psychoanalytic Society, 26

Object, transitional, 76–77
Object relations theory
  accommodations to, 120–21
  affects, 55
  American, 22–30
  Bacal's view of self psychology and, 92–94
  basic terminology, 53–60
  Bowlby's patterns of attachment, 60–61
  British, 30–40
  case example, 137–39
  comparison with self psychology, 45–47
  constancy, 63–64
  in couple and family treatment, 268
  definition, 7–10
  the ego, 55–56
  evolution of, 15–52
  Fairbairn's endopsychic structure, 73–75
  Guntrip's regressed ego and the schizoid problem, 75
  history of, 4–5
  introjection, identification, and internalization, 56–57
  Jacobson's view of early object loss and depression, 71–72
  Kernberg's stages of internalized object relations, 67–71
  Klein's paranoid/schizoid and depressive positions, 72–73
  Mahler's separation-individuation process, 61–67
  object and part-objects, 53–54
  pathology, 8
  primitive or lower level defenses, 57–58
  projection, 57
  real and fantasied object, 54
  relational matrix, 60
  self- and object-representations, 54–55
  self psychology and, 3–14
  structure, development, and psychopathology, 60–78
  the superego, 58–60

treatment, 96–109
  confrontation and interpretation, 100–104
  insight versus positive relationship experiences, 97–98
  modifying pathological structures, 97
  neutrality and abstinence versus meeting patients' needs, 98–100
  transference-countertransference dynamics, 104–9
  Winnicott's mother and self, 75–77
Obstacles, overcoming in forming positive relationships, 161–76
Oppression, 50–52
Ornstein, Anna, 42
Ornstein, Paul, 42, 48

Paranoid/schizoid
  concept development, 32
  Klein's positions on, 72–73
Pathological structures, modifying object relations treatment, 97
Perfection, case example of narcissistic vulnerability, 233–37
Person-in-situation perspective, 3
Power struggle, unresolved
  case example of, 197–200
Primary maternal preoccupation, 76
Projection, 57
  case example, 139–40
Projective identification, 57–58, 200–202
  case examples, 202–13, 280–81
"The Psychiatric Deluge," 4
Psychodynamic theory, 3–4
  assimilation into social work, 4
  expansion of, 4–7
Psychopathology, self psychology and, 84–88
Psychosexual stages, 17–18

Race, 51–52
Rage, 219–20
  as a disintegration product, 83–84
Rankian theory, 4
Reaction formation, 58–59
Reich, Wilhelm, 19
Rejecting object, 74
Relational matrix, 60

Relationships, external, 7
Religion, 51–52
Resentment, of the worker
  case example, 207–13
Resistance
  to selfobject transference, 181–82
  in treatment approaches, 6
Responsiveness, optimal, 83
Richmond, Mary, 4
Rivière, Joan, 35
Robinson, Virginia, 4
Role, loss of, 88

Schizoid tendencies, case example, 142–44
Schmideberg, Melitta, 31
Self
  bipolar, 82–83
  case example of prolonged grief involving
    the loss of, 224–28
  character types, 87
  cohesive, 80
  core nuclear, 80
  emergent, 89
  encouraging new relations and activities,
    222–23
  fragmenting, 87
  grandiose, 81–82
  grandiose-exhibitionist, 80
  narcissistic line of development, 79–80
  object representations and, 54–55
  overburdened, 87
  overstimulated, 87
  sense of core, 89–90
  Stern's four senses of, 89–91
  strengthening, 222–23
  subjective, 90
  tempering demands of the grandiose, 221
  true, 77
  understimulated, 87
  verbal, 90
  weakness in, 85
Self-affectivity, 90
Self-agency, 90
Self-coherence, 90
Self-concept
  case example of blow to, 228–31
  case example of negative, 150–53

Self disorders, classification, 85–87
Self-history, 90
Self-in-relation theory, 51
Selfobject needs, 80–81
  case example, 273–79
  case example of frustrated, 147–49
  interpretation and empathic failures,
    182–83
  mourning loss of, 220–21
  in therapeutic treatment, 177–79
Selfobject transference, 111–12
  repair of transference disruption, 115–16,
    186–89
    case examples, 189–200
Self psychology, 40–44
  Bacal's view as a form of object relations
    theory, 92–93, 92–94
  basic terminology, 79–84
  case example, 137–39
  comparison with object relations theory,
    45–47
  in couple and family treatment, 268–69
  definition, 7–10
  evolution of, 15–52
  history of, 4–5
  intersubjective field, 119–20
  object relations theory and, 3–14
  perspectives on psychopathology, 84–88
  research and theory, 88–92
  treatment, 109–21
    confrontation, limits, and structure,
      117–18
    disruption and repair of transference,
      114–16
    encouraging healthy narcissism, 116–17
    experience near empathy, 110
    goals, 110
    mental health attitude, 109
    optimal frustration or optimal
      responsiveness, 113–14
    overcoming resistance to the emergence
      of selfobject transferences, 112–13
    selfobject transferences, 111–12
    understanding and explaining, 113
  view of human development, 9
Self-punishment, 222
Sensual-sexual motivational system, 92

Separation, 28
Separation-individuation, 28
  autistic phase, 62
  differentiation subphase, 62
  interpretation in therapeutic treatment,
      180–81
  object constancy, 63–64
  practicing subphase, 62–63
  rapprochement subphase, 63
  subphase inadequacies and, 61–67
  symbiotic phase, 62
Sexual abuse, adult survivors of
  case example of intrusive thoughts and
      memories of, 262–66
  effects of, 248–49
  theoretical and clinical perspectives, 249–52
Shame, 219–20
Shane, Estelle, 10, 48
  two dimensions of intimacy, 93
Shane, Morton, 10, 48
  two dimensions of intimacy, 93
Social work
  practice significance, 10–11
  treatment
      approaches, 5–6
      Harry Guntrip's, 38–39
      assessment planning, 125–54
      beginning phase, 155–85
      of clients undergoing stressful life events,
          216–40
      of clients with special problems, 241–66
      couple and family treatment, 267–85
      middle phase issues, 186–215
      selective techniques, 176–84
Spitz, Rene, 22, 25–26
Splitting, 57–58, 69
  case examples, 139–40, 165–72, 280–81
  confronting, 165–72
Status, 88
Stern, Daniel, 10, 48, 49
  four senses of the self, 89–91
Stiver, Irene, 51
Stolorow, Robert, 10, 48
  theory of intersubjectivity, 93–94
Stone Center for Developmental Services and
      Studies, 51

Strachey, James, 35
Stress
  temporary reactions to, 88
  treatment, 216–40
Substance abuse
  case example, 253–58
  causes and treatment, 241–42
  theoretical and clinical perspectives, 242–44
Sullivan, Harry Stack, 22, 25
Superego, 58–60
  in stages of internalized object relations, 68
Surrey, Janet, 51

Taft, Jessie, 4
Therapist, treatment approaches, 5–6
Tolpin, Marian, 42
Tolpin, Paul, 42
Transference
  adversarial, 111
  as approach to treatment, 6
  of creativity, 111
  disruption and repair of, 114–16
  idealizing, 111
  interpretation of resistance to, 181–82
  Heinz Kohut and, 44
  mirror, 111
  in object relations treatment, 104–9
Trauma, 50
Twinship, 82
  transference, 111

Unattuned response, case example of, 194–97
Unemployment, 88

Weakness, 85
White, Robert, 21
Winnicott, D. W., 10, 35–37
  "good enough" mother and the true and
      false self, 75–77
  theory of "objective countertransference,"
      105–6
  object relations treatment, 104
Wolf, Ernest, 42, 48
Women, 50–51. *See also* Mothering
Worker, understanding similarities and
      differences between client and, 213–14